Justice and Rights

Justice and Rights

CHRISTIAN AND MUSLIM PERSPECTIVES

A record of the fifth "Building Bridges" seminar held in Washington, D.C., March 27–30, 2006

MICHAEL IPGRAVE, EDITOR

Georgetown University Press / Washington, DC

Georgetown University Press, Washington, D.C. www.press.georgetown.edu

Library of Congress Cataloging-in-Publication Data

Justice and rights : Christian and Muslim perspectives : a record of the fifth "Building bridges" seminar held in Washington, D.C., March 27–30, 2006 / Michael Ipgrave, editor.

p. cm.

Includes bibliographical references and index.

ISBN 978-1-58901-489-3 (pbk. : alk. paper)

1. Christianity and justice—Congresses. 2. Islam and justice.—Congresses. 3. Human rights—Religious aspects—Christianity—Congresses. 4. Human rights—Religious aspects—Islam—Congresses. I. Ipgrave, Michael.

BR115.J8J86 2009

261.2'7—dc22

2008051750

∞ This book is printed on acid-free paper meeting the requirements of the American National Standard for Permanence in Paper for Printed Library Materials.

15 14 13 12 11 10 09 9 8 7 6 5 4 3 2

First printing

Printed in the United States of America

Contents

Participants

Khaled Akasheh
Head Officer for Islam, Pontifical Council for Interreligious Dialogue, Vatican City

Seyed Amir Akrami
Lecturer, University of Tehran

Yousif Al-Khoei
Director, Imam Al-Khoei Foundation

Bishop Angaelos
General Bishop, Coptic Orthodox Church, United Kingdom

John Azumah
Lecturer of Islamic Studies, Director of the Centre for Islamic Studies and Muslim–Christian Relations, London School of Theology

Osman Bakar
Professor of Islamic Thought and Civilization, International Institute of Islamic Thought and Civilization, Malaysia

Vincent J. Cornell
Asa Griggs Candler Professor of Middle East and Islamic Studies, Emory University

Ahmad Dallal
Associate Professor of Arabic and Islamic Studies and Chair of the Arabic and Islamic Studies Department, Georgetown University

Ellen F. Davis
Professor of Bible and Practical Theology, Duke Divinity School

Lejla Demiri
Research Fellow in Divinity, Trinity Hall, University of Cambridge

Carolyn Evans
Associate Professor, Faculty of Law, University of Melbourne

Malcolm Evans
Dean, Faculty of Social Sciences and Law, School of Law, University of Bristol

Hugh Goddard
Professor of Christian–Muslim Relations, University of Nottingham

Yvonne Haddad
Professor of the History of Islam and Christian–Muslim Relations, Georgetown University

Michael Ipgrave
Archdeacon of Southwark,
Church of England

Mohammad Hashim Kamali
Chairman and CEO, International
Institute of Advanced Islamic Studies,
Malaysia

Fikret Karcic
Professor, Faculty of Law,
University of Sarajevo

John Langan
Joseph Cardinal Bernardin Professor
of Catholic Social Thought,
Georgetown University

Daniel A. Madigan
Jeanette W. and Otto J. Ruesch Family
Associate Professor of Theology,
Georgetown University

Maleiha Malik
Reader in Law, King's College,
University of London

Jane Dammen McAuliffe
President, Bryn Mawr College

Mustansir Mir
Professor of Islamic Studies,
Youngstown State University

Michael Nazir-Ali
Bishop of Rochester,
Church of England

Recep Senturk
Associate Professor of Sociology,
Fatih University, Turkey

Ataullah Siddiqui
Senior Research Fellow,
The Islamic Foundation, and
Director of the Markfield Institute of
Higher Education, Leicester,
United Kingdom

Mona Siddiqui
Professor of Islamic Studies and
Public Understanding and Director of
the Centre for the Study of Islam,
University of Glasgow

Nicholas Townsend
Director of Studies and Tutor for
Associate Students, South East Institute
for Theological Education,
University of Kent

Miroslav Volf
Director, Yale Center for Faith and
Culture, and Henry B. Wright
Professor of Theology,
Yale University Divinity School

Rowan Williams
Archbishop of Canterbury,
Church of England

Timothy J. Winter
Sheikh Zayed Lecturer in Islamic
Studies, Faculty of Divinity,
University of Cambridge

Introduction

Christian and Muslim Perspectives

Michael Ipgrave

This volume is a record of the fifth annual Building Bridges seminar of Christian and Muslim scholars, convened by the Archbishop of Canterbury at Georgetown University, Washington, D.C., in March 2006. In keeping with the pattern of earlier seminars, a theme of enduring and contemporary significance was addressed through lectures by scholars of both faiths, through study and reflection together on key texts, and through group and plenary discussion.[1] This volume presents the lectures and the texts with introductions and commentarial notes reflecting discussions at the seminar.

The theme chosen for this seminar was "Justice and Rights—Christian and Muslim Perspectives." As the material presented here demonstrates, this is a topic not only of immense relevance for both faiths in the modern world but also with deep roots in the core texts of both traditions. The very phrasing of the theme may suggest a tension in the way the material is approached. On the one hand, justice is recognized by Christians and Muslims as one of the defining characteristics of God and sought by them as his purpose for a world that is manifestly unjust; in other words, it is laid upon them as a mandate, and traditionally their first response to the vocation of justice has been to think of their obligations, both toward God and toward the other. On the other hand, the language of rights appears to embody and presuppose a principle of human autonomy and assertiveness that may fit uncomfortably with a traditional religious orientation. The situation is further complicated in that among the human rights generally recognized today is the freedom to practice and manifest religion or belief, whether that be Christianity, Islam, another faith, or the explicit absence of religious commitment. It is not surprising that "Justice and Rights" is a theme of serious contest and debate between Christian and Christian, Muslim and Muslim, and Christian and Muslim; between people of faith and those of no faith; and between religious communities and governments. What is remarkable about the material presented here is the extent to which it shows that Muslims and Christians are facing similar issues, even if the answers they give can differ quite radically.

This seminar and volume differ from predecessors in including among the texts studied not only scriptural material but also documents from the Christian and Islamic traditions, in both the premodern and the modern periods. Given the way in which the societies of Christendom and of the Islamic world have developed over the centuries, and given also the way in which both faiths have throughout their history exhibited many different patterns of relationship with political power, it did not seem possible to treat the subject adequately without reference to texts beyond the scriptures. This in turn provides the rationale for the simple structure of this volume, which follows the pattern of the seminar itself in looking first at the roots of thinking about divine justice in the scriptures, then moving on to survey the evolving traditions of both religions, with a particular focus on the relationship between religious and political authority, and finally reaching the modern context, where issues of rights and freedom come very much to the fore.[2] As this introduction indicates, the themes under consideration are vast in extent and contested in treatment; the hope is that this small selection of resources and collection of reflections can encourage Christians and Muslims to further dialogue on the issues.

Notes

1. For records of earlier Building Bridges seminars, see the following volumes, all edited by Michael Ipgrave: *The Road Ahead: A Christian–Muslim Dialogue* (London: Church House, 2002); *Scriptures in Dialogue: Christians and Muslims Studying the Qur'ān Together* (London: Church House, 2004); *Bearing the Word: Prophecy in Biblical and Qur'ānic Perspective* (London: Church House, 2005); *Building a Better Bridge: Muslims, Christians, and the Common Good* (Washington, DC: Georgetown University Press, 2008).
2. Here we understand "scriptures" in a wide sense to include Hebrew scriptures, the New Testament, the Qur'ān, and the ḥadīth collections.

PART I

Scriptural Foundations

For Christians and Muslims alike, justice is a concept and a vocation grounded in their scripturally shaped understanding of who God is and what his purposes are for humanity. In their respective overviews of the Qur'ānic and the Biblical teachings, Mohammad Hashim Kamali and Ellen F. Davis emphasize both the centrality of justice as a criterion for recognizing the nature of God and the urgency of justice as a divine command to be realized in the world: It is at once descriptive of the Creator and prescriptive for the creature.

The passages that follow show a selection of the ways in which core Christian and Islamic texts—from the Hebrew scriptures, the Qur'ān, the New Testament, and the ḥadīth collections—relate this divine characteristic and imperative of justice to the human exercise of power in society. The locus of that power is identified very differently in the separate texts; correspondingly, from the perspective of divine justice, very distinct appraisals are given of the authority of the powerful—ranging from a paean to the ideal of kingship mirroring divine rule, through accounts of political leadership seen as accountable either directly or indirectly to God, to the hostile image of a cosmic power actively warring against all that is holy. Through all the texts, however, runs the firm conviction that, whatever the human realities of power, the justice that is of God will eventually be established.

Chapter 1

The Ruler and the Ruled in Islam: A Brief Analysis of the Sources

Mohammad Hashim Kamali

In addressing this subject, I refer first to two Qur'ānic verses on the rights and duties of the *uli'l-amr* (those in charge of affairs).[1] The passage in question, known as the *āyāt al-umarā'* (the rulers' verse) occurs in sūra al-Nisā'.[2] Qur'ān commentators have spoken in detail about the meaning of these verses and their implications regarding the nature of an Islamic government and the relations of the ruler to the ruled. Some of the salient points discussed are the precise meaning of *uli'l-amr* and the various interpretations given to this key Qur'ānic term; the qualifications of the *uli'l-amr*; how the *uli'l-amr* are to be known and identified; the duty of obedience to the *uli'l-amr*; and the limits, if any, of such obedience.

The subject of how the *uli'l-amr* are entrusted with the power to rule is, of course, a wider subject that relates to the procedure and method of designation of the head of state into office through nomination and *bay'a* (pledge of allegiance), a subject that falls beyond my immediate concern. There are also other textual requirements that are integral in the relationship of ruler to ruled. Consultation (*shūrā*) is one of them, and so is the compliance of both the ruler and the ruled to the injunctions of Islam and its Sharī'a; however, I do not propose to delve into these issues here beyond any cursory references necessary to establish the context.

Uli'l-Amr in the Qur'ān

The Qur'ānic reference to *uli'l-amr* provides in an address to the Muslims to "obey Allah, and obey the Messenger and those in charge of the affairs (*uli'l-amr*) among you. If you have a dispute concerning any matter, refer it to Allah and the Messenger, if you believe in Allah and the Last Day. This is better and more becoming in the end" (al-Nisā' 4:59). The duty of the ruled to obey the ruler is thus the principal theme of this verse. The immediately preceding verse in the text is, conversely, concerned with the duty of the rulers themselves. This is as follows: "Allah commands you to render the trusts (*al-amānāt*) to whom they are due and when you judge among people, you judge with justice" (al-Nisā' 4:58). The two principal duties of the rulers expounded here are thus faithful discharge of the *amānāt* that are due to the people and administering justice among them. The following text then expounds on the citizen's duty of obedience to the *uli'l-amr*. This sequence of themes naturally implies that obedience is a duty to rulers who are just and who are observant of the *amānat al-ḥukm* (the trust of governance) they have undertaken.

The early Qur'ān commentator Muḥammad ibn Jarīr al-Ṭabarī (d. AH 310/930) applied the term *uli'l-amr* basically to the head of state, his deputies, and assistants. According to an alternative interpretation, *uli'l-amr* comprises two groups of people: leaders in temporal affairs (*al-umarā' wa'l-wullat*) and leaders in juridical affairs, the *'ulamā'*. Obedience to them is a requirement in all that is for the benefit and *maṣlaḥa* of the community.

Conversely, the jurists (*fuqahā'*) have discussed *uli'l-amr* in conjunction mainly with the institution of the caliphate. Writers on *al-aḥkam al-sulṭāniyya* (principles of government) have consistently used another term, *ahl al-hall wa'l-'aqd*, as a substitute to *uli'l-amr*. The juristic term here refers to the contract (*al-'aqd*) of *imāma*, which is concluded after nomination and *bay'a*. The *ahl-al-hall wa'l-'aqd* are influential community leaders who play a decisive role in the nomination of the head of state, and they combine the qualifications that the candidate for leadership must possess. These are, according to Abu'l-Ḥasan al-Mawardi (d. AH 458/1058), just character (*'adala*), knowledge (*'ilm*), and wisdom (*ḥikma*). The last of these qualifications means the ability of the person to discern the interest, or *maṣlaḥa*, of the community. Anyone who possesses these qualities can be included in the *ahl al-hall wa'l-'aqd* (also known as the *ahl al-shūrā*) and therefore qualify for leadership.

While relying on Fakhr al-Rāzī's interpretation, Muḥammad Rashīd Riḍā (d. 1935), the author of the twentieth-century Qur'ān commentary *Tafsīr al-Manār*, observed that the *uli'l-amr*, *ahl al-hall wa'l-'aqd*, and the *ahl al-shūrā* are different terms with the same meaning and that they all refer to persons of discernment and opinion who exercise the people's authority and are competent to give advice and counsel in public affairs. They are not necessarily the *'ulamā'* of jurisprudence, nor are they governors and commanders—although these are also included—but are influential persons who are qualified to give advice and counsel.

Two other twentieth-century Qur'ān commentators and jurists, Mustafa al-Maraghi and Maḥmud Shaltūt, both Shaykhs of the Azhar University, have in their respective Qur'ān commentaries concurred with this analysis but added that the *uli'l-amr* in every field are those who have specialized knowledge and are particularly qualified to give expert advice. Both expressed reservation over the tendency of past commentators to confine the *uli'l-amr* to *umarā'* and *'ulamā'* and noted that *uli'l-amr* in the Qur'ān occurs as a general (*'āmm*) term, and it need not therefore be confined to either of these two categories of people.

A large number of twentieth-century scholars have held that the *uli'l-amr* at the present time include the head of state, members of the legislative assemblies, and leading executive officials of government. Some have held that military leaders and other government functionaries who exercise delegated powers need not be included, as they actually follow the orders of the *uli'l-amr*.

Next, the Qur'ānic reference to *amānāt* in the text under review characterizes the Islamic system of government as an *amāna*, which means that government is a trust, and its leaders and officials are the bearers of that trust. *Amāna* is, in turn, signified by accountability to God Most High and the community. This is supported by at least two ḥadīths by two companions, in one of which Abū Hurayra, and in the other 'Abd al-Raḥman ibn Ghanam, asked the Prophet if they could be appointed to a government position. In both cases the Prophet, peace be on him, replied, while referring to government office, that "this is an *amāna*, and it involves accountability, even remorse."[3] Characterizing government as a trust is also supported in another ḥadīth, reported by al-Bukhārī and others: "Every one of you is a guardian and responsible for that which is in his custody. The Imam is a guardian and he is responsible for his subjects. A man is a guardian and he is responsible for his family. A woman is a guardian in the household of her husband."[4] Taqī al-Dīn ibn Taymiyya's (d. AH 748/1328) renowned book, *al-Siyāsa al-Shar'iyya fī Iṣlāḥ al-Rā'ī wa'l-Ra'iyya* ("Sharī'a compliant policy for the benefit of the ruler and ruled"), which is a commentary on the *āyāt al-umarā'*, highlighted two themes in his elaboration of *al-amānāt*: selection and appointment of officials, which must be based strictly on qualification and merit, and fair distribution of wealth in the community. But the fact that the reference to *al-'adl* (justice) occurs in the text immediately after *al-amānāt* indicates that justice is the most important of all *amānāt* in the Islamic conception of government.

With reference to the distribution of wealth in the community, ibn Taymiyya has quoted the second caliph 'Umar b. al-Khaṭṭāb to have said concerning the assets of the *bayt al-mal* (public treasury): "No one has a greater claim to these assets in preference to anyone else. Everyone's entitlement would be judged by his record (of service), his financial condition, his burdens, and his personal needs."

Amāna (trust) in government is also an integral part of representation. The head of state is a representative (*wakil*) of the community, by virtue of *wakala*, which is a fiduciary contract, and a *wakil* is simultaneously a trustee. The *wakil* derives his authority from the principal, the community in this case, and a serious breach of the terms of *wakala* entitles the community to terminate the contract. In the Islamic theory of caliphate, this is what the community is entitled to do in the event the head of state violates the Sharī'a and flouts the basic terms of his trust.

Other points of interpretation in the text before us may be summarized in the following manner. The term *uli'l-amr* that occurs in its plural form in the text under review implies that Islam upholds collective leadership and does not envisage concentration of political power in one individual. This is further substantiated by the Qur'ānic principle of *shūrā*, which by its nature requires participation and involvement of both the ruler and the ruled in the conduct of government.

The Qur'ānic phrase "those in charge of the affairs from among you," *uli'l-amr-e minkum*, refers to the community as a whole and not to any particular group or section thereof. What is implied here is that leadership in an Islamic polity must arise from the community itself. An imposition of power from outside the Muslim community cannot therefore be in conformity with the Qur'ānic vision of leadership.

The Limits of Obedience

The latter portion of the text under review also admits the possibility of disagreement (*tanāzu'*) arising between the ruler and the ruled, notwithstanding the fact that the main theme of the verse is obedience to the *uli'l-amr* (al-Nisā' 4:59). When a dispute arises between the citizen and the *uli'l-amr*, it should be referred to the Qur'ān and Sunna, and not to the *uli'l-amr*. This is why the reference to the *uli'l-amr* is omitted in the latter portion of the verse, for the *uli'l-amr* in that situation would be a party to the dispute, and it is only logical that they should not be the judge of their own case. From this analysis it would appear that the text under review also necessitates the existence of an independent judiciary that is powerful enough to adjudicate disputes between the citizen and the state. Such disputes must be determined and resolved within the framework and guidelines of the Qur'ān and Sunna. Both of these sources are emphatic on impartial justice, peace, and order in the community and submission to the rule of law.

Another duty of the ruled toward the ruler that textbook writers have discussed next to obedience (*ta'a*) to the *uli'l-amr* is that the latter should be given assistance (*naṣra*). The lawful ruler is thus entitled to cooperation from and assistance of the citizen in the due fulfillment of his duties. One of the instances of *naṣra* that is specifically mentioned in this connection is giving the ruler sincere advice (*naṣīḥa*) that leads to improvement, correction of a possible error on his part, or prevention of an impending danger to him.

There are a number of ḥadīths on the subject of obedience to the ruler, which are clearly emphatic and make obedience to the *uli'l-amr* a duty that is not to be taken lightly or dismissed even in the face of some reservation the citizen might have about the legitimacy of the ruler or the government in power. Juristic writing on the subject of *ta'a* has, however, tended to change focus, especially in the works of postclassical writers on caliphate such as al-Ghazālī (d. AH 508/1111), ibn Taymiyya, and others. The jurists of the later periods who witnessed tumultuous times and rebellions tended to lay greater emphasis on obedience to the ruler. Scholars who witnessed such events as the Mongol invasion of Baghdad went on record to say that sixty years of dictatorship was better than one night of chaos. Juristic discourse on this subject has consequently followed a different course than the one suggested in the original teachings of Islam and the precedent of the pious caliphs (*khulafā' rāshidūn*). The teaching of the ḥadīth is equally strong, for example, on opposition to an unjust government. It is never advised to condone tyranny and oppression. To note but two ḥadīths in this connection, it is provided, "When the people see a tyrant but fail to take him by the hand (to alert him), they come close to sharing the punishment that Allah assigns to that tyranny." "The best form of jihad is to tell a word of truth to a tyrannical ruler." Notwithstanding the emphasis that is found in the teachings of Islam on obedience to the ruler, the same does not apply to an oppressive ruler—as is clear in the previously discussed ḥadīths. But the legitimacy or otherwise of the dynastic caliphate and hereditary dictatorship is a wider subject that I do not propose to address here. What is necessary to stress here is that the limits of obedience to a lawful ruler and government became increasingly more complex when the jurists began to question legitimacy of the ruling authorities themselves. It became difficult, then, to draw clear conclusions on the limits of obedience and to determine exactly when an oppressive government loses its right to obedience. There is some evidence in a ḥadīth that mentions that the Muslims should obey their leader, regardless of whether they like or dislike the leader, so long as that leader has not indulged in transgression, which amounts to disbelief and *kufr*. Granted that the ḥadīth quoted here is authentic, it is possible that it has envisaged unusual circumstances of *fitna* and sedition where continuation of the political status quo, even an oppressive one, would take preference over civil strife and rebellion.

It would appear that in the absence of clear constitutional guidelines and procedures in earlier times to determine the legality of a government, instances of serious disagreement between the ruler and the ruled often led to armed rebellion and revolt. There were some attempts to regulate resolution of disputes between the ruler and the ruled through the introduction, for example, of a high-powered administrative tribunal, the *Diwān al-Mazālim* (the court of grievances), in the late second/eighth century of the 'Abbāsid rule. Prior to the setting up of the *Diwān al-Mazālim*, the caliph himself sat, on a certain day of the week, and received complaints against powerful individuals and high officers of government who had resorted to acts of injustice against the people. The audits department (*Diwān al-Azimma*) and the *Diwān al-Ḥisba* (office of the Muḥtasib) that were set up even earlier under the caliph al-Mahdī (d. AH 177/780) played a role in giving substance to the principle of accountability (*muḥasabat al-ḥukkam*). They had specified duties in bringing to light irregularities in the allocation and expenditure of public funds, supervision, and the smooth running of the marketplace. But further developments on these duties and the question of accountability as a whole came with the advent of constitutionalism and legal reforms of the nineteenth and twentieth centuries that opened opportunities for organized opposition and criticism of the government in power. The elected assembly that combined political party organization, including opposition political parties, the trade unions, and so on, has had the effect of alleviating to some extent the persistent problem of accountability in the relationship of the ruler to the ruled. Yet a greater challenge that many Muslim societies and governments face at the present time may be said to be over the faithful implementation of the constitutions and other instruments of accountability that are often available but remain ineffective. For a variety of reasons that cannot be addressed here, constitutionalism in the postcolonial period in the Muslim world has been less successful than it has been in the West.

Commitment to Justice

The Qur'ānic discourse on justice is general and comprehensive in that it seeks to transcend all barriers to impartial justice. There are more than fifty verses in the Qur'ān on justice and a much larger number of verses that denounce injustice and *zulm*. The overall effect of the Qur'ānic emphasis on this theme renders justice into a philosophy and worldview of Islam, especially in the relationship of the ruler to the ruled. Because justice is the overriding goal and objective of Islam, then it is also the criterion of legitimacy. A law, ruling, or command that is contrary to justice is therefore un-Islamic. Justice is also made applicable not only in the courtroom and in respect of a fair distribution of wealth in the community but also to the personal conduct of the individual in his vision of himself and in his relationship with others, his family, the environment, and the world at large. Muslims are thus enjoined "to speak with justice even if be to someone close to you" (al-An'ām 6:152). The emphasis on impartial justice and the unqualified scope of this demand is such that justice is demanded of everyone "even if it be against yourselves, your parents and your relatives, or whether it be against the rich or poor" (al-Nisā'4:135). Love and hatred can both jeopardize the cause of justice, which is why the text further impresses on Muslims not to let "the hatred of a people to swerve you away from justice. Be just as this is closest to (true) piety" (al-Mā'ida 5:8). The relationship of justice to piety here is seen in the just character of the Muslim personality. Justice as a virtue and attribute of the individual, be it the ruler or the ruled, is where all justice begins.

A rigid and inflexible approach to justice is not recommended. This can be seen in the juxtaposition of *'adl* and *iḥsān* in the verse that reads, "God commands justice and beneficence (*iḥsān*) and the giving of financial assistance to the family" (al-Naḥl 16:90). The requirement of justice is here moderated by considerations of *iḥsān*, which means being good to others. Whereas justice is mostly regulated by the Sharī'a, *iḥsān* is not constrained by conformity to formal rules. Justice is also something that is usually demanded by an aggrieved party, whereas *iḥsān* does not depend on a demand or a claim as such. It can be initiated within or outside the formalities of court litigation, evidence, and proof—indeed anywhere, anytime. *Iḥsān* can consist of leniency and forgiveness, just as it may mean an equitable judgment that delivers a fair solution in difficult cases where conformity to formal rules may lead to rigidity and harshness. The judge may exercise leniency, for example, in the case of a repentant, or a first-time, offender, just as he may resort to the rules of equity and fairness (in juristic terms, *istiḥsān*) in cases where conformity to existing rules does not deliver a fair solution.

The manner of the address in these and numerous other passages in the Qur'ān is such that makes justice an objective duty of the *uli'l-amr*, unrestrained by considerations of family, class, race, nationality, or religion. The judge in an Islamic court may not, for example, discriminate between a pious Muslim and one of questionable piety, between a Muslim and a non-Muslim, between friend and foe, or indeed between the ruler and the ruled. Islamic history provides many inspiring examples of cases in which the head of state sat before the court of Sharī'a in a private suit and the court issued judgment against him. Trial procedure and presentation of evidence in these courts facilitate vindication of truth and justice on neutral and, what may be said, positivist, grounds rather than dogmatic and theological considerations. Contrary to common perceptions whereby the Sharī'a courts are often identified as religious courts, I submit that, conceptually at least, the court of Sharī'a is substantially a civilian rather than a religious tribunal. Because justice in Islam transcends the barriers of religion and creed, the court that is committed to its administration need not therefore be characterized as a religious tribunal. The religious affiliation of litigants is not a factor to be taken into account in trial procedures, presentation of evidence, and adjudication. The Sharīʿa court may not discriminate against one or the other party simply because of his piety or religion. This is, in fact, the purport of the Qur'ānic verses just reviewed.

Freedom and the Moral Autonomy of the Individual

Freedom is an important theme in the relationship of ruler and ruled. Freedom has meant different things to different people. To a mystic, a Sufi, freedom has primarily signified freedom from the desires of the self and from dependency on the material world. The philosophers and theologians have discussed freedom in the context of predestination and free will and the interplay, so to speak, between the human will and the will of God Most High. But the jurist and the student of constitutional law have understood freedom in the context of the relationship of ruler to ruled, freedom from authority, and the ability to lead one's life away from the imposition of other individuals and the coercive power of the state.

Islam stands for freedom, which is why it is often characterized as *dīn al-fiṭra*, that is, a natural religion, which esteems a great deal of what is of value to human nature and the enlightened reason of man. Human nature is to a large extent influenced by human intellect, which is probably the most important part of the *fiṭra* of man. The Qur'ān declares that "God created mankind in the state of nature (or natural freedom). Let there be no change in God's creation" (al-Rūm 30:30). The Prophet Muhammad, peace be on him, added his voice to this discussion when he said in a ḥadīth that "every child is born in the natural state (of *fiṭra*)." Indeed one of the missions of the Prophet, as the Qur'ān puts it, was "to remove from the people the burdens and the fetters that were on them before" (al-A'rāf 7:157). The caliph ʿUmar b. al-Khaṭṭāb had occasion to pose a question that begged a negative answer: "Since when did you enslave the people whom their mothers gave birth to as free individuals?" In the matter of religious belief, the Qur'ān declares, "Let there be no compulsion in religion. Guidance had been made clear from misguidance," and it was for the individuals to accept it or to reject it (al-Baqara 2:256). Elsewhere in the text, the Prophet was instructed to tell the disbelievers, "To you is your religion and to me, mine" (al-Kāfirūn 99:6). And then, in a question that again begs a negative answer, the Qur'ān begins by stating that if God had willed, everyone would have embraced Islam, and then poses this question to the Prophet Muhammad: "Are you then forcing the people to become believers?" (Yūnus 10:99). To paraphrase, God tells his messenger, "I did not choose to compel any one; are you going to do what I did not?" Islam is the only great religion among the Abrahamic faiths that accepts religious pluralism, extends recognition to other faiths, gives the followers of other scriptures a recognized and protected status, and refuses compulsion as a basis of its own propagation.

The *fiqh* literature on the subject of apostasy has been questioned by many prominent *'ulamā'* themselves, and it calls for a corrective as it has perpetuated and generalized a circumstantial ḥadīth to the effect that "one who changes his religion shall be killed." This is obviously inconsistent with the impulse of the Qur'ān and its clear proclamation on the freedom of religion. For apostasy occurs in about twenty places in the Qur'ān, and nowhere has the holy text assigned a temporal punishment for it. Apostasy is again a wide subject, and my discussion of it here is brief, for I have addressed the subject in greater detail elsewhere.[5] It is important to note, however, that the Prophet of Islam lived in a continuous state of war with the Quraysh of Makkah, as they were engaged in active hostility over a number of years. There were no neutral grounds in those tumultuous relations. A Muslim who became apostate would flee to Makkah, join the enemy forces, and fight against Muslims, or else he engaged in active conspiracy against them. It was against this background that the Prophet uttered the ḥadīth in question. But the *fiqh* literature has almost turned a blind eye to this crucially important circumstantial factor. The result was that a solitary (*āḥād*) ḥadīth has been taken so far as to suppress the clear text of the Qur'ān on the freedom of religion.

Islam advocates a limited, as opposed to a totalitarian, government in which the individual enjoys considerable moral autonomy. Thus there are limitations on the legislative capabilities of government in Islam, which may accordingly not introduce law contrary to the injunctions of Sharī'a. Many of the contemporary constitutions of Muslim countries have consequently adopted the so-called repugnancy clause to ensure that statutory legislation does not violate the principles of Islam. In the event the *uli'l-amr* issues a command contrary to the injunctions of Islam, the citizen is not required to obey it—as is clear from the text of a ḥadīth that states, "There is no obedience in transgression. Obedience is required in righteousness."

Similarly, the Qur'ānic principle of *ḥisba*, that is, promotion of good and prevention of evil (*amr bi'l-ma'rūf wa nahy 'an al-munkar*), entitles the individual to promote what he or she deems to be good and beneficial and to prevent what he or she considers to be prejudicial and harmful. This can only be attempted by a free and morally autonomous individual. To combat manifest oppression is consequently a part of *ḥisba*, and the Muslim is entitled to speak or take action against it. The *fiqh* literature provides considerable detail regarding the proper implementation of *ḥisba*. Contrary to common perceptions, the Sharī'a does not seek to regulate all aspects of the personal lives of the individual.

Note, for example, the renowned scale of Five Values: the obligatory, recommended, permissible, reprehensible, and forbidden (*wājib, mandūb, mubāḥ, makrūh, ḥarām*). Only the first and the last of these are legally enforceable. The other three, which are much wider in scope, basically amount to moral advice, and it is advisable to observe it, as much of it has also been integrated in the mores and customs of Muslims. Yet no one can be taken to court on the basis of neglecting a *mandūb* or a *makrūh*. Without wishing to enter into details, it may be mentioned in passing that in the terminology of *fiqh*, *ibaḥa,* and *mubāh* are used synonymously with freedom, for a *mubāh* by definition is something over which the individual enjoys unrestricted freedom.

This element of respect for basic freedom of the individual is also seen in the distinction by Muslim jurists of two types of obligations, namely religious (*dīnī*) obligations and juridical (*qaḍa'ī*) obligations. Only the latter are enforceable in the courts of justice. Most of the purely religious duties of Islam, such as prayer, fasting, the *ḥajj*, and so on, fall under the category of *wājib dīnī*, which are not a fit subject for court proceedings. The *muḥtasib* may have a role to play in ensuring that the religious duties of Islam are properly observed, and so too have the state and the *uli'l-amr*, who are to facilitate their observance, yet they fall outside the proper jurisdiction of the court.

Furthermore, no government agency, nor even the Sharī'a courts, has powers to grant discretionary changes in the private rights and properties of individuals without the consent of the person concerned. Judges have no powers to create an offence, on discretionary grounds, without valid evidence in the sources. There is, moreover, no recognition in Islam of any privileged individual or class of individuals, and no one, including the head of state, enjoys any special immunity before the law. Everyone is accountable for what they do, and all one competent individual is normally entitled to do in respect of another is to offer him good advice (*naṣīḥa*).[6]

The Sharī'a also imposes limits on government power in respect to taxation and the manner in which taxes are collected and expended. Taxation must consequently aim at the minimum of what is deemed necessary to facilitate maintenance of law and order and must under no circumstances deprive the taxpayer of his essential needs. Tax is basically levied on profitable assets, a time period of one year or what may be necessary for the yield to materialize must be allowed, and all tax as a matter of principle must be moderate.

Modern constitutional law is entrenched in the idea of commitment to the rule of law and the imposition of limits on the coercive power of government, protection of civil liberties, and accountability in government. In this sense, constitutionalism is in substantial harmony with the value structure of Islam. Contemporary constitutions tend to embody, to a large extent, organized forms of consultation and *bay'a*, and laws and rules that are duly ratified by the people's elected representatives may be seen as the embodiment of the command of the *uli'l-amr*. Should there be a part or section in the constitution of a Muslim country that stands in disharmony with any of the basic values or principles of Islam, only that part should be isolated and not the whole of the constitution. For after all, one can find in the works and textbooks of *fiqh* rulings and opinions that may represent a mistaken interpretation, or an error in *ijtihād*, in which case only that opinion should be isolated, but not the whole of an otherwise valuable endeavor. This is, in fact, one of the basic guidelines of the theory of *ijtihād*; a ḥadīth on the subject entitles a person who makes an honest error in *ijtihād* to a reward, but one who reaches the correct result is entitled to two such rewards.

Chapter 2

Biblical Perspectives on Divine Justice and Political Authority

Ellen F. Davis

"Justice" is one of the root concepts of scripture, and so, as with most root systems, it is complex and multibranched. Justice is first of all a defining characteristic of Israel's God, and further, it is a divine gift that enters into our world through the human agents of God. Further yet, justice is a divine demand—or turning that concept around, it is a discipline, one that every servant or child of God, and the people of God as a political body, are expected to take on and follow for a lifetime: "*Tsedeq tsedeq tirdof;* Justice, justice you shall pursue" (Deut. 16:20). Perhaps the single most memorable thumbnail sketch of divine justice comes from the poet-prophet Isaiah of Jerusalem. In "the vision of Isaiah," justice is what makes God conspicuous in the world (*Niqdash bitsedaqah*, Isa. 1:1): "Lofty is YHWH of Hosts in justice (*mishpat*), and the Holy God is manifested-as-holy in righteousness" (Isa. 5:16). In Isaiah's eyes, justice and righteousness constitute God's holiness; that is, they mark as utterly distinct from the ordinary this One whom Isaiah designates *Qedosh Yisra'el*, the Holy One of Israel. The antonym of *qadosh*, "holy," is *hol*, "profane," and it is noteworthy that the latter is not a negative term; it simply means "ordinary." God's incomparable holiness is then God's absolute extraordinariness. These lines from Isaiah appear in the context of an oracle of doom. In the condensed language of poetry, they point to the core problem of our existence: If righteousness and justice make God completely distinctive, the ordinary unholy state of our existence is unrighteousness, injustice. The central problematic of Isaiah's prophecy, and perhaps that of the Bible altogether, is how to reverse our "normal" condition of injustice. The Bible as a whole expresses Israel's and the church's centuries-long yearning for something hoped for, something glimpsed in a vision but not yet clearly seen: "new heavens and a new earth according to God's promise, where righteousness is at home" (2 Pet. 3:13; cf. Isa. 65:17).

Yet already with my translation of that verse from Isaiah I have oversimplified the biblical understanding of divine justice. *Yigbah YHWH Tsva'ot bammishpat*, "Lofty is YHWH of Hosts in justice." I might equally have rendered that, "Lofty is YHWH of Hosts in judgment." But that also is an undertranslation. The only accurate translation in English is too awkward to gain acceptance: "Lofty is YHWH of Hosts in justice/judgment"—for the Hebrew word *mishpat* is double-sided; it is translated sometimes as "justice," sometimes as "judgment." Both are correct, and the problem is that, in English, we must choose between them, thereby missing the essential relationship between the two. Most broadly speaking (taking into account the whole wide semantic range of the word *mishpat*), the term here designates God's signature style. *Mishpat* is God's modus operandi, the characteristic and recognizable way God works with and in the world, both in the present and also in that indefinite future moment to which so much of the poetry (especially) of the Bible is oriented, when God will "come to judge (*lishpot*) the earth. He will judge the world with righteousness (*tsedeq*) and the nations equitably (*bemêsharîm*)" (Ps. 98:9, cf. 96:13). As these few lines suggest, the two sides of *mishpat*, judgment and justice, are indivisible. When God does *mishpat* in the "judgment" sense—"when he comes to judge the earth"—God does it "with righteousness," *tsedeq*, the word that is so often paired with and inseparable from *mishpat* in the "justice" sense.

I stress the bivalence of the word *mishpat*, because it seems to me that this bit of Hebrew philology highlights by way of contrast the difficulty that many in my own North American church (at least) have in reckoning with the biblical concept of justice. Most of us view "judgment" and "justice" as two different, even incompatible, theological concepts. Each of us, depending on our theological orientation and ecclesial location, is likely to focus on one or the other of those concepts, but not both. Christians in the contemporary West tend to be oriented either to God's judgment and the end time, *or* they are oriented to social and political justice. Yet for the Isaiah tradition—a vast expanse of prophetic vision, with multiple contributors, stretching over two centuries—such a separation between judgment and justice is nonsensical. One might say that the Hebrew language requires that the two aspects of *mishpat* be held together, but equally the scope of the vision set forth here requires it.

It is especially apt for us, meeting in this city (Washington, D.C.), to begin with the vision of Isaiah of Jerusalem, because he was a highly political figure who (in the eighth century BCE) served as adviser to two kings. So-called First Isaiah is also perhaps the greatest poet of social justice in the Bible.[7] In a divine love poem, God offers heartsick witness to the ruinous injustice spreading through Israel like an invasive vine wrecking a vineyard that has been tended with exquisite care: "The vineyard of YHWH of Hosts is the house of Israel and the population of Judah.

He planted his delights and waited eagerly for *mishpat*—and look! *mispach*, bloodshed; for *tsedaqah*, righteousness—and look! *tsa'aqah*, a wretched cry" (Isa. 5:7). Further, Isaiah is a political visionary in the fullest sense; his vision for the Davidic monarchy far transcends present experience and ordinary reality, yet does so without ceasing to be political: "For a child is born to us, a son is given to us; and the authority rests on his shoulder. They call his name 'Wondrous Counsellor,' 'Mighty God,' 'Father Forever'—denoting abundant authority and peace without end upon the throne of David and upon his kingdom, to establish it and to sustain it in justice and in righteousness, now and forever. The zeal of YHWH of Hosts will accomplish this" (Isa. 9:6–7). This superpolitical vision—a glimpse of the best that might yet be achieved in the political realm—serves a hortatory function. By showing human kingship conformed to divine sovereignty, it implies that any king who claims to be the anointed of God should be living in, or at least living toward, conformity to God's justice and righteousness. If this vision of an ideal kingship is *super*political, there may be also a *supra*political vision in the book of Isaiah as a whole, for it stretches our imagination to the end of the world as we know it. Indeed, from God's perspective, that end may not be far off, for the divine speech employs a grammatical form denoting imminence: "*Hin*ᵉ*nî*, look! I am about to create new heavens and a new earth" (Isa. 65:17)—a new reality "where righteousness is at home," as the Second Letter of Peter recapitulates that super- and suprapolitical vision given through Isaiah (2 Pet. 3:13).

I think it is fair to say that, along with the Psalms, the Isaiah tradition sets the terms for the wide range of biblical thinking about divine justice and political sovereignty. The biblical writers over centuries explore, on the one hand, the potential for justice's "homecoming," how it might enter into and operate within the human sphere. On the other hand, they relentlessly expose the lack of justice within Israel's political institutions and even most of its religious institutions. Interestingly, it is possible to trace a rough genre difference among the various biblical treatments of justice. It is primarily the poets—prophets and psalmists—who set forth hope-filled visions of justice residing in our world. The biblical poets are not naïvely optimistic; Isaiah and others often denounce the absence of justice. Nonetheless, the fullest exposé of unjust human political institutions occurs in narrative texts, and primarily in the long historical composition known as "the Deuteronomistic History."[8]

Poetic and narrative representations of Solomon's reign, popularly famed for its justice, illustrate something of the difference between the two genres of biblical literature—a difference that points to tension as well as complementary perspectives within biblical tradition. Psalm 72 is the great prayer for royal justice within the Bible. Significantly, it is the only Psalm whose superscription makes a specific association with Solomon. Here justice is conceived as divine gift: "O God, your *mishpat*—give it to the king, and your righteousness (*tsedaqah*) to the king's son, that he may judge your people with righteousness and your vulnerable ones with justice" (Ps. 72:1–2). Ideally speaking, the divine gift of justice enables the king to judge in a way that mimics God's own exercise of *mishpat*.

The narrative account of Solomon's reign gives a mixed report about the extent to which this prayer for Solomon was actually fulfilled. Most famously, the story of the two prostitutes fighting over the one surviving baby attests to Solomon's perspicacity (1 Kings 3:16–28). That story, which is the high-water mark of royal *mishpat*—judgment and justice—in biblical narrative, ends thus: "And all Israel heard of the *mishpat* that the king had accomplished-in-judgment (*shafat*), and they were in holy fear of the king, for they saw that the wisdom of God was within him, to do *mishpat*" (1 Kings 3:28). This instance of Solomon's good judgment occurs near the beginning of the account of his reign. Reading on, one encounters further references to his international reputation for wisdom, but the narrative reveals also deep, even fatal flaws in his exercise of justice (e.g., 1 Kings 5:14, 10:1–9). The outstanding instance of Solomon's injustice is the imposition of forced labor on his own people, resulting in such widespread misery that at his death a gathering of "the whole congregation of Israel" appeals thus to his son Rehoboam (1 Kings 5:13 [Hebrew 5:27]): "Your father made our yoke hard to bear—and you, now, lighten your father's labour-load and his heavy yoke that he set upon us, and we will serve you!" (1 Kings 12:4). Rehoboam tragically misses his opportunity for justice, and so the united kingdom of David and Solomon dissolves. Henceforth the history of the monarchy as recorded in the book of Kings is mostly a tour of the rogues' gallery, concluding with God's just judgment on the kingdoms of Israel and Judah: destruction of their elegant capital cities and exile of their peoples. The failure of royal *mishpat* (justice) makes it necessary for God to exercise *mishpat* (judgment) against the political-religious establishments of Israel and Judah.

The narrative tradition of the Bible in both testaments shows that the divine gift of justice is most often refused or perhaps not even recognized as a possibility by those who are meant to serve as God's representatives in the exercise of public responsibility. That point is perhaps most sharply made near the very end of the narrative tradition, in the book of Acts. The story of Paul's dealings with the Jewish and Roman authorities is the most fully articulated New Testament account of the operations of the political system. With respect to the question of divine justice, the crucial moment comes in Paul's interview with the Roman governor Felix. According to the evangelist and narrator Luke, Felix had an interest in religious matters; he "was rather well informed about the Way," as the new Christian faith was called (Acts 24:22). So when Paul was being kept in custody in Caesarea, Felix sent for him "and heard him speak concerning faith in Christ Jesus. And as he discussed justice, self-control (*enkrateia*), and the coming judgment, Felix became frightened" and sent Paul away (Acts 24:24–25 [NRSV]). Note that Paul's summary of the faith covers the same territory that I find included within the single Hebrew word *mishpat*: both justice (*dikaiosuni*) and the coming judgment (*krima*). It is a good Hebraic catechism.

Moreover, Paul introduces a third element into his teaching: *enkrateia*, "self-mastery." One could argue that the ordering of the three is deliberate, that self-mastery mediates between justice and the coming judgment. This would be a good biblical argument, for as I have discussed, the tradition steadily affirms that justice is far from a natural inclination. Though justice may ideally be received as a gift, as divine wisdom manifested in human life, nonetheless it must be practiced as a discipline (1 Kings 3:28). In other words, justice is always a learned behavior and must be relearned, year by year and generation by generation, not only by leaders but also by ordinary people in any community or society that purports to be just. Within biblical tradition the book of Proverbs gives the fullest account of education for justice, as its opening lines indicate: "The proverbs of Solomon son of David, king of Israel—for [the purpose of] knowing wisdom and discipline, for seeing into insightful speech; for acquiring a discipline of success: righteousness and *mishpat* and equity" (Prov. 1:1–3). The formula for success here is nothing like what we might expect to find in our own cultures. The "discipline of success," as the sages of Israel conceive it, has nothing to do with networking, dressing well, having a good investment portfolio, going to or teaching at prestigious schools—the various indices of success in our culture. In sum, success does not mean self-aggrandizement, maximizing and displaying my own power. Rather it means "righteousness and *mishpat* and equity." My success is judged on the basis of whether it secures the well-being of the other.

Moreover, this formulation of "a discipline of success"—*tsedeq ûmishpat ûmêsharîm*—does not stand alone within the tradition. It is noteworthy that exactly the same three terms occur in the lines we heard earlier from Psalm 98. The sage, the wisdom teacher of Proverbs, is quoting the psalmist: "[God] will judge (*yishpot*) the world with righteousness (*tsedeq*) and the nations equitably (*bemêsharîm*)" (Ps. 98:9). So the psalmist's description of God's judgment is present as a subtext within the sage's teaching, and the implication of its presence is this: Success means using our power in the same way God does, to advance the cause of those whose hands are weaker, whose voices are more muted than our own.

The book of Proverbs includes within the scope of its concerns and its audience both the powerful and the vulnerable: on the one hand, kings and their agents; on the other, the peasants who are subject to their actions. The genre of proverbial speech was part of the official literature cultivated by ancient Near Eastern monarchs; likely the proverbs were used in the education of young rulers and courtiers. Accordingly, there are several thumbnail sketches of just kingship: "Charmed speech is on a king's lips; in judgment his mouth does not commit treachery" (Prov. 16:10), and "It is an abomination for kings to act wickedly, for with righteousness is a throne established" (Prov. 16:12). "With righteousness is a throne established"—again, the language here is drawn from the psalms, which repeatedly assert that God's throne is established with righteousness and justice (Ps. 9:8, 89:15, 97:2). Here, as in Isaiah, the ideal for human kingship is conformity with the reality of divine kingship.

The biblical sages resemble the prophets in keeping that ideal alive while not propagating it naïvely. Their tradition preserves candid snapshots of bad monarchs: "A growling lion and an attacking bear is a wicked ruler over a helpless people. A leader lacking insight abounds in acts of oppression, but those who despise selfish gain prolong their days" (Prov. 28:15–16), and "When the righteous abound, the people rejoice; but when someone wicked is in power, a people groans" (Prov. 29:2). Altogether, the biblical view of political authority as represented in both testaments is realistic yet not cynical, and the fact that the tradition has that temper carries implications for the church's practice. If there is in the political sphere at least as much evil as good, then that is all the more reason to keep educating for justice, and also praying for it. It is a regular part of the fixed liturgy in Anglican tradition to pray "for those in positions of public trust, that they may serve justice, and promote the dignity and freedom of every person."[9] Doubtless many Christians regard such prayer with a measure of skepticism, even in the very act of saying "Amen." Certainly the news that comes from a city such as this one regularly makes prayer for justice in government seem like wishful thinking. Yet as we have seen, there are strong biblical grounds for praying thus. Moreover, if offered sincerely, those prayers may serve as a hedge against the sin of cynicism, the willful foreclosing of hope for ourselves and others. Some time ago, when a political scandal was receiving much press coverage here (frankly, I have forgotten which scandal it was), one of my friends, a citizen of another country, commented, "You Americans are so naïve. At home we just assume that anyone who runs for public office is a scoundrel." If we are tempted to reconcile ourselves to that assumption, then our continued prayers for those in public authority should move us to recognize that our situation is a tragic one. It is a tragedy of national and international proportions if we have become inured to the loss of a godly vision of justice in the political sphere.

Since we are meeting in this particular center of government, I will end by citing one especially moving expression of such a vision, located just a couple of miles away. Abraham Lincoln's words from his second inaugural address (1865), inscribed on the walls of his memorial, bespeak a hope for justice, a hope tested and refined perhaps through the most costly of American wars: "With malice toward none; with charity for all; with firmness in the right, as God gives us to see the right, let us strive on to finish the work we are in; to bind up the nation's wounds; . . . to do all which may achieve and cherish a just and lasting peace, among ourselves, and with all nations." The political visions of the biblical prophets, sages, and psalmists support us in the conviction that embracing such a vision, even against much evidence, is not naïve. Rather it represents a commitment to what "the zeal of YHWH of Hosts," working through human faithfulness, has yet to accomplish among us (Isa. 9:7).

Chapter 3

Scriptural Texts

3.1 Two Psalms

Ellen F. Davis

Psalm 72

> Psalm 72 conveys a positive vision of how Israel should be: a "kingdom of right relationships," the pattern set at the apex of political authority by the just judgment and compassionate priorities of the king himself. Through the king, God's justice is channeled into human society.[10]

This is the last of many psalms associated with the royal house of David, which cluster in the first half of the Psalter; an appended verse reads, "Here end the prayers of David son of Jesse" (20).[11] The psalm shows what might be called an "ecological" view of justice; it promotes a vision of *tsedeqah* ("right relationship, righteousness") and *shalom* ("well-being, peace") operative in both political and agricultural spheres. A challenge for interpreters, perhaps especially those in the contemporary context, is to discern the connection between those two spheres as envisioned by the psalmist.

Early in the psalm, royal justice is imaged as being "like rain on mown grass" (6), a metaphor that touches the core of existence in the semiarid uplands of Israel. By the end of the psalm, that metaphor is literalized as prayer for "an abundance of grain in the land; at the top of the mountains may it wave" (16). The connection between the metaphor of the king's justice, welcome as rain, and the literal reality of a maximally productive land is made by the psalm speaking of royal ideology or theology on two levels of operation: suprapolitical, or "mythic," and sociopolitical.

Several phrases seem exaggerated, pointing to a view of kingship that exceeds historical reality: "May they fear you as long as the sun exists, while there is a moon" (5), "May [the king's] name be forever, enduring with the sun" (17). Evocation of the heavenly bodies suggests the view, common throughout the ancient Near East, that the monarch is (or should be) the lynchpin of the cosmos, the "sacred bridge" connecting the divine and human realms. In Jerusalem, that ideal was represented in the placement of the royal house immediately adjacent to God's house, the temple; the king was to be a channel through which divine blessing flowed from God, into the sacred precinct, and out into the land in an almost physical sense. It is noteworthy that, while the topography of Jerusalem appears quite dry to ordinary eyes, it was in the sight of the psalmists well watered: "There is a river whose streams make glad the city of God" (Ps. 46:5); pilgrims drink "from [God's] torrent-stream of delights" (Ps. 36:9).

At the level of social-political-economic ideology, the king is viewed as the instantiation of divine wisdom. As in the story of Solomon's judging between two women who claimed one surviving baby, the king was charged by God to be the prime executor of justice in the land (1 Kings 3:16–28). The biblical narratives of kingship regularly show first early promise that a given monarch might fulfill that charge, then steady erosion of this hope. David first came to power supported by "everyone in distress and everyone in debt and everyone who was embittered" (1 Sam. 22:2)—all the peasants for whom Saul's administration of justice had failed. A generation later, David's son Absalom gained support for his own rebellion in exactly the same way, probably from children of peasants who had once supported his father (2 Sam. 15:1–6). Another generation later, Rehoboam had an opportunity to relieve the acute pressure his father, Solomon, had imposed on the peasant farmers through forced labor. When he failed to take that opportunity, the new king was abandoned by the ten tribes of the northern kingdom of Israel (1 Kings 12:1–19).

Multiple stories show that Israel's peasant farmers were acutely aware of the king's responsibility for justice and directly responsive to failures of justice. In an agrarian economy, when justice fails in high places peasants become highly vulnerable to land loss. The prominent inclusion in every biblical law code of provisions to limit long-term indebtedness, land forfeiture, and debt slavery makes clear that this complex of ills was a systemic problem that ancient Israel never overcame (Exod. 21:2–11; Lev. 25:13–55; Deut. 15:1–18). However, the poet of Psalm 72 shows what "the system" could look like: justice flowing from God, through the Israelite king and out into a land prospering under the hand of a people free to work it and committed to its care, generation after generation. Even foreign rulers honor this just monarch (11). The idea that fruitful fields require a just government on national and international scales gains power today in light of the contemporary global agricultural crisis resulting from industrial production practices that increasingly impoverish small farmers, damage or exhaust local water supplies, and drastically reduce the fertility of the arable soil.

In Christian tradition, this psalm, like others referring to Davidic kingship, is seen to be redolent with messianic imagery. The tribute of other kings (10–11) comes to be interpreted as a typological foreshadowing of the homage of the magi (Matt. 2:1–12), and the royal name enduring forever (17) as the name of Jesus.[12] The blessing of the nations is held to be realized in the universal fellowship of believers who confess this name, for which ever greater universality is desired; and it is in submission to his spiritual kingship that true and lasting justice is found. Implicit in such an account is the deeply held Christian belief that humans cannot simply grasp justice for themselves but must receive it as a gift of grace in love. The Old Testament too makes it clear that justice is not the normal modus operandi for humans but is rather behavior that must be taught by God. However, too sharp a contrast with Islamic views should not be drawn here: Christians also believe that it is a natural inclination of humans to long for justice and to accept it when it is given.

Of Solomon

72[1] Give the king your justice, O God,
and your righteousness to a king's son.
2 May he judge your people with righteousness,
and your poor with justice.
3 May the mountains yield prosperity for the people,
and the hills, in righteousness.
4 May he defend the cause of the poor of the people,
give deliverance to the needy,
and crush the oppressor.
5 May he live while the sun endures,
and as long as the moon, throughout all generations.
6 May he be like rain that falls on the mown grass,
like showers that water the earth.
7 In his days may righteousness flourish
and peace abound, until the moon is no more.
8 May he have dominion from sea to sea,
and from the River to the ends of the earth.
9 May his foes bow down before him,
and his enemies lick the dust.

10 May the kings of Tarshish and of the isles
render him tribute,
may the kings of Sheba and Seba
bring gifts.
11 May all kings fall down before him,
all nations give him service.
12 For he delivers the needy when they call,
the poor and those who have no helper.
13 He has pity on the weak and the needy,
and saves the lives of the needy.
14 From oppression and violence he redeems their life;
and precious is their blood in his sight.
15 Long may he live!
May gold of Sheba be given to him.
May prayer be made for him continually,
and blessings invoked for him all day long.
16 May there be abundance of grain in the land;
may it wave on the tops of the mountains;
may its fruit be like Lebanon;
and may people blossom in the cities
like the grass of the field.
17 May his name endure forever,
his fame continue as long as the sun.
May all nations be blessed in him;
may they pronounce him happy.
18 Blessed be the LORD, the God of Israel,
who alone does wondrous things.
19 Blessed be his glorious name forever;
may his glory fill the whole earth.
Amen and Amen.
20 The prayers of David son of Jesse are ended.

Psalm 82

Psalm 82 is a unique and surprising psalm, portraying divine justice dramatically through the scene of God's confronting other members of the "congregation of El," that is, the divine assembly (a concept rarely evoked in the Bible). The point of the confrontation is that rendering just judgment and thus granting deliverance to the poor and defenseless is the indispensable and nonnegotiable criterion by which the true God is recognized and acknowledged, in Israel and "among all the nations."

This psalm is unique in that its setting is the divine council, a mythic concept at home in the ancient Near East but only rarely evoked in the Bible. When it is evoked, it seems to be done so for its shock value. The psalmist uses it to make a point in the strongest possible terms: that justice is fundamental to God's "identity" and self-manifestation to humanity. The verb *shafat* ("exercise judgment, do justice") occurs four times. First, Israel's God "exercises judgment in the midst of the divine beings" (1). Further, justice is the substance of the challenge he addresses to them: "How long will you judge unjustly?" (2); "Do justice for the poor." (3). But they fail to rise to the challenge: "They don't know; they don't discern." The consequences of their darkness are so great that "all the foundations of the earth are shaken" (5).

The message of this remarkable psalm, with its risky rhetoric teetering on the edge of pagan myth, is that the great differential in the cosmos is between the proper working of the world when the powerful are responsive to the claims of justice and the fundamental threat to the whole created order when they are not. Therefore the gods who do not "get it" are deposed, toppled from their eminence: "You will die like a human, fall like one of the rulers" (7). God's pronouncement of doom in the heavenly realm is obliquely addressed to us humans; the powerful among us are subject to the same judgment as the fallen deities.

A human voice erupts suddenly at the end of the psalm: "Rise, O God; judge the earth! For you are the One who will inherit all the nations" (8). That demand expresses the deep longing that generates—or perhaps is receptive to—such a strange vision of the divine. The longing for God's just kingdom has intense and lingering resonance in Christian scripture and prayer, ringing through the Lord's Prayer ("Your kingdom come") and persisting to the penultimate verse of the New Testament, which is another urgent plea: "Come, Lord Jesus!" (Rev. 22:20).

A Psalm of Asaph

82 1 God has taken his place in the divine council;
in the midst of the gods he holds judgment:
2 "How long will you judge unjustly
and show partiality to the wicked? *Selah*
3 Give justice to the weak and the orphan;
maintain the right of the lowly and the destitute.
4 Rescue the weak and the needy;
deliver them from the hand of the wicked."
5 They have neither knowledge nor understanding,
they walk around in darkness;
all the foundations of the earth are shaken.

6 I say, "You are gods,
children of the Most High, all of you;
7 nevertheless, you shall die like mortals,
and fall like any prince."
8 Rise up, O God, judge the earth;
for all the nations belong to you!

3.2 Twelve Verses from the Qur'ān

Mustansir Mir

There are more than fifty verses in the Qur'ān on justice and rights; all occur in short passages and none seem to summarize the rest. Hence a selection of verses needs to be discussed in order to convey the substance of the Qur'ānic perspective on the subject. The first two verses (al-Nisā' 4:58, 59), the *āyāt al-umarā'*, or rulers' verses, designate justice as an obligation of rulers and refer to a duty of the ruled to obey just rulers and those who manage community affairs in accordance with the Qur'ān and the exemplary guidance (Sunna) of the Prophet. These verses also characterize justice as an integral part of *amāna*, the trust of governance. The following ten verses visualize justice in three domains: justice to oneself, justice in one's relationship with God, and justice to one's fellow humans. The first two domains are indicated in al-An'ām 6:152, al-Ṭalāq 65:1, and al-Baqara 2:229, whereas the last domain is the theme of a larger number of verses. The three clusters of verses also serve to determine the basic attributes of the Qur'ānic conception of justice, its sphere of application, and its near total commitment to impartiality.[13]

The Qur'ān offers no explicit definition of either "justice" or "rights," yet these are by no means unknown concepts in the scripture. It is recognized that human beings have an innate understanding of fairness, and the Qur'ānic imperative to establish a just basis for action therefore involves a constant reminding or refreshing of the memory, *dhikr*. Law in the Qur'ān is not mere prescription, but intimately linked to—indeed a subset of—ethics (al-Nisā' 4:135) and is typically expressed in hortatory and admonitory modes. The call to justice is an invitation to explore its meaning in relationship to practical situations; indeed, the Qur'ān is averse to theorizing in isolation from practice. The purpose of its injunctions is to bring justice through a moral reform that is built on *taqwa*, self-restraint through the reverential fear of a merciful and just God (al-Mā'ida 5:8).

Although not available as an abstract definition, but rather cast as an invitation, the Qur'ānic understanding of justice is not without substance. A just order is one that is properly ordered in mutuality and equilibrium, where each element is in its proper and bounded place (al-Ṭalāq 65:1; al-Baqara 2:229). There must be reciprocity between rights and duties, between humans as recipients and as agents of fair dealing; a key term in the Qur'ānic vocabulary of justice is that of the *mīzān*, the "balance" (al-Ḥadīd 57:25; al-Muṭaffifīn 83:1–3).

In some ways, it may appear that the Qur'ānic balance is weighted differently from that of post-Enlightenment thinking about justice. Rooted in a God-oriented emphasis on an ethic of obedience to duties (al-Nisā' 4:59), it can be argued that in the Qur'ān human rights arise from, and in this respect are secondary to, obligations owed to God and, under God, to other humans. Important in this regard is the concept of *amāna*, "entrustment," in the sense of something that belongs to somebody else but is given temporarily into one's keeping with a recognition that it will need to be returned eventually to its owner (al-Nisā' 4:58). If all fulfill this entrusted accountability by carrying out their duties, justice will be established as the rights of all are upheld. Thus, in most cases, rights and duties are correlative in the Qur'ān, though some human rights—for example, the right to inheritance, or maintenance of a family—have an existence of their own irrespective of the fulfillment of obligations. Human rights and obligations (*ḥaqq al-'abd*) alike, though, are subject to the *ḥaqq Allāh*, the rights of God, which are also God's prerogatives exercised over humans; God Himself owes no obligation to creatures.[14]

al-Nisā' 4:58, 59

The two *āyāt al-umarā'* address the rights and responsibilities of those who are "in charge of affairs" (*uli'l-amr*). The phrase refers to those who "have" authority rather than those who "are charged" with authority; it does not necessarily imply a specific designation of people either by God or by the people. The precise interpretation of *uli'l-amr* has been much discussed within the Islamic exegetical tradition: whether, for example, it refers simply to state authorities or in a dual sense to leaders in temporal affairs and to leaders in Islamic law. It is clear, though, that the two verses complement one another: The first speaks of the duties of rulers, while its sequel teaches the need for the ruled to obey the rulers. The second verse is the only occasion that the Qur'ān enjoins obedience to the *amr*, in contrast to the numerous injunctions to obey God and the Prophet.[15]

> 4[58] God commands you to render the trusts to whom they are due, and, when you rule between people, to rule with justice.

> [59] Obey God and obey the Messenger and those charged with authority among you. Should you dispute over a matter among yourselves, refer it to God and the Messenger—if you do believe in God and the Last Day.

al-An'ām 6:152

The injunction in this verse to speak truly (which may refer particularly to giving evidence) immediately follows a reminder of the importance of fair dealing in commercial transactions.

> 6[152] When you speak, speak with justice, even if it be to someone close to you.

al-Ṭalāq 65:1; al-Baqara 2:229

Both these verses locate justice in the due observance of the limits, *ḥudūd*, established by God. This term came to be used technically for the penalties ascribed to certain crimes that were subsequently elaborated on by jurists on the basis of indications in the Qur'ān, but the meaning here is set more broadly within a view of justice as depending on the right ordering of social space. The first verse also makes clear that justice is inbuilt within the human being.

> 65[1] Whoever transgresses the limits of God does verily wrong his own soul.

> 2[229] These are the limits ordained by God. So do not violate them. If any do violate the God-ordained limits, verily they are the transgressors.

al-Nisā' 4:135

This verse exemplifies the exhortation by which the Qur'ān presents the imperative of justice, warning against the waywardness or capriciousness (*hawa*) that can lead believers astray.

> 4[135] O you who believe! Stand out firmly for justice as witnesses to God even if it be against yourselves, your parents and your relatives, and whether it be (against) rich or poor. For God can best protect both. And follow not the desire (of your hearts) lest you swerve. If you distort or decline to do justice, God is well aware of all that you do.

al-Mā'ida 5:8; al-Mumtaḥana 60:8; al-An'ām 6:115

These three verses each link the practice of justice to the purposes of God and the believers' relationship with him. The first, where justice is seen to approximate *taqwa* (reverential fear of God) resonates with the Qur'ānic belief that "good and evil are not equal" and that injustice should be repelled by "that which is better."[16] In the second verse, the negation of divine proscription should be interpreted as a positive exhortation to equitable dealing. The third verse teaches that justice and righteousness constitute God's holiness.

> 5^{8} Let not the hatred of a people make you swerve away from justice. Be just, for it is closest to righteousness, and fear God, for God is well aware of all that you do.
>
> 60^{8} God forbids you not from dealing kindly and justly with those who have not fought you over your faith nor evicted you from your homes. For God loves those who are just.
>
> 6^{115} And the words of thy Lord find fulfillment in truth and justice. None can change His words.

al-Naḥl 16:90

This verse juxtaposes justice, *'adl*, with beneficence, *iḥsān*, which means being good to others. Set alongside and able to modify the formal structures of legal justice, the method of *istiḥsān* enables a flexible approach to be adopted in situations where the rules may lead to unfairness. Whereas justice is mostly regulated by the Sharī'a, *istiḥsān* is not constrained by conformity to formal rules, though it is expressive of the values of the Sharī'a.[17]

> 16^{90} God commands justice and beneficence, and giving (of your wealth) to kith and kin, and He forbids indecency, lawlessness and evil.

al-Ḥadīd 57:25; al-Muṭaffifīn 83:1–3

Both these verses epitomize justice in terms of the balance, *mīzān*, signifying both equilibrium and a standard to judge between right and wrong. This relates also to divine judgment: God will himself set up a *mīzān* to weigh the souls of humans on Judgment Day.[18]

57 25 We sent Our Messengers with clear signs and sent down with them the
book and the balance in order to establish justice among people.

83 1 Woe to those that deal in fraud; 2 when they receive by measure from others, they exact full measure, 3 but when they have to give by full measure to
others, they give less than due.

3.3 Two New Testament Texts

Michael Ipgrave

These two widely disparate New Testament texts are often referred to together as expressing contrasting attitudes to the state—in the first, acceptance of the Roman imperium as an order established by God; in the second, triumphant celebration of its anticipated overthrow by God—yet they also share three features. Both speak specifically to the Christian community; neither text is directly addressed to those with political responsibilities—that would be a development which had to wait until the postbiblical, and especially the post-Constantinian, tradition. The two texts also agree in stressing that a just God is the ultimate source of authority in the political sphere: In Romans, the ruling powers are seen as worthy of obedience because they are part of an order instituted by God, while in Revelation the same powers are to be judged for having usurped the place of God. Finally, both are governed by the fervent Christian hope that the just God would shortly establish his justice through the triumphant coming of Christ to reign in glory; against this horizon, all earthly rule is ephemeral.

Romans 12:14–13:14

In the context of a wider discussion of the life of the church, Paul addresses the responsibilities of members of the church to the state authorities, which are seen as existing by God's permission and to serve God's purposes. The core text that Christian tradition has isolated in discussions of church–state relations is 13:1–7, but this must be relocated in the wider context of the whole passage to understand its significance within Paul's view of Christian discipleship.

The core text's teaching of obedience to governing authorities can be analyzed in three parts: a general injunction to submission (1a), a rationale for submission (1b–5), and a practical illustration of the meaning of submission (6–7).

The general injunction is expressed through a verb in the third person and has a potentially universal reference ("every person," *pasa psuchē*) as its subject; it appears in principle to refer to all human beings, though Paul clearly has the

Roman Christians primarily in mind. The "governing authorities," *exousiai huperchousai*, are in the first place the structures of the Roman Empire, particularly as they impact on the everyday life of Christians. Some commentators have raised the question whether Paul may also be making an allusion to angelic *exousiai* that control the life of nations, but this remains unproven and unlikely. The attitude to the authorities that is taught by the text is that of "subjection." The verb used for this, *hupotassō*, is one of a series in this passage that all derive from the root *tag-*, indicating an overall ordering of affairs. "Subjection" in this sense means the acceptance of a particular place within a scheme of things; it is distinguished from the stronger concept of "obedience" (*hupakouō*), which implies beyond external compliance an interior assent to authority. Thus Paul leaves open a space for dissent in the *forum internum* of the human soul.

The rationale for this subjection is developed in two stages: one that rests directly on a theological foundation (1b–2a), and one that begins from prudential considerations, though the argument here too returns to a theological point (2b–5). In the theologically grounded rationale, the *tag-* roots feature prominently to emphasize an "appointment" by God that reflects the language of the prophetic tradition, for example, Deutero-Isaiah on Cyrus, or Jeremiah on Nebuchadnezzar (Isa. 45:1–7; Jer. 43:10).[19] The argument is based on an acceptance of God's sovereignty and teaches the validation of political authority through its location within the divine order. It is unwarranted to draw from this a general principle of invariable and absolute submission to the state; on the contrary, if the existing authorities transgress this divine order, it would follow that they are no longer worthy of submission. The transition to a prudential argument is marked by the threat of "judgment" (*krima*) in 2b; it is more plausible to interpret this as the judgment of the state rather than that of God. Similarly, the reference to the authority as God's "servant," *diakonos* (4), should be taken to indicate the ruler's subservience to God rather than as a suggestion that through his governance he is carrying out God's will in a form of Christian ministry.[20]

The core text concludes with an insistence on the importance of paying taxes (6–7). The assumption here is that these are in fact being paid by the Roman Christians; Paul seems to be echoing Jesus's teaching on the respective payments due to God and to Caesar.[21] Like Jesus, his argument leads him to a general conclusion that draws a distinction between rendering the outward marks of submission ("taxes," *opheilai*; "revenue," *phoros*) and demonstrating a submission that is from within ("respect," *phobos*; "honor," *timē*); the latter is due especially to God.[22]

If the central verses 13:1–7 are linked to those that provide their preceding and following context, it becomes increasingly implausible to see them as teaching in any abstract sense the divine institution of the state. The entire passage 12:1–13:14 is a description of the transformation that is associated with being God's people in Christian discipleship. Political responsibility is indeed part of this, but Paul also speaks of overcoming evil with good (12:14–21) and of love as fulfilling the law (13:8–10). It is then possible to develop this contextual reading to say that the political authorities of this text are not so much "ordained" by God as they are placed within his order as challenges precisely to test the quality of Christian discipleship.

Such a reading can then also be applied to another key New Testament passage. While Paul's Roman Christians are living peaceably under Roman rule, in the First Letter of Peter the same injunction to submission (*hupotagēte*) is addressed to the church in a situation of suffering, where the challenge to Christians is to continue to practice good in the face of evil (1 Pet. 4:12ff). While Paul himself does not explicitly address the question of what a Christian response should be when the authorities exceed the bounds of God's "ordering," *diatagē* (a silence perhaps not unconnected with his status as a Roman citizen), 1 Peter enjoins passive obedience for the faithful in a situation of "fiery ordeal."[23] Nevertheless, this too is not an absolute submission: We know in particular from the early martyrological record that it did not extend to acquiescence in the state-ordained cult of the divine emperor. Even within the teaching of submission to human authority, limits had to be set to safeguard and honor God's exclusive rights.

In terms of the Christian community's own positioning, the situation addressed by Romans 13 is one where the ruling authorities are seen as "them," but a "them" set within the ordering of "our God" (unlike Rev. 18, where the authorities are a "them" actively opposed to and by "us" and "our God"). When the Roman imperium eventually formed an alliance with the Christian Church, it was then easy to reread the text in that changed situation as referring no longer to "them" but to another aspect of "us." That is to say, it provided a theological validation of "our" state expressed through the ministry of the Christian emperor; in subsequent periods, the authority so endorsed was the "godly magistrate" or, in our own times, the modern democracy seeking a common good.

If Romans 13 is heard as a transformational call to Christians living in the context of a state that, whatever its character, is subject to the higher authority of God, then it seems that three ways of interaction are open to the Christian community. The usual pattern will be one of obedience to the state set within the institution of God, an expression of the peace and order that God wills for his world. Whenever possible, Christians are also called to participation in civil society through the promotion of gospel values and through working together with others to seek the common good, "taking thought for what is noble in the sight of all," *kala enōpion pantōn* (12:17) Exceptionally, Christians will be called on to show disobedience to the state when it steps beyond or acts contrary to the divine institution or closes down the civil space within which the common good may be sought; in the New Testament, this disobedience seems always to be passive for humans; but there may also be times when active resistance is called for.[24]

> 12[14] Bless those who persecute you; bless and do not curse them. [15] Rejoice with those who rejoice, weep with those who weep. [16] Live in harmony with one another; do not be haughty, but associate with the lowly; do not claim to be wiser than you are. [17] Do not repay anyone evil for evil, but take thought for what is noble in the sight of all. [18] If it is possible, so far as it depends on you, live peaceably with all. [19] Beloved, never avenge yourselves, but leave room for the wrath of God; for it is written, "Vengeance is mine, I will repay, says the Lord." [20] No, "if your enemies are hungry, feed them; if they are thirsty, give them something to drink; for by doing this you will heap burning coals on their heads." [21] Do not be overcome by evil, but overcome evil with good.

> 13[1] Let every person be subject to the governing authorities; for there is no authority except from God, and those authorities that exist have been instituted by God. [2] Therefore whoever resists authority resists what God has appointed, and those who resist will incur judgment. [3] For rulers are not a terror to good conduct, but to bad. Do you wish to have no fear of the authority? Then do what is good, and you will receive its approval; [4] for it is God's servant for your good. But if you do what is wrong, you should be afraid, for the authority does not bear the sword in vain! It is the servant of God to execute wrath on the wrongdoer. [5] Therefore one must be subject, not only because of wrath but also because of conscience. [6] For the same reason you also pay taxes, for the authorities are God's servants, busy with this very thing. [7] Pay to all what is due them—taxes to whom taxes are due, revenue to whom revenue is due, respect to whom respect is due, honor to whom honor is due.
>
> [8] Owe no one anything, except to love one another; for the one who loves another has fulfilled the law. [9] The commandments, "You shall not commit adultery; You shall not murder; You shall not steal; You shall not covet"; and any other commandment, are summed up in this word, "Love your neighbor as yourself." [10] Love does no wrong to a neighbor; therefore, love is the fulfilling of the law.
>
> [11] Besides this, you know what time it is, how it is now the moment for you to wake from sleep. For salvation is nearer to us now than when we became believers; [12] the night is far gone, the day is near. Let us then lay aside the works of darkness and put on the amour of light; [13] let us live honorably as in the day, not in reveling and drunkenness, not in debauchery and licentiousness, not in quarrelling and jealousy. [14] Instead, put on the Lord Jesus Christ, and make no provision for the flesh, to gratify its desires.

Revelation 18

This text, in marked contrast to Romans 13, declares that Rome ("Babylon"), with all its economic and commercial power, stands condemned in the light of God's justice. It is less ambiguous than the earlier text and also is far less influential in Christian history. Indeed, it is easy to see Revelation as marginal to the tradition, though its ferocious imagery of destruction and judgment powerfully represents an apocalyptic strand that has resurfaced from time to time.

The text takes the form of a taunting song over the imagined fall of Rome, which is identified with Babylon as the oppressor of God's people. As for the Hebrew prophets, luxury and oppression are linked together, particularly in the "trade in human lives" (13) of slavery. The action of judgment and punishment is throughout taken not by humans but by God, as a punishment for Rome's arrogance, her usurpation of the place of God: "I rule as a queen" (7). There is no call on Christians to revolt or even to disobey, but simply to "come out of her" (4), that is, to be separate from a sinful society, and also to "rejoice" (20) in God's judgment.[25]

> 18[1] After this I saw another angel coming down from heaven, having great authority; and the earth was made bright with his splendour. [2] He called out with a mighty voice,
>
> Fallen, fallen is Babylon the great!
> It has become a dwelling place of demons,
> a haunt of every foul spirit,
> a haunt of every foul bird,
> a haunt of every foul and hateful beast.
> [3] For all the nations have drunk
> of the wine of the wrath of her fornication,
> and the kings of the earth have committed fornication with her,
> and the merchants of the earth have grown rich from the power of her luxury.
>
> [4] Then I heard another voice from heaven saying,
> Come out of her, my people,
> so that you do not take part in her sins,
> and so that you do not share in her plagues;
> [5] for her sins are heaped high as heaven,
> and God has remembered her iniquities.
> [6] Render to her as she herself has rendered,
> and repay her double for her deeds;
> mix a double draught for her in the cup she mixed.
> [7] As she glorified herself and lived luxuriously,

so give her a like measure of torment and grief.
Since in her heart she says,
"I rule as a queen;
I am no widow,
and I will never see grief,"
8 therefore her plagues will come in a single day—
pestilence and mourning and famine—
and she will be burned with fire;
for mighty is the Lord God who judges her.
9 And the kings of the earth, who committed fornication and lived in luxury
with her, will weep and wail over her when they see the smoke of her burning; 10 they will stand far off, in fear of her torment, and say,
Alas, alas, the great city,
Babylon, the mighty city!
For in one hour your judgment has come.
11 And the merchants of the earth weep and mourn for her, since no one buys
their cargo anymore, 12 cargo of gold, silver, jewels and pearls, fine linen, purple, silk and scarlet, all kinds of scented wood, all articles of ivory, all articles
of costly wood, bronze, iron, and marble, 13 cinnamon, spice, incense, myrrh,
frankincense, wine, olive oil, choice flour and wheat, cattle and sheep, horses
and chariots, slaves—and human lives.
14 The fruit for which your soul longed
has gone from you,
and all your dainties and your splendour
are lost to you,
never to be found again!
15 The merchants of these wares, who gained wealth from her, will stand far
off, in fear of her torment, weeping and mourning aloud,
16 Alas, alas, the great city,
clothed in fine linen,
in purple and scarlet,
adorned with gold,
with jewels, and with pearls!
17 For in one hour all this wealth has been laid waste!
And all shipmasters and seafarers, sailors and all whose trade is on the sea, stood
far off 18 and cried out as they saw the smoke of her burning
What city was like the great city?
19 And they threw dust on their heads, as they wept and mourned, crying out,
Alas, alas, the great city,
where all who had ships at sea
grew rich by her wealth!
For in one hour she has been laid waste.

[20] Rejoice over her, O heaven,
you saints and apostles and prophets!
For God has given judgment for you against her.
[21] Then a mighty angel took up a stone like a great millstone and threw it
into the sea, saying,
With such violence Babylon the great city
will be thrown down,
and will be found no more;
[22] and the sound of harpists and minstrels and of flutists and trumpeters
will be heard in you no more;
and an artisan of any trade
will be found in you no more;
and the sound of the millstone
will be heard in you no more;
[23] and the light of a lamp
will shine in you no more;
and the voice of bridegroom and bride
will be heard in you no more;
for your merchants were the magnates of the earth,
and all nations were deceived by your sorcery.
[24] And in you was found the blood of prophets and of saints,
and of all who have been slaughtered on earth.

3.4 Seven aḥādīth

Timothy J. Winter

The aḥādīth (plural; singular, ḥadīth), regarded as the second scripture of Islam, are records of the words and actions of the Prophet Muhammad, as distinct from the word of God recorded in the Qur'ān. They are of immense bulk, totaling perhaps a million separate reports. A subcategory, represented by one of the texts here, is the *ḥadīth qudsī*, "holy ḥadīth," where the Prophet conveys the words of God in a narrative not in the Qur'ān.[26] Although, as with the Qur'ānic text, political matters take up only a small proportion of the ḥadīth literature, the Prophet's situation as a ruler provides them with a context rooted in the real-life situation of a political community.

The aḥādīth demonstrate the transformation brought about in Arabian society through the Prophet's ministry. Against the Arabian background, it is clear that he represented not continuity with what was before so much as radical opposition to his people's previous values: He required his listeners to reject all that had been familiar to them, to shift from one end of the religious spectrum to the other, as they were called to focus their beliefs on the reality of the life that God gave beyond death.

> "The Prophet, upon whom be peace, prayed for pardon for his people, and received the reply: 'I have forgiven them all but acts of oppression, for I shall exact recompense for the one who is wronged, from his oppressor.'"[27]

In the Qur'ān, God is just and requires justice; but he is also forgiving and requires forgiveness; in fact, the Qur'ān's references to the latter property outnumber those on justice by a ratio of approximately ten to one.[28] Islamic theology has not always been clear on how the ensuing tension is to be resolved. "My Mercy outstrips My wrath" is a well-known divine saying, but one that nonetheless is far from abolishing God's wrath.[29] Indeed, a righteous indignation about injustice is integral to the prophetic representation of God's qualities, and from the earliest moments of its revelation the Qur'ān links God's expectations of his creatures to justice toward the weak. Often the same texts are explicitly eschatological, affirming that those who do not uphold God's justice in this world will be at its receiving end in the next.

Indigenous Arab religion can expect a stern retribution, given that its demands are for tribal solidarity, not for the upholding of universal canons of justice.[30] The idol cannot demand justice, only retribution (*tha'r*); the prophetic vocation therefore links the destruction of paganism with the establishment of a code of justice overturning Arab norms by refusing to discriminate between the tribes. This ḥadīth is to be read against the background of clan vendettas: Instead of seeking collective retaliation against a miscreant's tribe, the victim of injustice should appeal to the new law and to recall that all apparent imbalances will have a just settlement at the judgment seat.

> "There is an act of charity (*ṣadaqa*) to be given for every joint of the human body; and for every day over which the sun rises there is a reward of a *ṣadaqa* for the one who establishes justice among people."[31]

Justice (*'adl*) is due balance (*i'tidāl*), impartiality—the same word used to describe the balance of the body's four humors. When these are in balance, right thinking and health are the consequence; when they are not, the Qur'ān speaks of the last day when "their tongues, their hands and their feet will bear witness to what they used to do" (al-Nūr 24:24).

To purify the body from the disorders that both engender and result from sin, a system of worship is gifted in revelation, which culminates in the placing of the forehead, the symbol of human pride and self-oriented thought, upon the earth. The tongue "gives charity" by praising God and by speaking words of reconciliation. The hands do so by working to earn a lawful income and by striving to right wrongs in society. Taken together, the purifying "charity" offered by the parts of the believer's body always has a social impact, the highest aspect of which must be to "establish justice," not only by avoiding unbalanced temptations, but also by working to establish a political order in which justice is safeguarded. Political work is thus conceived as a sacrifice. Political authority is not "sought" in the conventional profane understanding, for a ḥadīth says, "Do not seek political power, for if you obtain it by seeking it, it will be given power over you."[32] This refers to a selfish, egotistic pursuit (*ḥirṣ*) of power rather than to the selfless seeking of power for the sake of the establishment of justice for others.[33] The model is the Prophet, who endangers himself in order to establish God's justice in a feuding Arabia and who ends his life in holy poverty, despite the advantages he could have gained from having been born into the aristocracy:

> "I have forbidden injustice for Myself, and have made it forbidden amongst you, so do not oppress one another."[34]

Here God himself is speaking: This is a so-called holy ḥadīth (*ḥadīth qudsī*).[35] The text establishes that the "political" life is not dissociated from the "religious," not just because the believer should recognize an integrated set of values in all he or she does, but also because by cultivating the political virtues we conform ourselves to the "qualities of God." Hence the often-cited ḥadīth, "Emulate the qualities of God."[36] In this somewhat Platonic understanding, the ground of ethics is in God, whose detailed moral excellences are the source of human values.

The alternative is seen, at least by Ashʿarīs, as a form of dualism. The ruler's subjects may thus recognize his actions as moral by reference to revelation and will consider any injustice as a blasphemy against God. Leaving political decisions to individuals who reject justice as a blessing grounded in a heavenly archetype is to cultivate the mentality of Pharaoh, who "exalts himself in the land" and "divides its people into groups" (al-Qaṣaṣ 28:4).

> "Umm Salama narrated, 'God's Messenger, upon him be peace, never went out of my house without raising his eye to the sky and saying, "O Lord God! I seek refuge in You lest I stray or be led astray, or slip or be made to slip, or cause injustice or suffer injustice, or do wrong or have wrong done to me." ' "[37]

The Prophet, as a saintly being who has "emulated God's qualities," must manifest his justice as well as his mercy. Here Islam and Christianity tread very different paths. The Christ of the Gospels, despite incidents such as the "cleansing of the Temple," preaches a passive witness; the Prophet of Islam also receives persecution patiently, yet strives to establish justice politically, with a mercy that may come through rigor.[38] No doubt this is not the result of a deep clash between ideals, but rather the consequence of incommensurable contexts: Islam too advocates nonconfrontation when believers are oppressed by a massively powerful empire, and Christians have moved away from the pacifism of the Gospels, fearful of the consequences of failing to control tyrants.[39] Yet in the founding stories the differing emphasis is clear. Some Muslims have regarded this as grounds for reproach: According to Shabbir Akhtar, "a Muslim face to face with a Pilate would have given the Roman chap a lot more to do than merely wash his hands," a view that neglects the cautious stance of classical Muslim jurists over resistance against overwhelming odds.[40]

But a characteristically Muslim optimism about the reformability of structures is also, no doubt, at work.[41]

> "God's Messenger (upon him be peace) said: 'Whoever sees something he dislikes in his ruler (*amīr*) should be patient, because whoever leaves the community (*jamāʿa*) even by one fraction, and then dies, has died the death of the Age of Ignorance (*jāhiliyya*).' "[42]

This ḥadīth forms part of a substantial body of revealed texts that seem to insist on political quietism in the face of misconduct by rulers. Unsurprisingly, it lay at the center of a storm of controversy. Most Sunnī scholars maintained the view that once a caliph had been chosen (*ikhtiyār*), it became unlawful for Muslims to rebel against him. For the Ḥanafīs (the most widespread school of law), "if the ruler is oppressive, or corrupt, he is not to be deposed"; this was due to the fear of civil war (*fitna*), the besetting evil of the Age of Ignorance before Islam. This quietism was resisted by the Muʿtazilite and Khārijite sects, by many Twelver Shīʿites, and also by some Shāfiʿī Sunnīs.[43] The institutional separation of the *ʿulamāʾ* class (*ahl al-qalam*), who were funded by their own mortmain endowments (*awqāf*), from the ruling family and its military formations (*ahl al-sayf*), which reached its peak in the Ottoman theory and practice of religious statecraft, nonetheless gave the preachers the duty of condemning the sultan's abuses and defending the interests of the poor and weak.[44]

In the late twentieth century the classical Sunnī view came under fire from radical reformers. Khomeini, departing from Sunnī and Shīʿī tradition, advanced a theory of governance by the religious scholar (*vilāyet-e faqīh*), while in the Sunnī world, individuals frustrated by the religious establishment's reluctance to challenge abuses by postcolonial regimes repudiated the old quietism and advocated militant struggle against governments that, they held, were answerable to Western powers rather than to the values of their own subjects and were hence unworthy of Muslim allegiance. Typically, and ironically, it seems that this sea change in Muslim political thought is the result of Western influence.[45]

> God's Messenger, upon him be peace, then made the rounds of the House, and prayed two *rakʿas* of prayer. Then he went to the Kaʿba, and, holding its door-jamb, said: "What do you think I will do?" They replied: "The son of a brother, and the nephew of a mild and merciful man!" [This exchange was repeated three times.] Then God's Messenger, upon him be peace, said: "I declare, as did Joseph: 'There is no blame upon you this day. God shall forgive you; and He is the most merciful of the merciful.'" And they left the mosque as though they had been raised from their graves.[46]

The tension between justice and forgiveness is given an iconic representation by this account of the Prophet's approach to the defeated Meccans, a moment that is the political culmination of his career. The Meccan elite had sought to assassinate him and to eliminate his fledgling community in Medina. Now helplessly in his power, they must have expected annihilation, in accordance with the accepted Arab principles of vendetta. Instead, they are freed and are not taken to task for their actions. Even Hind, wife of the Meccan leader Abū Sufyān, a woman who had paid for the assassination of the Prophet's uncle Ḥamza and had then chewed on his liver on the battlefield of Uḥud, was not punished. Instead, the Prophet chooses to quote Joseph's words, spoken as he forgave his errant brothers who were finally in his power in Egypt. Such a scene recalls the moral arguments that surrounded Nelson Mandela's Truth and Justice Commission in South Africa.[47] The rule of a corrupt ethnic elite was at an end; the policy of fomenting discord between tribal groups was terminated. As the Prophet goes on to say, "People are all the children of Adam, and Adam is of dust."[48] What purpose would be served by strict justice?

Major symbolic moments in the history of Mecca are often given eschatological significance. The city itself is a sanctuary (*ḥaram*), declared such "on the day God created heaven and earth."[49] As such it stands a little outside human justice. For many jurists, those who seek asylum in the city's mosque may not be dislodged, whatever their crime. And the *ḥajj* is clearly an anticipation of the Judgment, when all shall congregate to stand before God. Muslim eschatology represents the same tension between justice and forgiveness. On the one hand, it insists that "whoever has done an atom's weight of good, or evil, shall see it" (al-Zalzala 99:7–8), for "there is no injustice on that day" (Ghāfir 40:17). Yet on the other hand, justice is tempered. The principle that God's mercy outstrips his wrath dominates the scene, and, as with the conquest of Mecca, the figure who represents the inclusion of forgiveness in God's justice is the Prophet. Just as he offers an amnesty to the sinners of Mecca, Muslim orthodoxy believes that he intercedes for humanity before the judgment seat. Terrified of God's justice, humanity takes refuge beneath the Prophet's banner, as he is the only one who is not saying "Myself! Myself!" Instead, he cries, "My Lord! Save! Save!" and the strict application of God's justice appears to be set aside in favor of mercy. The Muʿtazilites, preoccupied with justice above all other divine qualities, were obliged to reject these aḥādīth.[50] But for mainstream Sunnī sources, it is thus, supremely, that the Prophet becomes "God's Beloved" (*Ḥabīb Allāh*).[51]

> God's Messenger, upon him be peace, said: "I smile because of two men from my nation, who shall kneel in the presence of the Lord of Power. One of them says, 'O my Lord, grant me retaliation for the wrong which my brother did to me.' And God says: 'Give your brother that in which he was wronged.' 'O Lord,' he says, 'none of my righteous works remain.' Then God the Exalted says to the man who made the demand: 'What shall you do with your brother, seeing that none of his righteous works remain?' And he replies: 'O my Lord! Let him bear some of my burdens in my stead!'" And God's Messenger wept, as he said: "Truly, that shall be a fearsome Day, a Day when men have need of others to bear their burdens!" Then he said: "God shall say to one who made the request: 'Lift up your head, and look to the Gardens!' This he does, and he says, 'O my Lord! I see high cities of silver, and

> golden palaces wreathed about with pearls! For which Prophet shall they be, or which saint or martyr?' And he said: 'They belong to whomsoever pays me their price.' 'O my Lord,' he says, 'And who possesses such a price?' 'You possess it,' he replies. 'And what might it be?' he asks, and He says: 'Your forgiveness of your brother.' 'O my Lord!' he says, 'I have forgiven him!' Then God the Exalted says: 'Take your brother's hand and bring him into Heaven.'" Then God's Messenger recited His word: "Fear God, and make reconciliation among yourselves."[52]

The last of the aḥādīth presented here is also an eschatological text, in this case explicitly so as it describes a scenario at the final judgment seat. It starts from the principle that everybody will be required to give restitution to victims for the wrongs they have caused, envisaging in effect a kind of trading of actions in the next world. However, in this text the strict workings of justice are transcended, as somebody with no good deeds to trade in still is granted entry into heaven through his brother's forgiveness. Once again, the metajustice of God is activated through a readiness to forgo retaliation: In Islam, justice is always serious, but mercy can never be set aside.

Adjacent to the doctrine of intercession in the classical theology manuals is the concept of *radd al-maẓālim*, the "Restoration of Wrongs." We shall be burdened, not only with direct punishment from God, but also with the sins that others are relieved of in order to compensate them for our wrongdoing against them. On that day, "God shall take the horned sheep's case against the hornless one."[53] Here, according to this well-attested ḥadīth, humans as well as God have an opportunity to forgive.

Toward the close of the classical Friday sermon, the preacher recites the Qur'ānic passage, "God enjoins justice and goodness" (al-Naḥl 16:90). The first is clearly not sufficient or the second would not have been mentioned. Islam's is a God of justice but also of mercy. The extent to which the latter virtue can override the former in political life can only be defined in a very limited way in books of law. In Islamic legal culture, which grants the judge more discretion than the heavily statutory jurisdictions of the West, the judge has much room for mercy. In the religion of wisdom and compassion, which deeply trusts human beings, it is no surprise that the judge should have been given this privilege. But his responsibility is grave, and if he is to escape God's own rigor, he must first defeat his ego. Sufism, the schoolroom of the selfless virtues, thus becomes the most fundamental juristic science.

Notes to Part I

1. This essay is based on the inaugural Multaqa Sultan Haji Ahmad Shah Lecture, Kuantan, October 14, 2002, an event organized by the Institute of Islamic Understanding, Malaysia.
2. See also the comments on these verses by Mustansir Mir in chapter 3.2 in this volume; al-Nisā' 4:58, 59.
3. E.g., an-Nawawi, Riyadh as-Salīhin, 81:679, in Muhammad Zafrulla Khan, ed., *Gardens of the Righteous* (Manchester: Routledge, 1995), 137.
4. al-Bukhārī, 3:592.
5. See, e.g., Mohammad Hashim Kamali, *Islamic Law in Malaysia: Issues and Developments* (Kuala Lumpur: Ilmiah, 2000), 203–20; and, Kamali, *Freedom of Expression in Islam* (Cambridge: Islamic Texts Society, 1997), 87–106, 212–50.
6. Further comments on *ḥisba* and *naṣīha* can be found in Kamali, *Freedom of Expression in Islam.*
7. It is no coincidence that activist poet-priest Daniel Berrigan is one of Isaiah's more perceptive modern interpreters. See his *Isaiah: Spirit of Courage, Gift of Tears* (Minneapolis, MN: Fortress, 1996).
8. The books of Joshua through Kings.
9. *The Book of Common Prayer*, 390; cf. 384, 387, 820–22.
10. Biblical translations both here and for the New Testament texts later are from the New Revised Standard Version.
11. As in Isaac Watts's hymn: "Jesus shall reign where'er the sun / Does his successive journeys run; / His kingdom stretch from shore to shore, / Till moons shall wax and wane no more."
12. Translations are from Abdullah Yusuf Ali, *The Holy Qur'an: English Translation and Commentary* (Lahore: Shaikh Muhammad Ashraf, 1934), with minor idiomatic modifications by Mohammad Hashim Kamali.
13. Citations to psalms will be made parenthetically in text.
14. Mohammad Hashim Kamali, *Principles of Islamic Jurisprudence* (Cambridge: Islamic Texts Society, 1991), 348, explains the distinction: "The Right of God is so called not because it is of any benefit to God, but because it is beneficial to the community at large and not merely to a particular individual."
15. In Shī'a interpretation, obedience to "God and the Messenger" also involves obedience to the imams.
16. Fuṣṣilat 41:34. The principle of "repelling [evil] by that which is better," *idfa billatī hiya aḥsan*, expresses the Islamic belief that good deeds have the capacity to erase bad deeds and can be applied even to limit the application of just retaliation (*qiṣāṣ*), albeit the latter already has built into

it the limitation of proportionality as compared with the pre-Islamic blood feud.

17. Kamali, *Principles of Islamic Jurisprudence*, 245, translates *istiḥsān* as "equity in Islamic law" but notes a distinction between this and Western conceptions of equity based on natural law: "*Istiḥsān* . . . is an integral part of the Sharī'a, and differs with equity in that the latter recognises a natural law apart from, and superior to, positive law."
18. al-Anbiyā' 21:47; al-A'rāf 7:8–9. Al-Muṭaffifīn 83:1–3 itself leads immediately to a mention of "the Day."
19. "Instituted," *tassō* (1b); "resist," *antitassō* (2a); "appointment," *diatagē* (2a).
20. *Diakonos* is unlikely to have any technical Christian meaning here, and Ernst Käsemann shows that throughout this passage Paul is using the "vocabulary of Hellenistic administration." Käsemann, *Commentary on Romans*, trans. G. W. Bromiley (London: SCM, 1980), 353.
21. Mark 12:17, and parallels—the same verb *apodidōmi* occurs in both the Gospels and the Epistle.
22. *Phobos* and *timē* in the New Testament are generally reserved for God.
23. Acts 16:37, 22:25–28, though against this must be set Philippians 3:20: "our citizenship is in heaven." *Purōsis*—the same word as in Revelation 18 for divine punishment of the enemies of God's people.
24. Even in Revelation 18, the resistance to the state enjoined for humans is passive—though it correlates with an active opposition to Rome on the part of God.
25. Cf. Jeremiah 51:45, where the prophet in God's name summons his people out of Babylon.
26. Other aḥādīth are referred to as ḥadīth *nabawī*, utterances of the Prophet himself.
27. al-Tirmidhī, *Īmān*, 59.
28. Muḥammad Fu'ād 'Abd al-Bāqī, *al-Mu'jam al-Mufahras li-alfāz al-Qur'ān al-Karīm* (Cairo: Dar al-Kutub al-Miṣriyya, 1939), 234, occurrences of the root *gh-f-r*, contrasted with 28, for *'-d-l*. The ḥadīth literature also suggests a major disparity: A. J. Wensinck and J. P. Mensing, *Concordance et indices de la tradition musulmane* (Leiden: E. J. Brill, 1936–88), 4:528–40 (*gh-f-r*); 4:151–55 (*'-d-l*). Despite the crudity of this statistical exercise, the discrepancy is suggestive.
29. al-Bukhārī, *Tawḥīd*, 13; Muslim, *Tawba*, 14.
30. Cf. the pagan tribesman's cry: "I am of Ghaziyya; if she be in error, then I will err; And if Ghaziyya is guided aright, I go right with her!" Toshihiko Izutsu, *Ethico-Religious Concepts in the Qur'ān* (Montreal: McGill-Queens University Press, 1966), 55. This is precisely the "my country right or wrong" of twentieth-century *jāhiliyya*. For Arabian tribalism, see further ibid., 55–72; M. M. Bravmann, *The Spiritual Background of Early Islam: Studies in Ancient Arab Concepts* (Leiden: E. J. Brill, 1972), 67.

31. al-Bukhārī, *Ṣulḥ*, 11.
32. al-Bukhārī, *Aḥkām*, 6; Muslim, *Imāra*, 13.
33. Yaḥyā ibn Sharaf al-Nawawī, *al-Minhāj fī sharh Ṣaḥīḥ Muslim ibn al-Ḥajjāj* (Cairo: al-Maṭba'a al-Miṣriyya, n.d.), 12:207.
34. Ḥadīth *qudsī* narrated by al-Bukhārī, *Aḥkām*, 6; Muslim, *Imāra*, 13.
35. For this genre, see William A. Graham, *Divine Word and Prophetic Word in Early Islam* (The Hague: Mouton, 1977).
36. al-Ghazālī, *Disciplining the Soul*, trans. T. J. Winter (Cambridge: Islamic Texts Society, 1995), 68.
37. Abū Dā'ūd, *Witr*, 32.
38. Étienne Trocmé, "L'expulsion des marchands du Temple," in *New Testament Studies* 15 (1968): 1–17, proposes this as evidence that Jesus had active Zealot connections.
39. Majid Khadduri, *War and Peace in the Law of Islam* (Baltimore: Johns Hopkins University Press, 1955), 135–36.
40. Shabbir Akhtar, *The Final Imperative: An Islamic Theology of Liberation* (London: Bellew, 1991), 45.
41. Cf. Ahmet Davutoğlu, *Alternative Paradigms: The Impact of Islamic and Western Weltanschauungs on Political Theory* (Lanham, MD: University Press of America, 1994), 102: "The necessity of human cooperation has been explained by Muslim thinkers on the basis of the virtue of love rather than the natural feeling of competition as the basic psychological stimulus."
42. Muslim, *Imāra*, 40.
43. Abu'l-Yusr Muḥammad al-Pazdawī, *Uṣūl al-Dīn*, ed. Hans Lins (Cairo: Dār Ihyā' al-Kutub al-'Arabiyya, 1383/1963), 190–91.
44. For medieval Islamic separations of religious and political institutions, see Ilkay Sunar, "Civil Society and Islam," in *Civil Society, Democracy and the Muslim World*, ed. Elisabether Özdalga and Sune Persson (Istanbul: Swedish Research Institute, 1997), 14–15. A few exceptions (usually Sufis) to this rule nonetheless bear mentioning. Perhaps the clearest example is Qāḍī Burhān al-Dīn of Sivas (d. 1398), a religious scholar who by a series of promotions in the state's administration became prince of a sizable territory. Vehbi Cem Aşkun, *Kadi Burhanettin: Sivas sultani* (Eskiflehir: Akdeniz Matbaai, 1964); William Chittick, "Sultan Burhān al-dīn's Sufi Correspondence," *Wiener Zeitschift für die Kunde des Morgenlandes* 73 (1981): 33–45. Other examples would include the Emir 'Abd al-Qādir of Algeria and 'Uthmān dan Fodio in Hausaland.
45. The case is made, for instance, by John Gray, *Al-Qaeda and What It Means to Be Modern* (London: Faber, 2003); also L. Carl Brown, *Religion and State: The Muslim Approach to Politics* (New York: Columbia University Press, 2000), 41: "The political ideology advanced by Ayatollah Khomeini and the political reality of a government actually led by mullahs, represents a sharp break with tradition."

46. Bayhaqī, *Dalā'il al-nubuwwa*, cited in Samīra al-Zāyid, *al-Jāmi' fī al-sīra al-nabawiyya* (n.p.: al-Maṭba'a al-'Ilmiyya, n.d.), 3:465.
47. South Africa's policy was, significantly, largely designed by the country's justice minister, the Muslim jurist Dullah Omar.
48. al-Zāyid, *al-Jāmi' fī al-sīra al-nabawiyya*, 3:464.
49. Ibn Hishām, *Sīrat Rasūl Allāh* (Cairo: Dār al-Fikr, 1980), 2:1257–58. As is so often the case, the parallel with the Jerusalem sanctuary, which was created "before the world," is striking. Geza Vermes, *Jesus the Jew: A Historian's Reading of the Gospels*, new. ed. (London: SCM Press, 2001), 117.
50. 'Abd al-Karīm Tattan and Kaylani, *'Awn al-murīd li-sharḥ Jawharat al-tawḥīd* (Damascus: Dār al-Bashā'ir, 1415/1994), 2:1125.
51. al-Ghazālī, *The Remembrance of Death and the Afterlife*, trans. T. J. Winter (Cambridge: Islamic Texts Society, 1989), 210–16.
52. al-Anfāl 8:1; ḥadīth from al-Ḥākim al-Nīsābūrī, *al-Mustadrak 'alā al-ṣaḥīḥayn* (Hyderabad: Dā'irat al-Ma'ārif al-'Uthmāniyye, 1915), 4:576.
53. al-Ghazālī, *Remembrance of Death*, 200; for the principle of *radd al-maẓālim*, see 198–205.

PART II

Evolving Traditions

What were the pressures that generated the continuing development of Muslim and Christian reflection on justice and rights? As the following presentations by Vincent Cornell and John Langan show, the primary horizons in both traditions were intrareligious conflicts rather than the external presence of the true "religious other." It was the urge to define and contain heresy or schism, the challenge of relating political and religious authority, and—conflating these two—the felt need for unity to be apparent in both church and state, in both *dīn* and *dawla*, that motivated theologians' thinking and writing in this area. Cornell and Langan, respectively, stress that for Muslims the main problem was posed by other Muslims, and for Christians by other Christians.

This point is largely borne out in the four texts of chapter 6, unambiguously so in the first, third, and fourth. Thus Augustine is seen struggling theologically with the political realities of the Donatist schism; al-Ghazālī seeks a way of recognizing and delimiting the scope of heresy within a fiercely contested Islamic space; Luther tries to identify the role under God of political government in a Christendom whose unity is shattered by the Reformation. Only the second text, ibn Lubb's responsum from fourteenth-century Spain, is set in an interreligious rather than an intrareligious context; yet here too the argument is directed toward an internal Islamic disputation, and it is quite possible that no real *dhimmī* is involved, that the "religious other" is just a theoretical construct.

Chapter 4

Religious Orthodoxy and Religious Rights in Medieval Islam: A Reality Check on the Road to Religious Toleration

Vincent J. Cornell

Allah, Allah!
Save the Muslim way of life!
The accursed enemy has overcome us
And Qarmaṭī propaganda has spread throughout the land!

According to several historical sources, this urgent plea was sent in 1058 CE by the ʿAbbāsid caliph al-Qāʾim bi-Amrillah to the Turkish warlord Tughril Beg (d. 1063), the founder of the Seljuq dynasty of sultans. It refers to the capture of Baghdad by forces loyal to the Fāṭimid caliph al-Mustanṣir (d. 1094), a Shīʿite Muslim of the Ismāʿīlī sect, who ruled Egypt, part of the Arabian Peninsula, and a significant portion of the Levant. Upon their conquest of Baghdad, the Ismāʿīlī forces mandated the Shīʿite call to prayer and proclaimed the name of the Fāṭimid caliph in the Friday sermon. The vizier of the ʿAbbāsid caliph and many of his officials were executed in a gruesome manner. More than a century later, ʿImād al-Dīn al-Kātib al-Iṣfahānī (d. 1201), the personal secretary of the Ayyūbid sultan Salāḥ al-Dīn, who eliminated the last vestiges of the Fāṭimid state, wrote of these events: "The *sunna* of [the Fāṭimid general] was a hideous one, and almost extinguished the divine light. This was because he insisted on calling people to follow the bastard in Egypt."[1]

The capture of Baghdad by a Shīʿite army is important because it led to Tughril Beg's reconquest of the city and the establishment of the Seljuq sultanate, which dominated Iran and Iraq for nearly a century. The Seljuq period is important for Islamic political history because it witnessed the legitimation of the sultanate, which became the dominant form of the Islamic state from the eleventh century until modern times. It is also important for economic history because it witnessed the spread of the *iqta'* (parcel) system of land tenure that dominated the rural economies of the Muslim world until modern times. Finally, it was a key period in the establishment of the ideology of Sunnī orthodoxy, which remains important to this day. Although both Muslim and non-Muslim scholars have claimed that there is no orthodoxy in Islam, the concept of Sunnī orthodoxy was central to Seljuq ideology. State (*dawla*), political order (*niẓām*), and religion (*dīn*) were all interconnected under the Seljuqs, and the defense of Sunnī Islam provided a major rationale for Seljuq rule. In Arabic, the term *sulṭān* literally means "holder of power." Typically, a sultan was a person who came to power by force of arms. Hence the office of sultan enjoyed less legitimacy than that of caliph or imam. This is why sultans before the fall of the ʿAbbāsid caliphate in 1258 had to be sanctioned by the caliph and why, even after the fall of the caliphate, the Mamlūk sultans of Egypt kept ʿAbbāsid descendants on hand in Cairo to legitimize their rule. Histories of the Seljuq state make it clear that the sultan was expected to provide five functions in return for his power: (a) to be obedient to Sunnī Islamic principles; (b) to express loyalty to the ʿAbbāsid caliph; (c) to promote social order throughout the realm and protect Muslim lives and property; (d) to patronize Sunnī religious scholarship; and (e) to put down heretics and social deviants, who followed "bad religion" (Persian *bad-dīn*).[2] Historians of the Seljuq period are nearly unanimous in noting that the Seljuq rulers were required to maintain "pure religion" (Persian *pāk-dīn*) and a concept called in Persian *niku-iʿtiqād*, literally "*ortho-doxa*" or "right belief." The historian Mustawfi Qazwini (d. before 1339), who wrote in the Mongol period and looked back on the Seljuq period nostalgically, compared the creedal purity of the Seljuqs with their predecessors and with certain of their successors, whose morals and religion he described as *mulawwath*, literally "sullied."[3] He even described Tughril Beg, who in reality had only a bare minimum of religious knowledge and did not speak Arabic, as "pure of belief and pure of creed" (*iʿtiqād-i pāk wa safa-yi ʿaqidāt*).[4]

The great vizier and organizer of the Seljuq state, Niẓām al-Mulk (d. 1092)—literally, "Organizer of the Kingdom"—was noted for being of "pure religion" and for having a "Muslim heart" (*musalman-dil*).[5] He established madrasas, such as the great Niẓāmiyya madrasas of Nishapur and Baghdad, for the propagation of Shāfiʿī jurisprudence and patronized the Sufis, who were useful to him in spreading Shāfiʿī law, Ashʿarī theology, and Sunnī principles among the public. The first vizier of the Seljuqs, ʿAmīd al-Mulk ("Support of the Kingdom") al-Kundurī (d. 1064), was noted for his doctrinal partisanship (*ta'assub*). He asked Tughril Beg to have Shīʿite Islam cursed from the pulpits of Khurasan. He also asked that a curse be made from the pulpits against Ash'arī theologians. As a methodological sectarian of the Ḥanafī rite, he was strongly biased against Shāfi'ī jurisprudence. For a time, he succeeded in having both Shāfi'ī jurists and Ash'arī theologians banished from Khurasan.[6] After the assassination of the pro-Shāfi'ī vizier Niẓām al-Mulk in 1092, the Ḥanafī of the Seljuq regime launched another inquisition that led to the purge and execution of many Shāfi'ī jurists. The famous Sunnī theologian, Abū Ḥāmid al-Ghazālī (d. 1111), was a product of this environment. The sectarian conflict between Sunnī Muslim and Sunnī Muslim led him to write *Fayṣal al-tafriqa bayn al-Islām wa al-zandaqa* ("The Sword of Discrimination between Islam and Heresy").[7] Despite the fact that the Seljuq era was one of the most influential periods of Islamic history in the development of law, theology, and Sufism, one could still be persecuted or killed for belonging to the wrong faction, having the wrong theology, or following the wrong school of law.

The point of this introduction to the politics of religion in the Seljuq period is to demonstrate that theology and law both matter in Islam and that theological issues cannot be artificially separated from legal and political conflicts. The determination of whether one's religion was "pure" or "soiled" was all too often an issue of policy that was overseen by jurists. This is why the Ḥanbalī jurist and theologian ibn Taymiyya (d. 1328) felt so strongly that religious doctrine should not be adjudicated in courts. When discussing traditional Islamic resources for pluralism, it is important to remember that few if any of the premodern theories of the just state in Islam were realized and that such models represented the hopes and dreams of their authors more than the reality on the ground. Models of the state that corresponded more or less to reality, such as al-Ghazālī's apologia for the sultanate, tended to be exercises in realpolitik that sought to make the best of a bad situation. In the medieval Islamic world as in medieval Europe, rulers were often mercurial, judges often served the interest of their patrons more than the general interest, and officials such as *muftīs*, who were ostensibly independent, could lose their jobs or even their lives if they questioned the system. Islamic history is replete with examples of the misfortunes that befell jurists and religious leaders who became too independent.

The stark and often embarrassing realities of Islamic history are an important corrective to two types of anachronism. The first anachronism is fundamentalism, which artificially collapses the distance between the religious present and the religious time of origin. A typically fundamentalist approach is to take modern concepts such as civil society or human rights and project them back onto the scriptural sources of Islam without regard for accuracy or for institutional developments that would call the anachronistic use of such concepts into question. The sign of the fundamentalist approach is a reified statement about normative religion, such as "Islam supports human rights." Besides ignoring the question of how the concept of right is expressed in the Qur'ān, the Sunna, and Islamic history, such a statement presumes there is a "correct" Islam that is discernible in the scriptures and that the "wrong" Islam of the historical tradition can be ignored. One does not need to read Foucault to realize that this modern version of the Seljuq notions of *pāk-dīn* and *bad-dīn* is a tool of authoritarianism and a product of the politics of knowledge.

The second type of anachronism is apologetics, which similarly takes modern Western concepts such as pluralism or freedom of expression and seeks to find examples of these notions in the writings and practices of the historical tradition of Islam. For example, an apologist could counter my description of sectarian intolerance in the Seljuq period by pointing out that in Mamlūk Egypt a petitioner could consult Ḥanafī, Mālikī, Shāfi'ī, and Ḥanbalī jurists one after the other and follow the decision of whichever jurist one wanted. This is true, but this counterexample does not prove the existence of the Western concepts of pluralism or freedom of expression in Mamlūk Egypt. The same state that maintained tolerance among the schools of Islamic law allowed the exoteric theologian ibn Taymiyya to be persecuted at the behest of the Sufis. Before discussing whether the "right" to religious freedom was present in medieval Islam, one must first understand what the concept of "right" means (both then and now) and how the differences between the medieval Islamic and modern notions of right affect the application of the concept today.

According to John Rawls in *A Theory of Justice*, a conception of right "is a set of principles, general in form and universal in application, that is to be publicly recognized as a final court of appeal for organizing the conflicting claims of moral persons."[8] Although it has sometimes been asserted that premodern Islam did not have a theory of rights, a concept of right can be found in the Qur'ān. One place where such a concept can be found is in the following verse: "Oh humankind! Respect your Lord, who created you from a single soul, and created its mate from it and from which issued forth many men and women. So respect God and the wombs, by which you ask recompense of one another" (al-Nisā' 4:1). In other verses, the concept of right, which is designated by the Arabic term *ḥaqq*, is more explicit, as in the following: "Do not take a human life, which God has made sacred, other than as a right (*illā bi-l-ḥaqq*); this He has enjoined upon you so that you might think rationally" (al-An'ām 6:151). Moral philosophers and legal theorists agree that the concept of right does not stand alone but that it also involves the concepts of duty and obligation. All three of these notions—right, duty, and obligation—are found in the Qur'ānic treatment of rights. The Arabic term *ḥaqq* can mean "right," "truth," or "justice." The idea that all created things possess rights as part of their ontological nature is fundamental to the Qur'ānic conception of justice. As such, the rights that are mentioned in the Qur'ān call forth specific obligations as corollaries to the acknowledgment of their status as a right. The semantic range of *ḥaqq* involves both a *right to* a particular good and a *right against* someone in the pursuit of that good. Both of these notions are implicit in the concept of *'adl*, another term for justice in the Qur'ān. The Qur'ānic meaning of *'adl* corresponds closely to the Aristotelian notion of justice, which carries the connotation of "fairness" or "equity."[9] In a previously published article, I suggested that the Qur'ān affirms the God-given natural rights of life, dignity, and freedom of choice, along with the corollary duty of mercy and the reciprocal obligation of justice.[10]

However, as Jeremy Bentham stated, "Right is with me the child of the law. . . . A natural right is a son that never had a father."[11] Rights in practice do not exist in a vacuum; each right that is enjoyed by a person requires a specific obligation from another. In addition, the granting of a right to a person implies the restriction of the rights of the other—at least to the extent that the other is prevented from violating the rights of the right holder. The mere fact that the concept of right exists in the Qur'ān does not necessarily mean that it has been employed adequately in Islamic practice. Nor does it necessarily mean that the concept of right in Islam means the same thing that it does in Western political philosophy. To make a proper comparison, one must first look at the concept of legal rights in the West, where most of the pioneering philosophical work on rights has been done. A greater understanding of the philosophical notion of legal rights can shed light on apparent contradictions and ambiguities in the treatment of the right of religious dissent in Islam.

For the purposes of this discussion, let us look at just one example of how a philosophically clearer understanding of legal rights can sharpen our understanding of the right of religious freedom in Islam. In the Anglo-American legal tradition, one of the most influential definitional treatments of legal rights can be found in the work of Wesley N. Hohfeld.[12] According to Hohfeld, the phrase "P has a right to X" has four possible meanings. These possibilities are logical possibilities and are not considered culture bound. In contemporary legal theory, they are called Hohfeldian categories:

1. A right may be a *privilege*, or a *bare liberty*. In the context of the right to religious freedom, this means that a Christian subject of an Islamic state has no duty not to go to church on Sunday, or that a Shī'ite subject of a Sunnī state has no duty not to include the phrase "Ali is the Friend of God" in his call to prayer. This is the minimal category of legal rights.
2. A right may be a *claim-right*. In the context of religious freedom, this means that officials of the Islamic state have a duty to allow Christians and Jews to worship as they please. Legal philosophers

further distinguish between claim-rights *in personam* and claim-rights *in rem*. Claim-rights *in personam* are duties that are assignable to particular persons because of a stipulated right, such as the duties incumbent on a signatory to a contract. A treaty or compact that allows Christian subjects of an Islamic state to build churches or sell pork in their own butcher shops is an example of a claim-right *in personam*. Claim-rights *in rem* are duties that are incumbent in principle on everyone. Religious freedom as a claim-right *in rem* would mean that the Islamic state would have an obligation to actively assist Christians or Jews in the practice of their religion. This might include providing state funds for the construction of churches or synagogues or the prosecution of Muslim subjects for desecrating Christian or Jewish places of worship. In Western societies, violations of claim-rights are often punishable by law in this way.

3. A right may involve the ability or *power* of an individual to alter existing legal arrangements. Rights that involve powers are usually powers of office, as in the U.S. president's right to cast a veto, or rights of trusteeship, in which one has the right to act contractually in the interest of another person. In the context of premodern Islamic society, this right may include the power of the sultan to renegotiate the terms of the agreement between the state and the Jewish or Christian *millets,* internally autonomous religious communities. Within a millet, it refers to the power of designated religious leaders to determine the affairs of their followers. In Western democratic societies, this right may potentially come into conflict with rights of individual autonomy, such as freedom of expression.
4. A right may constitute a type of *immunity* from legal change. In the context of religious expression in premodern Islam, this right was most consistently applied with regard to Qur'ānic provisions that allowed the worship of the People of the Book (*ahl al-kitāb*). Interestingly, it was less consistently applied with regard to ḥadīth accounts that mandated respect for the People of the Book and related prohibitions against molestation. Rulers who disrespected the rights of their Muslim subjects tended to treat this right lightly as well, up to Qur'ānic limits.

The claim-right is most commonly regarded as the Hohfeldian category that is closest to the notion of an individual right in political philosophy. A difficulty with Hohfeld's schema, however, is that it is narrow in scope and does not specify the place of moral duties within the concept of legal rights. For example, a well-known verse of the Qur'ān states with regard to religious freedom, "There is no compulsion in religion; true guidance is distinct from error; he who rejects false deities and believes in God has grasped a firm handhold that will never break. God is All-Hearing and All-Knowing" (al-Baqara 2:256). Muslim apologists frequently overlook how ambiguous this verse is. There is no compulsion in religion; however, because true guidance is distinct from error, the believer in an incorrect religion might be expected to find guidance eventually. What happens if she does not do so?

In most interfaith discussions, the phrase "there is no compulsion in religion" is defined as implying a claim-right *in rem*. In this understanding, every Muslim has a moral duty to let a Christian or a Jew practice her religion. However, is this really a claim-right? There is no stipulation as such in the text of the Qur'ān. Furthermore, the remainder of the verse strongly implies that God expects Christians and Jews to see the light and become Muslims. Therefore it is just as logical to conclude that this verse implies a mere privilege or a bare liberty and not a claim-right. Unlike a claim-right, which obliges Muslims to actively support Jews and Christians in the practice of their religion, a bare liberty requires nothing but minimal tolerance or indifference: Christians and Jews are free to practice their religion, but Muslims have no obligation to help them do so. Even more, worship may be construed as the only practice they are entitled to perform. A bare liberty confers no right to build churches or to accommodate religious minorities in specific ways.

The effects of such ambiguities can be viewed historically in the different approaches toward religious minorities in premodern Islamic states. It can also explain the variety of interpretations of the concept of *ahl al-dhimma* (protected or exempted groups) by Muslim jurists. The Ḥanafī jurist Abū Yūsuf (d. 808), who was legal advisor to the caliph Hārūn al-Rashīd and who viewed the rights of *dhimmīs* as claim-rights, was unequivocal in requiring that Jewish and Christian subjects of the ʿAbbāsid state be treated with respect and leniency. The later Muʿtazilite Qur'ān commentator Zamakhsharī (d. 1144), however, saw the right of Jews and Christians to practice their religion as a bare liberty. Not only did he counsel against the use of state resources in constructing and maintaining churches and synagogues, but he also advised treating *dhimmīs* with contempt when they paid their *jizya* taxes, hoping that "in the end they will come to believe in God and His Messenger, and thus be delivered from this shameful yoke."[13] The view of the Muftī of Granada, ibn Lubb (d. 1381), appears to follow Zamakhsharī's logic.[14] For ibn Lubb, too, the right of Jews to practice their religion appears to be a bare liberty and not a claim-right. He differs, however, from Zamakhsharī mainly in being more disengaged. Seeing the infidelity of the

Jews as unlikely to change, he seems unconcerned with their eventual conversion to Islam and instead falls back on the formula of the Qur'ān: "To you your religion and to me mine" (al-Kāfirūn 109:6).

A different interpretation is provided by ibn Taymiyya, who concentrates on the contractual relations between the Islamic state and the *dhimmīs*. In his legal opinions on the subject of religious minorities, ibn Taymiyya takes as a precedent the seventh-century "Covenant of the Caliph 'Umar" with the Christians of Syria. According to the terms of this covenant, the *dhimmīs* of Syria were granted security of their persons, their families, and their possessions, although they did not enjoy the same rights as the Muslims. This stress on the contractual nature of the relations between the Islamic state and its religious minorities suggests that for ibn Taymiyya the primary right of the Christians of Syria was a right of immunity from legal change. In other words, subsequent rulers of Syria were contractually bound by the Covenant of 'Umar and thus lacked the power to change the legal position of the Christians of Syria even if they wanted to do so. But this was not all: The provisions of the contract of immunity also included two specific claim-rights *in personam*. One was the right to demand from the state the ransom of Christian and Jewish prisoners of war along with the ransom of Muslims. This duty of the state was seen as a "most serious obligation" (*'azam al-wājiba*) by ibn Taymiyya, who negotiated with the Tatars to ransom *dhimmī* prisoners as full subjects of the Mamlūk state of Syria. Another claim-right *in personam* was the right of the *dhimmīs* to free themselves from the Covenant of 'Umar and claim equal status with the Muslims if they enlisted in the army of the state and fought alongside the Muslims in battle. This last right was highly unusual for ibn Taymiyya's time and illustrates the close attention that Ḥanbalī jurists like ibn Taymiyya paid to the letter of the law with regard to contractual obligations.[15]

However, ibn Taymiyya was no liberal. He was extremely worried about the effect of religious freedom on the Muslim public and the influence of Christianity on Islam. This can be seen in the following statement by Victor Makari, who summarizes ibn Taymiyya's views on religious minorities as they are expressed in his letters and *fatwās*:

> [The Christians] managed to abscond from dutiful taxation; they intermingled with the rest of the population; they blazed about in an insolent light. They succeeded in occupying positions of power within the high places of government, of financial administration and of national security. They put their experienced skills for profit, and their crafty amiability to work for their self-enrichment to the detriment of the Muslims. . . . The Jews, too, sell wine to the Muslims in Cairo. In the public ceremonies of their cult, they jostle

> one another ostentatiously where the banners of Islam are unfurled. Their religious practices, and even their edifices which were becoming increasingly numerous, were dangerously encroaching.[16]

In short, ibn Taymiyya was caught between his fear of *dhimmī* influence and his respect as a jurist for the claim-rights of the Christians and Jews of Syria in personam. He personally agreed with the caliph 'Umar, who said of the *dhimmīs*: "Humiliate them, but do no injustice to them" (*adhilluhum wa lā tazlimuhum*).[17] This would imply a bare liberty with respect to religious freedom. However, he could not bring himself to overlook the agreement drawn up between 'Umar and the Christians of Syria. The Prophet Muhammad said of such agreements: "As for one who oppresses a covenanter (*mu'ahidan*), diminishes his right (*intaqasahu ḥaqqahu*), charges him with a burden he cannot fulfill (*aw kallafahu fawqa taqatihi*), or takes something from him without his consent, I will be the proof against him on the Day of Judgment."[18] According to the principles of Ḥanbalī jurisprudence followed by ibn Taymiyya, the opinion of the Prophet trumps the opinion of the caliph 'Umar. However, the Sunna of the Prophet did not trump the opinion of 'Umar to the extent that ibn Taymiyya advocated the claim-rights of *dhimmīs in rem*. Relations with *dhimmīs*, he said, were to be held strictly to the limits of their contract and no further. There was no question of the Mamlūk state's supporting religious minorities, even to the extent that they had done so far.

Ibn Taymiyya's moral dilemma brings us back to the problem of religious difference among Muslims discussed at the beginning of this essay. For ibn Taymiyya blames the "insolence" of the Christians on the Fāṭimid Shī'ites, who gave them unwonted power in the first place. He blames the entry of *dhimmīs* into the most important circles of governmental and economic life on the Fāṭimid caliph al-Mu'izz (r. 953–75), the founder of Cairo, who consulted with advisers of Christian origin.[19] Using a classic example of the "slippery slope" argument, ibn Taymiyya maintains that indulgence toward the Christians by the Fāṭimids, and other religiously lax regimes, promoted the undermining of Islamic values by allowing the adoption of Christian religious practices in Islam, such as celibacy, monasticism, and pilgrimages to the tombs of saints. These practices were picked up by the Sufis, who unwittingly acted as a fifth-column element that diverted Muslims away from the teachings of the Prophet Muhammad. Such innovations weakened Islam and made it susceptible to the dangers it now faced from the Tatars and other external enemies.[20] Similar arguments are made by Salafī and Wahhābī reformists today, who still rely on ibn Taymiyya's *fatwās*. Arguments of this type are also made by Muslim modernists, who otherwise have little to do with ibn Taymiyya.

In conclusion, what lessons can be learned from the preceding discussion? First, the example of the Seljuqs and the moral dilemma of ibn Taymiyya demonstrate that doctrinal and legal issues cannot be separated in the search for strategies of toleration in Islam. The problem of acceptance with regard to other religions is closely related to the problem of the acceptance of diversity within the House of Islam itself. Theology does matter, although it tends to be ignored by many contemporary Muslim intellectuals. I disagree with a senior colleague from the Dar al-Islam Center in New Mexico, who said, when referring to the subject of Islamic reform, "It is all about the Sharī'a." Much is indeed about the Sharī'a in Islam, and notions of the Sharī'a have an undeniably major role to play in Islamic reform. However, Islam is also about theology, as it always has been. In the premodern period, Sufis in North Africa and Muslim Spain were expected to produce formal statements of doctrinal orthodoxy (*'aqīda*) to prove that they remained within the pale of Sunni Islam. *Uṣūlī* reformists in Morocco, who are closer to Sufism than are other Salafī Muslims, are fond of saying, "It is all about *'aqīda*." The concept of *'aqīda* is at the intersection between law and theology. It is a reminder that both are relevant to the direction that Islamic thought will take in the coming years. Law and theology are the checks and balances of Islamic discourse. Theology protects Islamic thought from legal casuistry, and the law prevents theologians from second-guessing God.

Second, you will probably have guessed by now that I also disagree with our friend and colleague Tariq Ramadan, who said in his latest book, "There is no theology in Islam." I believe that attention to Islamic theology is particularly important because, with respect to the right to dissent and the right to religious freedom, the record of Islamic law (i.e., the tradition of *fiqh*) is so equivocal. It is not sufficient to respond, like the Muslim Brotherhood, that the historical tradition of *fiqh* does not follow "real" Islam. At worst, such a statement is guilty of the fundamentalist fallacy; at best, it falls into the fallacy of emotivism, where claims and counterclaims are made with insufficient grounds to back them up. If religious intolerance is not part of "real" Islam, then it is incumbent upon Muslims to make this statement true by reinterpreting Islam in a way that condemns intolerance specifically. Such a project requires new hermeneutical strategies. I propose that such strategies may be more easily found in the theological traditions of premodern Islam than in its legal traditions.[21]

Third, I believe that Muslims need to devote much more time than they have so far to the study of Western moral philosophy. I have tried to show how useful this can be by focusing on just one way of sharpening our understanding of the concept of rights. We need to know what rights are before we can talk about them meaningfully, and we need to know how concepts of rights differ conceptually and over time before we can compare them. Otherwise, we fall prey to ideologues like Sayyid Qutb, who defined "freedom of conscience" as "freedom of consciousness"—that is, the "right" to be conscious of the ideology of Islam as he saw it.[22] In fact, I would go so far as to say that, today, the study of Western legal and moral philosophy is more important for Muslims than the study of classical Islamic philosophy. For me, Jeffrey Stout's *Ethics after Babel* is more relevant to the place of Islam in a world of pluralism than is al-Farabi's *Views of the Inhabitants of the Virtuous City.*

Finally, I remain a strong believer in the virtues of Islamic tradition when it comes to issues of worship and spirituality. I am more pessimistic, however, with regard to the chances of finding traditional Islamic solutions to the social and political problems of our times. Muslims should be concerned about authenticity and should do their best to find resources in the traditions of the past to help them solve the problems of the present. However, when such resources are not available, Muslims should be empowered to find new sources outside of Islamic tradition or create them themselves. If Sharīʿa and *fiqh* are to have continued relevance today, Muslims may need a new school of Islamic jurisprudence to guide their methodologies of legal practice. If Islam is to have a meaningful theology, pace Tariq Ramadan, Muslims need new theological approaches to supplement the efforts of figures such as Ashʿarī or Māturīdī. Only thus can Muslims develop an Islamic theology of toleration that is more than merely emotive.

Chapter 5

Une Foi, Une Loi, Un Roi: Political Authority and Religious Freedom in the West, from Constantine to Jefferson

John Langan

The period from Constantine to Jefferson is complex and rich; within the limits of this essay, the challenge is to find some key, a focus to enable us to order our perceptions of this vast, contentious, and immensely important block of time, which includes what are commonly characterized as the medieval and early modern periods of European or Western history. A starting point can be found in the famous slogan *Une foi, une loi, un roi*, which expressed the aspirations of monarchist conservative Catholics in France during the Wars of Religion between Catholics and Protestants, which lasted for almost forty years in the late sixteenth century.

In his opening address to the Estates General meeting in Orleans in December 1560, Michel de l'Hôpital, the newly appointed chancellor of France, observed that "no sentiment is so deeply rooted in the heart of man as the religious sentiment, and none separates one man more deeply from another." After thus acknowledging the importance of religion and the potential for social conflict that it contained, he went on, "It is not the division of languages that separates kingdoms, but that of religion and law which makes two kingdoms out of one. Hence the old proverb: One faith, one law, one king."[23] De l'Hôpital was addressing a nation on the brink of civil war and was trying to satisfy widespread desires for political peace and religious reform at a moment when political authority had been gravely weakened by the death of two kings in the preceding year and a half. But the maxim that he offered was presented as part of received wisdom, an "old proverb," not as an original reflection.[24] It should be seen as expressing a widely felt aspiration to live in a political unit that would be a coherent and harmonious social whole following one set of normative principles. This aspiration was not confined to France but was common in Western Christianity. Speaking of the sixteenth century, Joseph Lecler writes, "The Christian world of that time, though already divided into nations, preserved in the main the sociological structure of Christendom. The unity of faith remained the universal rule; it was also considered the most solid foundation for the unity of the State."[25]

In the vision of Christendom, the political unit is to be led by an individual who possesses ultimate decision-making power and authority (the king) and who rules in accordance with fair and generally recognized norms of justice (the law). The state and society would be shaped by a common body of beliefs and norms (the faith). It would thus be able to act as one body, but with a functional differentiation of parts to accomplish different tasks and with some differences of status. The moral and spiritual equality of persons before God affirmed in the central Christian narrative and in numerous passages of the Gospels would be interpreted so as to allow and even require different treatment of men and women, of children and parents, of insiders and outsiders, of high and low born. Law itself would be a differentiated but harmonious structure in which the norms of church or canon law, natural law, divine or scriptural law, human law, and custom would direct people to the common good and the ultimate end of happiness found in union with God. The enormous costs—humanitarian, political, economic—of a prolonged period of civil war, costs that could easily be foreseen by those who had observed the conflicts in Germany since Luther fixed his theses to the door of the university church in Wittenberg in 1517, would be avoided and replaced by the benefits of a period of religious, civic, and dynastic harmony. The sources of legitimacy for political authority (popular consent, dynastic descent, legal enactments, and the religious blessing of the coronation ceremony) would be aligned so that they converged on a single individual who would exhibit the appropriate kingly virtues. But religious freedom as exercised both by dissident communities and by autonomous individuals would be suppressed, at least in the public forum. The kingdom would be populated by believing and (more or less) practicing Catholics, who would be subjects of the Most Christian King and who would believe and act in obedience to the religious teachings of the bishop of Rome.[26] They would be subjects, not citizens; people of faith, not philosophical skeptics.

We should pause to recognize the appeal of this unitary paradigm, not merely to French conservatives who viewed the spread of the Reformation with dread, but also to societies that yearn for unambiguous legitimacy in their core institutions and that are averse to uncertainty and normative conflict. The yearning for a society free from normative dissonance is not confined to late medieval Christians. It can be found in contemporary religious conservatives and in many who look back on the Soviet Union, as well as among Islamic radicals. To large numbers of people, it will seem morally superior to the combination of ideals from Babel, Vanity Fair, Jonestown, Waco, Las Vegas, and Hollywood, the never-ending struggle of interest groups and the continuing barrage of conflicting opinions and forms of propaganda offered by the contemporary media, which are taken to be the characteristic expressions of modern liberal society.

Let this brief account of the unitary paradigm stand as an idealized sketch of the dominant conception of social order in Christendom from the late fourth century to the late eighteenth century. Let us admit the incompleteness of the sketch, which leaves out the economic structures of society and the ways in which they might influence the normative superstructure and which also leaves out the continuing presence of minority and dissident groups, among whom the Jews were particularly persistent and significant. The sketch brackets the persistent failure of Christendom to produce an enduring centralization of political power, to realize the dreams and the hopes of Charlemagne and those latter rulers down to the Habsburgs who dreamt of establishing a "universal monarchy."

There was normally one king in France—usually in contest with the ruler of the Holy Roman Empire of the German nation and with the king of England—who was frequently attempting to expand French influence into Italy and the Low Countries. But there were also many other kings in other parts of Europe, from Scotland to Hungary, and from Portugal to Sweden, as well as numerous princedoms and urban republics, especially in Italy and Germany, that had effective self-governance and that pursued more or less ambitious foreign policies. There was both one king and many kings, one sovereign ruling over his (rarely her) subjects, and often ready to quarrel with other kings and peoples. The plurality of monarchies in the formative period of Western civilization and the plurality of nation-states in the subsequent period of modern nationalism and imperialism were facts that protected diversity and probably encouraged cultural creativity along with political anarchy and violence.

Support for the ideal of *un roi* affirmed both the appeal of political unity within the monarchy and the separateness of this particular political unit as one in a pluralistic world of states. *Une loi* flowed from the decisions and choices of the unitary authority exercised by the king, and authority that was not absolute and beyond legal challenge (at least in the period before the rise of Renaissance absolutism) and that depended for its secure exercise on the military ability and the political skills of the monarch and his court. In line with the tradition of Roman law, the king was the source of law and the protector of justice for all his subjects. In carrying out these responsibilities, the king did not have arbitrary and unlimited power; he was to be guided by other and higher laws—the law of God, the law of nature, the law of the church—laws that he could neither ignore nor suspend. While not achieving the stable guarantees of a constitutional political order, early European societies were not totalitarian. For one thing, they lacked the systems of communication and control that would have enabled their rulers to exercise the comprehensive control that totalitarian regimes in more recent years have aimed at. Conversely, there was a strong normative basis for restricting royal and imperial power, which was not to be obeyed when it conflicted with divine commands.

The difficult task of reining in royal power in a predemocratic and largely illiterate society was in a special way the responsibility of the leaders of the church, which provided the alternative form of power and authority during most of the period we are examining. From the time of the famous rebuke of the Christian emperor Theodosius I (379–95) by St. Ambrose, the bishop of Milan (which was then the imperial capital), it was the task of church leadership to reprove the monarch, to defend the liberty of the church, to offer protection to the victims of abuses of political authority, and to proclaim the teachings of the Gospel and the church as well as to consecrate the holders of royal power.[27] In various emergencies, this last responsibility could be extended to include choosing and deposing the monarch. The classical statement of this separation of powers in the Christianized Roman Empire is found in the letter of Pope Gelasius I (492–96) to the emperor Anastasius in Constantinople: "There are two, August Emperor, by which this world is ruled: the consecrated authority of priests and the royal power. Of these the priests have the greater responsibility, in that they will have to give account before God's judgment seat for those who have been kings of men."[28] The assumption of this letter—which was written at a time when the main religious divisions in the increasingly disrupted Roman Empire were within the newly dominant Christian community over Christological issues—is that there is one community of faithful being led and governed by "the priests," and especially by the highest of the bishops, the bishop of Rome, and that this community effectively coincides with the community ruled by the emperor, or "the royal power." This, with considerable simplification and idealization, is an early form of the situation of one king, one faith, and one law. But it is also a situation of two fundamentally distinct powers, or "swords," that are intended to be in harmony with each other but that can come into sharp disagreement.

In this form of the unitary paradigm we have been examining, there is a distinction of institutions (church and state) and of authorities (religious and political). But, as we shall see, affirmation of a separate religious authority does not in itself lead to religious freedom. What it led to in the course of the Middle Ages was a series of conflicts over how to coordinate these two sorts of authorities, both in the emerging nation states and in the more comprehensive realm of imperial politics. Popes and bishops contended for *libertas ecclesiae*, the freedom of the church from secular control. Neither they nor the secular authorities were ready to accept the religious freedom of individuals who held divergent or heretical views or who proposed to interpret God's commands on their own authority and according to the dictates of their own consciences. The schism between Eastern and Western Christianity, between Constantinople and Rome, did not alter the fundamental structure of the unitary paradigm; rather, it complemented the division of political authority with a parallel division of religious authority. Though religious authority was more clearly and reliably subordinate to political authority in the Byzantine Empire of "New Rome," its relation to political authority was drastically altered in those regions of the East that had fallen under Muslim control. In the West, after the Gregorian reform of the eleventh century, a strengthened papacy was able to make its authority felt in the many kingdoms of the West so that the effective range of its power was wider than that of any particular monarch. In addition, the papacy also had both the resources and the vulnerabilities that resulted from its rule of the territories in central Italy commonly referred to as the "papal states."

What is fundamental for the Christian tradition in its various forms is the existence of a separate normative and institutional structure that could not be completely absorbed within the realm of the state and that accustomed Christian people to think of the religious life of the community as proceeding under a distinctively religious authority. We can think of the medieval papacy under such redoubtable leaders as Gregory VII (1073–85) and Innocent III (1198–1216) as the preeminent embodiment of such religious authority. But we should note that the belief that religious authority should govern the lives and beliefs of Christians, and that this authority should prevail over the demands of the state when these conflict with the teachings of the religious community or with the demands of God laid down in scripture, is powerful even in forms of Protestantism that were highly critical of Rome and all its works and pomp, including its centralization of authority and its reliance on juridical models in governing the community of Christ's followers. Both Catholicism and Protestantism produced numerous martyrs who were willing to resist the powers of this earth, even to shedding their blood and laying down their lives. They conceived of themselves not as affirming their own rights and their beliefs and preferences but as acting in obedience to God, and not to men and human institutions. They were acting in obedience to the authority of God and Christ and the Bible and the church (which they linked to each other in different ways, depending on their ecclesial identity and their theological positions); they were also acting in accordance with their consciences.

One way of conceiving this diversity of types of religious authority is suggested by the canonical distinction between the external forum and the internal forum. The external forum is a realm of behavior, of acts whose validity depends on conformity to publicly established laws and norms. This is the forum that is of most pressing interest to legislators and political leaders. The internal forum is a realm in which the believer attempts to discern the will of God and to respond to the complex moral demands of a situation in light of his or her conscience. Religious authority is appropriate in both fora, even though Protestants have been inclined to dismiss the religious character and the religious weight of authority in the external forum, and Catholics have often shown a tendency to regard reliance on appeals to conscience as an assertion of personal freedom and preference against authority.[29] The conscientious and faithful believer acts in a certain way because he or she sees the judgment reached by conscience as itself authoritative. The committed members of a religious body following the command of a superior or pastor act because they see both the command and the disposition to obey as having religious value.

The commitment to a duality or more of authorities is deeply embedded in the Western tradition. The primary alternative (i.e., nonpolitical) form of authority—religious authority—has presented itself in both prophetic and priestly forms, that is, in forms that cherish and even emphasize critical independence from political authority and in forms that model themselves in significant ways on political authority. Religious authority is thus exercised in ways that range in their social manifestations from enthusiastic anarchy to hierarchical and bureaucratic theocracy. Religious authority has resisted, not always successfully, the recurring desire of the state to reduce it to a quiescent and instrumental role. It has frequently been ready to ask for special standing and protection when doing so seemed to be to its advantage, but it has also been ready to resist the implications of the unitary paradigm when these would deny it freedom of self-governance, of open witness to the message of the Gospel, and of defining its belief and its membership. For most thoughtful Christians, a situation in which the church functions as no more than a department of the state is felt to be dishonorable and disgraceful. For Christians concerned primarily with religious truth and religious values, the core of the French dictum is *une foi*, not *un roi*. In many cases, they were willing to accept division of the political realm and even expulsion from it.

Down through the centuries, Christianity has been fruitful in generating sectarian bodies, groups of believers who were able to fashion stable and continuing communities that had their own distinctive conceptions of religious authority. They gave up the aspiration to have *une loi* and *un roi*, that is, a political regime corresponding to their articulation of faith. The existence of such sectarian churches or denominations, which have been especially numerous and important in the English-speaking world—a fact that Voltaire noted in his famous description of England as a land of one sauce and sixty sects[30]—is a rejection and a diminution of the religious authority of a highly institutionalized church, whether that be Catholic, Anglican, Lutheran, or Reformed. But it is often at the same time an affirmation of the religious authority of personal conscience, of charismatic leadership, and of dedicated witness. For those who live and have been formed within them, such bodies come closer in ethos to the primitive church described in the New Testament and also to the heroic founding phases of Catholic religious orders, which often moved beyond the scope of the hierarchy to meet emerging religious problems and needs. After the Reformation, the West became the territory of many churches and religious bodies as well as of many kingdoms. The proponents of the unitary paradigm, especially those for whom the consolidation of political authority in a unitary state was of primary importance, were generally unwilling to accept the socially divisive implications of this development. Many European states took repressive measures against sectarian religious movements, even when these were apolitical and had renounced any prospect of shaping the larger society. In this they were joined and supported by established or dominant churches, which were willing to exercise their religious authority in ways that restricted the religious freedom of dissident or sectarian groups and that were also ready to turn to the state for the protection of their privileged position in a social order that was becoming increasingly less enclosed and less stable.

This was a stance that was highly vulnerable to moral criticism, because it left these churches, of which the Catholic Church was the largest and most visible, in the position of demanding freedom for themselves as a matter of religious right and denying it to other religious groups. This meant calling on the state to make a determination of what constituted religious truth and a determination of where this was to be found. Seeking such determinations would lead both to an effective concession of religious authority by the church to the state (which happened more obviously in Protestant regimes than Catholic) and to a diminution of religious freedom for all. Insisting on religious unity in a strong form in which all would believe and practice their faith in the same way would require state assistance and state enforcement, even against the authority of conscience, and would put the dominant church on the side of persecution rather than toleration, in effect on the side of the Romans and the lions against the Christians. The expulsion of the Huguenots from France that followed the revocation of the Edict of Nantes by Louis XIV in 1685 was the most widely criticized example of this sort of imposed religious uniformity. This was a situation that was unacceptable for moral and religious reasons both to the sects that descended from the Protestant Reformation and to the liberal intellectuals and philosophers who wanted to free both the state and themselves from religious authority. In the United States, both these groups helped to shape the constitutional framework that both separated church and state and protected the free exercise of religion and that has left us with comparatively high levels of religious observance and of interreligious civility.

What conclusions can be drawn from this compressed meditation on the ways in which the Western Christian world struggled with issues of religious and political freedom during the long period in which the Christian Church, and later

Christian churches, were dominant social institutions? First, we need to acknowledge the power and the appeal of the unitary paradigm proposed by the dictum *Une foi, une loi, un roi.* However archaic it may now seem, and however uncomfortable it may make us, it has been very important and influential, both as a reality being constructed and as a goal being desired and hoped for. Contemporary Christians who ignore this aspect of our history, and the ways in which it influences the relations of Christian churches with other religious bodies, run the risk of self-deception. The replacement of the unitary paradigm in its Christian form with the pluralistic paradigm found in Western liberal societies was the result of long historical struggle; it is more than the application of obvious principles.

Second, the Christian version of the unitary paradigm is marked by an internal division between religious and political authority. Religious authority in the West in both its external and internal forms has shown vitality and persistence in the face of political authority.

Third, the Western forms of religious authority have had mixed consequences for religious freedom. Especially in the period reviewed here, Catholicism was, on the one hand, quite willing to restrict religious freedom, to persecute deviant or heretical Christians, to subordinate religious freedom (understood as a universal human right exercised by individuals) to both religious and political authority. On the other hand, its insistence on its own freedom as a religious body meant that it was also contributing to the creation of political and social spaces that were not fully under the control of the state and that would eventually allow greater religious freedom for both communities and individuals.

Fourth, once societies accept that there is no possibility of restoring religious uniformity, either by persuasion or by force, the task of forming one law becomes even more urgent. This problem can be dealt with in several different ways: by subordinating and marginalizing the dissident religious groups; by privileging the wider range of normative possibilities for freedom and dissent that were countenanced in Protestantism while denying inclusion to more disparaged groups such as Catholics, Jews, and Muslims; by emphasizing the decisive importance of constitutional procedures and compacts; and by turning to the philosophical ancestors of what John Rawls discusses as "public reason." Varying mixtures of these strategies were employed in the "northern countries" (the Netherlands, Great Britain, the United States). The last two of these strategies are still of great practical and theoretical importance; the first two have fallen before moral, political, and legal demands for equality, liberty, and impartiality.

Fifth, in a world where religious authority will continue to speak vigorously but with many voices, political authority needs to be restrained within the bounds of justice, both by being divided and controlled in a constitutional regime and by religious authority's using persuasive but not coercive means of educating both those who obey it within the religious community and those who hear it from outside in the public square. In these circumstances, religious authority needs to become and to remain the friend of religious freedom.

Sixth, after the long embrace of religion, specifically Christianity, by political authority in the West, the end of Christendom and its aftermath of religious division and pluralism produces a situation in which the relationship of the Christian churches to political authority is distant, while the contemporary churches' similarity to the early church may be more pronounced. On the political side, Europe is increasingly one body of law, even though Charlemagne would hardly recognize either the forms of government or the diversity of faiths that are to be found there now. But here we begin to encroach on current events and our time, with its problems and opportunities rooted in a long tradition of searching for unity and living fruitfully in a cherished plurality.

Chapter 6

Traditional Texts

6.1 A Letter of St. Augustine

Rowan Williams

Augustine of Hippo, writing in North Africa in the early fifth century, defends the policy of using political authority to compel Donatists (schismatic Christians) to enter the Catholic Church. Augustine's stance was to prove highly influential in succeeding centuries, though those who invoked his authority did not always note the nuances in his position.[31]

The origins of the Donatist schism lay in controversy over Christian leaders who had collaborated with secular authorities during the persecution of the church; some of the more rigorist believers condemned these as *traditores* who had lost their spiritual authority and separated from their communion to form a supposedly pure and untainted church.[32] The Donatists, claiming to be the true church of Christ, sought recognition first from the Roman see and then from the Emperor Constantine but were rejected by both.[33] The schism drew on grassroots support, fed by class divisions and by nationalist sentiment; in its extreme paramilitary wing, the *circumcelliones*, it took on something of the nature of a national revolt against the elite represented by the Catholic Church. When Augustine was appointed bishop, he inherited a situation of embittered and violent conflict, with Donatists a majority in many cities. As the state authorities moved to close down the Donatist congregations, confiscate their property, and fine attenders, however, the balance of membership shifted back to Catholicism.

Writing against this background, Augustine frankly admits to the Donatists that he has changed his mind on the use of coercive state pressure to bring them back into the Catholic Church.[34] Originally he had believed that there was no place for compulsion in religion but had been led to a different view by the evident success of imperial policy in bringing people back to Catholicism. He seems to have viewed this not simply in terms of coercion but also, more subtly, as creating the conditions under which individuals could freely enjoy the opportunity to return to the faith—Donatism, particularly in its extreme form, was for Augustine a coercive force keeping people from the truth.

This letter of Augustine represents a new development not only in his own thought but in that of Christianity as a whole: the first recorded justification in Christian literature of state force exercised against a Christian minority. As such it stands at the beginning of the tradition that "error has no rights," because the obligation to truth of society as a whole must overrule the liberty of individuals to choose that which is false. This represents a very significant moment in Christian thinking, as it initiates and validates partnership between church and state for the crushing of minority religious viewpoints.

It is important to recognize the context within which Augustine was writing, which in some ways mitigates the starkness of his arguments. Against a background of local violence and separatist activity, he insisted that it was improper to kill or to torture members of the Christian minority. On the one hand, the Donatists had themselves already appealed, unsuccessfully, to the state; had they been able to, they would have suppressed the Catholic community and therefore had in principle already conceded the point that they were trying to score against Augustine. Indeed, as he reminded them, like the Catholics they too believed that it was quite right for the authorities to ban disruptive religions such as paganism: In Augustine's time, the offering of pagan sacrifices was a crime punishable by death. On the other hand, it could also be argued that, as there was little or no difference of theological belief between Catholics and Donatists, what was at stake in this argument was not so much an issue of freedom as a matter of public actions permissible by the state. It is clear that Augustine was irritated by the claim of the Donatists to represent a community of conviction when they appeared to be little more than a group of people held together by a local custom of resentment—"frogs croaking in their own pond," as he memorably described them.[35]

Nevertheless, these factors notwithstanding, there is no doubt that Augustine's argument in this letter marks an unhappy moment in the history of Christian thought and opened the door to still unhappier chapters of Christian history, as the state was called on physically to support the church in coercive ways that led to the violation of human conscience, and so to the corruption of the church. Augustine himself came to have second thoughts over the approach he had developed here. While the following extract begins with a theory of Christian kingship prefigured by Nebuchadnezzar, within a decade Augustine had become skeptical about the idea of a Christian ruler who is always able to discern and enforce the truth; in the *City of God*, the highest praise is reserved for the Emperor Theodosius, who demonstrates his true piety by knowing how to repent when he has acted unjustly.[36] From this develops the tradition of the *Mirror of Princes* literary genre, in which the justice of the ruler is shown above all by its humility and readiness to share power received from on high.

> III.9.[37] You say that no example is found in the writings of evangelists and apostles, of any petition presented on behalf of the church to the kings of the earth against her enemies. Who denies this? None such is found. But at that time the prophecy, "Be wise now, therefore, O ye kings; be instructed ye judges of the earth; serve the Lord with fear" [Ps. 2:10–11], was not yet fulfilled. Up to that time the words which we find at the beginning of the same Psalm were receiving their fulfillment, "Why do the heathen rage, and the people imagine a vain thing? The kings of the earth set themselves, and the rulers take counsel together against the Lord and against his anointed" [Ps. 2:1–2]. Truly, if past events recorded in the prophetic books were figures of the future, there was given under King Nebuchadnezzar a figure both of the time of the church under the apostles, and of her present time. In the age of the apostles and martyrs that was fulfilled which was prefigured when the aforesaid king compelled pious and just men to bow down to his image and cast into the flames all who refused. Now, however, is fulfilled that which was prefigured soon after in the same king, when, being converted to the worship of the true God, he made a decree throughout his empire that whosoever should speak against the God of Shadrach, Meshach and Abednego, should suffer the penalty which their crime deserved [Dan. 3:29]. The earlier time of that king represented the former age of emperors who did not believe in Christ, at whose hands the Christians suffered because of the wicked; but the later time represented the age of the successors to the imperial throne, now believing in Christ, at whose hands the wicked suffer because of the Christians.
>
> 10. It is manifest, however, that towards those who, under the Christian name, have been led astray by perverse men, a moderate severity (*temperata severitas*), or rather clemency, is carefully observed, lest Christ's sheep be among the wandering who by such measures must be brought back to the flock; so that by punishments such as exile and fines they are admonished to consider what they suffer and why, and are taught to prefer the Scriptures which they read to human legends and calumnies. For which of us, yea, which of you, does not speak well of the laws issued by the emperors against heathen sacrifices? In these, assuredly, a penalty much more severe has been appointed, for the punishment of that impiety is death. But in repressing and restraining you the thing aimed at has been rather that you should be admonished to depart from evil, than that you should be punished for a crime.

V.16.[38] You see, therefore, I suppose, that the thing to be considered when anyone is coerced is not the mere fact of the coercion (*quod cogitur*) but the nature of that to which he is coerced (*illud quo cogitur*), whether it be good or bad; not that any one can be good in spite of his own will, but that, through fear of suffering what he does not desire, he either renounces his hostile prejudices or is compelled to examine the truth of which he had been contentedly ignorant; and under the influence of this fear he repudiates the error which he was wont to defend, or seeks the truth of which he formerly knew nothing, and now willingly holds what he formerly rejected. Perhaps it would be utterly useless to assert this in words if it were not demonstrated by so many examples. We see not a few men here and there, but many cities, once Donatist now Catholic, vehemently detesting the diabolical schism and ardently loving the unity of the church; and these became Catholic under the influence of that fear which so offends you, by the laws of emperors from Constantine, before whom your party of its own accord impeached Caecilianus, down to the emperors of our own time, who most justly decree that the decision of the judge whom your own party chose and whom they preferred to a tribunal of bishops should be maintained in force against you.

17. I have therefore yielded to the evidence afforded by these instances which my colleagues have laid before me. For originally my opinion was that no one should be coerced into the unity of Christ, that we must act only by words, fight only by arguments and prevail by force of reason, lest we should have those whom we knew as avowed heretics feigning themselves to be Catholics. But this opinion of mine was overcome not by the words of those who controverted it, but by the conclusive instances to which they could point. For in the first place there was set over against my opinion my own town, which, although it was once wholly on the side of Donatus, was brought over to the Catholic unity by fear of the imperial edicts, and which we now see filled with such detestation of your ruinous perversity that it would scarcely be believed that it had ever been involved in your error. There were so many others which were mentioned to me by name, that from facts themselves I was made to own that to this matter the word of Scripture might be understood as applying: "Give opportunity to a wise man, and he will be yet wiser" [Prov. 9:9]. For how many were already, as we assuredly know, willing to be Catholics, being moved by the indisputable plainness of truth, but daily putting off their avowal of this through fear of offending their own party! How many were bound, not by truth—for you never pretended to that as yours—but by the heavy chains of inveterate custom, so that in them was fulfilled the divine saying: "By mere words a servant who is hardened will not be disciplined; for though he understand, he will not give heed" [Prov. 29:19]. How many supposed the sect of Donatus to be the true church merely because ease had made them too listless, or conceited, or sluggish to take pains to examine Catholic truth! How many would have entered earlier had

not the calumnies of slanderers, who declared that we offered something else than we do upon the altar of God, shut them out! How many, believing that it mattered not to which party a Christian might belong, remained in the schism of Donatus only because they had been born in it, and no one was compelling (*cogebat*) them to forsake it and pass over into the Catholic church!

XII.50.[39] We disapprove of every one who, taking advantage of this imperial edict, persecutes you, not with loving concern for your correction, but with the malice of an enemy. Moreover, although, since every earthly possession can be rightly retained only on the ground either of divine right, according to which all things belong to the righteous, or of human right, which is in the jurisdiction of the kings of the earth, you are mistaken in calling those things yours which you do not possess as righteous persons and which you have forfeited by the laws of earthly sovereigns, and plead in vain, "We have laboured to gather them," seeing that you may read what is written, "The wealth of the sinner is laid up for the just" [Prov. 13:22]; nevertheless we disapprove of any one who, availing himself of this law which the kings of the earth, doing homage to Christ, have published in order to correct your impiety, covetously seeks to possess himself of your property. Also we disapprove of any one who, on the ground not of justice but of avarice, seizes and retains the provision pertaining to the poor, or the chapels in which you meet for worship, which you once occupied in the name of the church, and which are by all means the rightful property only of that church which is the true church of Christ. We disapprove of any one who receives a person that has been expelled by you for some disgraceful action or crime on the same terms on which those are received who have lived among you chargeable with no other crime beyond the error through which you are separated from us. But these are things which you cannot easily prove; and although you can prove them, we bear with some whom we are unable to correct or even to punish; and we do not quit the Lord's threshing-floor because of the chaff which is there, nor break the Lord's net because of the bad fishes enclosed therein, nor desert the Lord's flock because of goats which are to be in the end separated from it, nor go forth from the Lord's house because in it there are vessels destined to dishonor.

6.2 A Response of ibn Lubb

Vincent J. Cornell

This text, presented here for the first time, comprises a petition by an unnamed Jew of fourteenth-century Granada and the response given by Abū Sa'īd Faraj ibn Lubb (d. AH 782/1381), the *muftī* (jurisconsult) of that city. Both petition and response are written in poetical form, which indicates that they may have been composed for one of the literary or philosophical salons that were common in Nasrid Granada.[40]

This text revolves around the issue of personal responsibility in adherence to Islam or unbelief, focusing on the concept of *kasb*, literally, "earnings." This key term from Ash'arite theology is variously translated in the following text as "fate," "accrued destiny," or "accrued responsibility," according to the context in which it appears. The Jewish petitioner uses the concept of *kasb* to depict Islamic theology as predestinarian and presents his predicament as a double bind: God's desire that he live as an unbeliever precludes his salvation in a way that denies even a modicum of free will. Ibn Lubb's response refutes this objection by explaining the nuances of the Ash'arite position on destiny, which posits a parallelism between human choice and divine predestination. The elaboration of the text is such that it reads like a carefully considered policy statement rather than the record of an actual exchange; indeed, it is quite possible that there was no real *dhimmī* involved, but the whole text is a theoretical exercise designed to illustrate ibn Lubb's point.[41]

The "Verses of the *Dhimmī*" and the explanation by ibn Lubb are presented as an example of the possible theological barriers posed by traditional Islamic thought to the modern notions of religious pluralism and global civil society. Both the latter concepts are dependent on the notion of the autonomous moral individual, whose choice of religious allegiance is personal and privatized. Moral autonomy and the privatization of belief are both called into question by the Ash'arite theological position outlined by ibn Lubb. For him, as for much in traditional Islam, an acceptance at the level of truth of alternate theologies would go against a natural order in which theology, law, and society are woven together in a totalistic way.[42]

The Verses of the Dhimmī:

Oh scholars of religion, a *dhimmī*[43] of your religion[44]
Is perplexed. So guide him with the clearest proof:

If my Lord has decreed, in your opinion, my unbelief
And then does not accept it of me, what is my recourse?

He decrees my misguidance and says, "Be satisfied with your fate."
But how am I to be satisfied with that which leads to my damnation?[45]

He curses me and then shuts the door against me. Is there any
Way out at all for me? Show me the outcome!

For if, oh people, I were to be satisfied with my current fate,
Then my Lord would not be pleased with my evil calamity.

How am I to be satisfied with what does not please my Master?
Thus, I am perplexed. So guide me to the solution of my perplexity.

If my Lord wills my unbelief as a matter of destiny,
How can I be disobedient in following his will?

Do I even have the choice of going against his ruling?
So by God, cure my malady with clear arguments!

When the Great and Glorious Teacher and Counsellor Abū Saʿīd Faraj ibn Lubb, God be pleased with him, came upon this petition, he said in response:[46]

The Lord has decreed the unbelief of the unbelievers, but he was not
Content for it to be a responsibility (*taklīf*) for every religious community.[47]

He denied His creation [choice] in what He wished to make happen
And implement. His dominion [over destiny] is the strongest proof of this.

When we are pleased with the Lord's decree, we take it as a law (*ḥukm*).
However, our dislike of it leads us into wrongdoing.

Do not be content with an act that [God's] law has forbidden,
But submit to the determination and ruling of His will.

He calls everything to account, but leads certain ones
To success through His special favor. The call, however, is general.[48]

You disobey when you do not follow the road map of His law,
Even if you seem to be proceeding along the way of His will.[49]

The choice of your fate (*kasb*) is yours, but the Lord is the Creator,
Who dispenses it among His creation as He wills.

What God does not will, will not exist.
Exalted and glorified is God, the Lord of Creation!

This is an answer to the petition of a questioner
Who speaks out of ignorance and is completely blind.

"Oh scholars of religion, a *dhimmī* of your religion
Is perplexed. So guide him with the clearest proof!"

The scholar Abū Saʿīd said: The first verse of what I have written is taken from the statement of God Most High, "Say: With God is the decisive proof. Had He willed, He could have guided all of you" [al-Anʿām 6:149]. It also refers to the statement, "Had Allah willed, they would not have assigned partners to God" [al-Anʿām 6:107] and the statement, "If your Lord had willed, they would not have done this" [al-Anʿām 6:112], and the statement, "He does not accept unbelief from His worshippers" [al-Zumar 39:7].

The second verse is also taken from the statement of God Most High, "With God is the decisive proof; had He willed, He could have guided all of you" [al-Anʿām 6:149]. What He means by the "decisive proof" is the proof of God's ownership of acts, as in the noted ḥadīth from *Ṣaḥīh Muslim*:

ʿImrān ibn Ḥusayn asked Abū Aswad al-Du'lī whether the unbelief of an unbeliever is predetermined. [ʿImrān] asked, "Is this [predetermination] not a form of oppression?" Said Abū al-Aswad, "I was greatly shocked by this question. Then I said, 'All that exists is the creation of God and belongs to Him. He will not be questioned about what He does, but they will be questioned'" [al-Anbiyā' 21:23]. ʿImrān said to him, "You are correct. I just wanted to assess the soundness of your intellect." Then he related to him the full text of the ḥadīth of the Messenger of God (may God bless and preserve him) on this subject.

The third and fourth verses both refer to the statement of God Most High, "Verily God ordains what He wills" [al-Māʾida 5:1], and His statement, "God has made unbelief, lewdness, and rebellion hateful to you" [al-Ḥujurāt 49:7].

The fifth verse refers to the statement of the Most High, "Beware of those who conspire to evade His command" [al-Nūr 24:63], along with the statement, "Allah summons unto the Abode of Peace, and leads whom He will to a straight path" [Yūnus 10:25]. Thus, He calls everyone to Heaven but only selects some to be guided toward His way.

The sixth verse refers to the statement of the Most High, "Beware of those who conspire to evade His command" [al-Nūr 24:63], along with the statement of the Most High, "God causes whomever He wills to go astray" [al-An'ām 6:39], and "Whomever God causes to go astray has no guidance" [al-A'rāf 7:186].

The seventh verse refers to the statement of the Most High, "Allah created you and that which you do" [al-Ṣāffāt 37:96.], and "God creates everything" [al-Zumar 39:62].

The eighth verse draws its inspiration from the statement of the Most High, "You do not will but God wills" [al-Insān 76:30], and "Even if you desire their right guidance, still Allah will not guide the one that misleads. Such people have no helpers" [al-Naḥl 16:37.], and "Verily you cannot guide those whom you love, but Allah guides whomever He wills." This finishes what was recorded about this subject at that time. All praise belongs to God.

The scholar Abū Sa'īd, may God be pleased with him, said: I realized that I needed to clarify the meaning of the seventh verse of my response:

The choice of your fate (*kasb*) is yours, but the Lord is the Creator,
Who dispenses it among His creation as He wills.

What prompted me to do this was that I came upon the statement of another respondent to the verses of the *dhimmī* who misinterpreted the intended meaning of my verse.[50] After he mentioned the verse, he stated in his text: "The [verse of the *dhimmī*] does not need to be answered in this way. When God obliges a person to be an unbeliever, it is decreed by God throughout one's life until one's death. Therefore, it should not be said that one has a choice in the accrued destiny (*kasb*) of his faith or unbelief. This would amount to contesting the fate (*qadar*) decreed by God Most High and opposing the rulings (*aḥkām*) of His will. How is it possible for one with a sane mind, a clear conscience, and a sound imagination to grant the right of choosing one's faith or otherwise to a person for whom God has decreed unbelief throughout his life? Especially one whose unbelief is imprinted on his heart and has been denied God's mercy? As the Most High says in the unambiguous verses of His Book (*fi muḥkam kitābihi*): 'And he whom Allah guides, is led aright'" [al-Isrā' 17:97].

[Said ibn Lubb:] The intent of this respondent, when he discusses moral accountability (*ḥisab*) in his answer and is asked to provide proof of his opinion, is to say: "[Ibn Lubb's verse] is the statement of a scholar who holds an intermediate position between the methodology of the advocates of free will (*al-Qadariyya*) and the advocates of predestination (*al-Jabriyya*)." Then he comes up with another statement, the gist of which is the following. "What is confirmed by a clear mind and a sound intellect should not be opposed or argued against by statements that are not confirmed as unassailable or are based on an account (*riwāya*), a tradition (*naql*), or an authoritative teaching (*taqlīd mahd*), unless there is proof to the contrary."

[Said ibn Lubb:] First, the above-mentioned verse [of my poem] is a response to the verse of the *dhimmī*: "Do I even have the choice of going against [God's] ruling?" The meaning of this response is that the accrued responsibility (*kasb*) of a person with regard to good or evil is dependent on what one chooses or wishes at the time the act issues from him, knowing that the Lord (may He be glorified) desires the occurrence of that act to be in conformity with the desire of the person. God creates through His power the desire and the act at the same time in accordance with His will. This is the meaning of my statement in the poem: "The Lord is the Creator and the Dispenser." Now the will that God Most High has created in the person through His power is created from God's power. At the same time, [the human will] is the basis of moral responsibility (*taklīf*) and the foundation of command and prohibition, the promise of reward, and the threat of punishment. All of this is the creation of the Lord Most High. What God desires negates the tendency [of the human being] to contest fate and contradict rules that are valid eternally. For nothing enters into existence except what God Most High creates in conformity with His will. So how can one deny that a person has responsibility for the contradictory and disputational choices he makes, even though this is what God has decided for him and created for him? To say otherwise would be to adopt the position of the *Qadariyya*, who advocated personal freedom of will and the creation of one's own acts without attributing them to the Lord. In fact, they believed that one could even go against God's will. This is because one of their tenets was that God does not will misguidance or disobedience. Exalted is He beyond allowing what He does not will to ever occur in His Dominion or that anyone should be independent of him or that anyone but him should be the creator of anything!

The intended meaning of the seventh verse is completed and expressed in the eighth verse of my poem as follows:

What God does not will, will not exist.
Exalted and glorified is God, the Lord of Creation!

This meaning is expressed in its entirety in the statement of the Most High in His recollection of the Prophet Noah's address to the unbelievers among his people, "My counsel will not profit you even if I wanted to advise you, if Allah's will is to keep you astray" [Hūd 11:34]; this is because God created [the desire for misguidance] in the human being. God Most High confirms His will that the human being [be misguided] in the statement: "if Allah's will is to keep you astray." Then He delegates a choice to the human being, which is the personal desire expressed in the statement, "If I wanted." Then he renders the will of the human being ineffective in contrast to the will of the Creator Most High in the statement, "My counsel will not profit you." One should then consider the statement of the Most High that follows this: "He is your Lord" [Hūd 11:34]. This alludes to the following deductive argument: In other words, how could the command be otherwise, when [God] is the Lord and we are the slaves? God's warning to [Noah's people] caused them to be afraid because of their unbelief, as in His statement, "And unto Him you will be brought back" [Hūd 11:34]. Thus, the meaning of my two aforementioned verses did not deviate from the context of this verse or any other verse of the Qur'ān in any way. The Qur'ān is full of verses with the same meaning.

It is therefore incorrect to say about the response in my verses, while alluding to the places where these meanings are mentioned in the Qur'ān, that it amounts to using the Qur'ān to demonstrate that one may deny God and not submit to him, which is what the *dhimmī* says in his verses. I only meant to refute the *dhimmī*'s purpose in intending to demonstrate opposition and enmity toward the creed of the people of Islam. Then I demonstrated in my answer the refutation of his critique and the correctness of the method [of the people of Islam] according to established rules of rational argumentation. Next, I pointed out the places where he presumed to find arguments for his critique in the Qur'ān. The Most High has presented many intellectual arguments as unassailable proofs for the assertion of divine unity: "If there were therein gods beside Allah, then verily both (the heavens and the earth) would be ruined" [al-Anbiyā' 21:22]. God Most High also said: "We have neglected nothing in the Book" [al-An'ām 6:38]. Were it not for consideration of length, I would have demonstrated my objectives in composing all of these verses, one by one.

My argument in the remainder of the verse, "Who dispenses it among His creation," has two aspects. The first alludes to the fact that God's determination of the fate of the human being is conditional on the relationship between the immediate outcome and the ultimate result [of an act]. God Most High says: "Surely, We will ease his way unto the state of ease" [al-Layl 92:7]; and He says about the other party: Surely, "We will ease his way unto adversity" [al-Layl 92:10]. He says in the ḥadīth: "Work, for everyone finds his way easily to what was created for him."[51] The second aspect of my statement alludes to the fact that God Most High determines the act for which the person is responsible (*al-fi'l al-kasbi*). This is commensurate with the will to act that is created by God for the responsible person (*al-'abd al-muktasib*) and what is appropriate to that person's ability. If not, it might be said that if the responsibility for the fate (*kasb*) of the human being belonged entirely to the Lord as has been established, then a person could never jump over the sea, for example, or fly through the air, such that it would become a habitual affair for him. This is because God's power prevents all of this from happening. However, it is [more correctly] said that the linking of accrued destiny to the limited created ability of the person is what prevents this from happening. Thus, if ever this parallelism were to break down, it would be a miracle and not a behavior for which one would be responsible. Because of this parallelism, some people differ in their ability to jump and others differ in their destinies. For the Most High has created destinies without fixed proportion and everyone earns the destiny that is fated for him. "Say: Each person acts according to his own manner" [al-Isrā' 17:84].

After this, I say: The denial of the addition of choice to the actions of the human being amounts to a repudiation of necessity and is in opposition to the Sharī'a. As for necessity, the human being senses desires, aims, and intentions within his soul, and then distinguishes between his states either purposefully or absent-mindedly, willingly or unwillingly. As for the difference [in choices], this goes back to the relationship between the existence and nonexistence of desire. Responsibility with respect to command and prohibition is not validated except by means of the desire and ability that God has created in the human being. However, when God deprives him of this, the human being is not held responsible, for "God does not burden a soul with what it cannot bear" [al-Baqara 2:286]. The premise of absolute predestination does not take into account what the Sharī'a has confirmed about the will and ability of the human being. The Most High states: "For whomever among you desires to follow the straight path" [al-Takwīr 81:28], "he who wishes will choose a way unto his Lord" [al-Insān 76:29], "yet you will not do so, unless Allah wills it" [al-Insān 76:30]. Thus, [human] wanting is the same as [divine] willing. The Most High also states: "So be conscious of Allah as much as you can" [al-Taghābun 64:16]. Thus, capability is the same as ability.

In his *Sunan*, Abū Dā'ūd cites the following ḥadīth from ibn Shihab: "It was reported to us that the Messenger of God (may God bless and preserve him) used to say when he preached: 'That which is coming is near, but it is farther than what is coming. God does not hasten it because of one's hastiness and He does not lighten it for people's convenience. What God wills is not what people want. People want one thing, and God wants another. What God wills, will be, even if people dislike it. There is no putting off what God brings near and there is no bringing near what God wants to put off. Nothing exists without the permission of God.'"

It is said among the Sunni Muslims that this is "predestination," in the sense that whatever belongs to the human being of will, capability, and accrued destiny is the creation of God. It is likened to predestination in this sense. However, this statement takes into account God's preference with respect to reward, justice, and punishment according to the proof of dominion that the Most High possesses over human affairs. "Say—and belonging to God is the decisive proof—had He willed, he could indeed have guided all of you" [al-An'ām 6:149]. In respect of this is the statement: "Say: The matter belongs to God alone [Āl 'Imrān 3:154], for verily, to Him belong the creation and the command" [al-A'rāf 7:54]. On this matter was revealed the divinely inspired statement that is one of the treasures of heaven, as is mentioned in the ḥadīth: "There is no power and ability but through God." In other words, one does not have the power to disobey God nor does one have the ability to obey God, except through God. The essence of the meaning that is derived from this statement is that there is no power to turn away from a thing or ability to do a thing except through God. Thus, the statement links disobedience to obedience, just as it otherwise links actions to their opposites.

Now see how the speaker contrives an argument from my verse when I state, "The choice of your fate is yours," intending by this the infidel author of the verses of the petition. Our intention, however, was to address any responsible person. So how does he understand from what was intended by the verse that the infidel, who is supposedly imprinted with his unbelief, has the choice of being responsible for his faith, despite the fact that faith is not mentioned in the verse? However, he did mention accrued destiny (*kasb*) in it, and the accrued destiny of the unbeliever is in fact his unbelief. He links this to his act of choice, and the verse continues on the subject of personal right as it continues to discuss the right of the believer to own responsibility for his belief. Look how [the second respondent] added to the meaning of the verse and to the position of the people of the Middle Way, who are the Folk of the Sunna: that it is permissible for the aforementioned infidel to choose responsibility for his faith and that he could utter this, while taking into consideration that God would not accept it of him! Thus, he made the contestation of fate and opposition to the divine will allowable, although there was no expression of this in the verse. For the accrued fate of every person is through his own act and that of his sect. The folk of the Methodology of the Middle Way are not to be blamed for obliging the unbeliever to take such a course. Those with knowledge of God did speak about the way of Abū Lahab and said:[52] His responsibility for his faith was from the standpoint of a responsibility that could not be borne and was understood only in this sense, because the occurrence of the opposite of what is already known and willed by God is impossible. Thus, Abū Lahab's faith was neither a matter of accrued destiny nor of choice. However, the critic added this to the verse in answer to the following question: "Do I even have the choice of going against his ruling?" In other words, of going against God's decree upon [the infidel]. He juxtaposed this with my statement, "The choice of your fate is yours," in the sense, "You will receive what you have asked for." Then he ignored the remainder of the verse and the following verse. All that I have said in the two verses is: You have the choice of the accrued destiny that God has created for you and has willed for you, existing as it has always existed. The occurrence of what God does not want from you or from anyone else is impossible. May God, Lord of All, be exalted and glorified above the occurrence of something that goes against His will and His decree within His Dominion!

Here ends the statement of what I wanted to clarify, may God be praised.

The author (may God be pleased with him) recorded this at the beginning of Rabi' al-Thani in the year 762/1361.

6.3 A Treatise of al-Ghazālī

Vincent J. Cornell

Abū Ḥāmid Muḥammad al-Ghazālī's (d. 1111) *Fayṣal al-tafriqa bayn al-Islām wa al-zandaqa* (The Decisive Criterion for Distinguishing Islam from Heresy) was written to counteract the tendency of partisan Muslim scholars to condemn their opponents as unbelievers or heretics. Al-Ghazālī belonged to the Ash'arite school of theology, which taught that one could not call oneself a Muslim unless one could rationally justify why one believed the way one did.[53]

According to al-Ghazālī's text, statements of the Qur'ān and the Sunna may be interpreted on five different levels: (a) ontologically-existentially (*dhātī*), (b) experientially (*ḥissī*), (c) conceptually (*khayālī*), (d) intellectually (*'aqlī*), and (e) metaphorically (*shabahī* or *majāzī*). These five levels constitute the boundaries of interpretive space, and all five are valid as long as they do not lead to the conclusion that God or the Prophet is lying, that is, as long as they rest on an acceptance of the text as such. It should be noted that to defend the validity of all five ways is not the same as to assert the correctness of them all, but rather to affirm that somebody following them cannot be condemned as a heretic. Nevertheless, al-Ghazālī's rules of hermeneutics do imply that the theologian will at times be compelled to acknowledge "the logical impossibility of the apparent meaning of a [sacred] text." Once this becomes the case, hermeneutical space is opened for a variety of alternative explanations. According to the epistemological standard held by al-Ghazālī, all hermeneutics constitute informed speculation (*ẓann*) and not truth (*ḥaqq*). Thus no one may claim an exclusive right of interpretation, and no single interpretation of a text is definitive.

Al-Ghazālī's approach clearly defines the limits of an enlarged space within which difference is possible in the Islamic community. In this respect, his method is irenic, defending a freedom based on our inability fully to know the will of God. This very epistemological reticence, though, can equally lead to skeptical tendencies, which in the case of the multifaceted al-Ghazālī were countered by the dimension of direct knowledge that he believed could be derived from Sufism.

VIII. Listen now to the Rule of Figurative Interpretation. You already know that all of the parties agree on the aforementioned five levels of figurative interpretation, and that none of these levels falls within the scope of "deeming a statement to be a lie." They also agree, however, that the permissibility of engaging in figurative interpretation is contingent upon having established the logical impossibility of the apparent meaning (*ẓāhir*) of a text. The first level of apparent meaning corresponds to ontological (*dhātī*) existence. Whenever this is conceded, the remaining levels are entailed. If this proves (logically) impossible, however, one moves to the level of sensory existence (*ḥissī*), for it too embraces those levels below it. If this proves impossible, one moves to the level of conceptual (*khayālī*) or noetic (*ʿaqlī*) existence. And if this proves impossible, one moves to the level of analogous, allegorical existence (*al-wujūd al-shabahī, al-majāzī*).

Now, no one is permitted to move from one level (of interpretation) to a level beneath it without being compelled by logical proof (*burhān*).[54] Thus, in reality, the differences among the various parties revert to (differences regarding) logical proofs. In other words, the Ḥanbalite says that there is no logical proof affirming the impossibility of aboveness being the domain of the Creator. And the Ashʿarite says that there is no logical proof affirming the impossibility of the beatific vision. In other words, it is as if each party is simply dissatisfied with the justification adduced by its opponent and does not deem it to constitute a definitive proof. But however the matter may be, neither party should brand its opponent an Unbeliever simply because it deems the latter to be mistaken in what it holds to be a logical proof. Granted, one party may hold the other to be misguided (*ḍāll*) or to be guilty of unsanctioned innovation (*mubtadiʿ*). As for being misguided, this may be said inasmuch as they veer away from what the one (judging them) holds to be the right path. As for being guilty of unsanctioned innovation, this may be said inasmuch as they (may be understood to have) innovated a doctrine that the Pious Ancestors were not known to have openly advocated, it being well-known, for example, that the Pious Ancestors held that God will be seen in the Hereafter. Thus, for anyone to say that He will not be seen is for them to be guilty of unsanctioned innovation. So is it for them to advocate openly a figurative interpretation of the beatific vision. In fact, if it should appear to one that the meaning of this beatific vision is simply a seeing that takes place in the heart, one should neither disclose nor mention this, because the Ancestors did not mention it.

At this point, however, the Ḥanbalite might say: Affirming the aboveness (*al-fawq*) of God is well-known among the Ancestors, as is the fact that none of them ever said that the Creator of the universe is neither connected to nor disconnected from the universe, nor (that He is) neither within nor outside of it. Nor (did they say) that the six directions are devoid of Him, or that His relationship to the direction of up is like His relationship to the direction of down. All of these statements constitute, therefore, unsanctioned innovations, since "unsanctioned innovation" (*bid'a*) refers to the origination of a doctrine that has not been handed down on the authority of the Ancestors.

It is here that it should be made clear to you that there are two vantage-points (from which these matters might be considered).

The first is that of the masses (*'awamm al-khalq*). The proper thing for them to do is to follow (established doctrine) and to desist forthwith from altering the apparent meanings of texts. They should beware of innovating proclamations of figurative interpretations that were not so proclaimed by the Companions; and they should close the door at once to raising questions about such things. They should refrain from delving into speculative discussions and inquiries and from following the ambiguous passages of the Qur'ān and Sunna. Indeed, it was related in this regard on the authority of 'Umar, may God be pleased with him, that a man once asked him about the meaning of two (apparently) contradictory verses, to which 'Umar responded by striking him with a whip. And it was related on the authority of Mālik, God show him mercy, that he was once asked about mounting (the Throne), to which he responded: "(The fact of) mounting is known; acknowledging it is obligatory; its modality is unknown; and asking about it is unsanctioned innovation."[55]

The second vantage-point is that of the speculative theoreticians (*al-nuzzar*) who come to harbor misgivings about inherited theological doctrines handed down from the past. Their investigations should not go beyond what is absolutely necessary. And they should only abandon the apparent meaning of a text upon being compelled by some definitive logical proof. Moreover, none of them should condemn the others as Unbelievers because he holds the latter to be mistaken in what they hold to be a logical proof; for rendering such judgments is no trifling matter that is easily substantiated. Instead, let them establish among themselves a mutually agreed-upon criterion for determining the validity of logical proofs that enjoys the recognition of them all. For if they do not agree on the scale by which a thing is to be measured, they will not be able to terminate disputes over its weight. We have cited the five (probative) scales in our book, *al-Qisṭās al-mustaqīm*.[56] These are the scales regarding the validity of which it is inconceivable that anyone disagree, assuming that they have been properly understood. Indeed, everyone who understands these scales acknowledges them to be an absolute means to certainty. And for those who have mastered them, dispensing and exacting fairness, exposing (the subtleties of difficult) matters, and terminating disputes become matters of ease.

None of this precludes, of course, the possibility that the various parties may (continue to) differ with each other. For such may result from a failure of some of them to satisfy all the prerequisites (to the use of these scales). Or it may be due to their abandoning these scales and measures during the course of inquiry in favor of a strict reliance upon natural talent and disposition, like one who, after mastering the meters of poetry, returns to relying upon his innate sense of taste in order to escape the drudgery of having to calibrate the meter of each individual line. Such a person will be prone to making mistakes. Or it may be due to differences in (the level of mastery of) the various sciences relied upon in forming the propositions of logical syllogisms. Indeed, among the sciences that are basic to logical syllogisms are empirical (*tajrībī*)[57] sciences, sciences that are based on diffuse and congruent reports (*tawāturī*)[58] and other sciences. And people differ in terms of their experience and exposure to diffusely congruent reports from the past. Indeed, one person may deem a report to be diffuse and congruent while another person does not; and one person may experience a thing that another does not. Or it may be due to a confusion between suppositious (*wahmī*) and rational (*ʿaqlī*) assumptions. Or it may be due to the tendency to confuse words that are widespread, commonly used, and positive in meaning, with *a priori* categories and first principles, as we have explained in detail in our book, *Miḥakk al-naẓar*.[59]

In the end, however, if they master these scales and carefully perfect their use, they will be able to identify mistakes with ease, assuming, that is, that they are willing to abandon obstinacy.

IX. There are, on the other hand, people who rush to figurative interpretation under the influence of speculative presumptions rather than on the basis of definitive logical proofs. Even these people, however, should not in every instance be immediately branded Unbelievers. Rather, one should observe. If their figurative interpretation pertains to a matter that is not connected with the basic principles and requirements of creed, we do not brand them Unbelievers. An example of this would be the statement of some Sufis to the effect that what is meant by (the prophet) Abraham's seeing the stars, moon, and sun, along with his statement, "This is my lord" [al-Anʿām 6:76–78], is not the apparent meaning of these things but rather angelic, luminous essences, whose luminosity is noetic rather than perceptual and whose essences are characterized by ascending levels of perfection, the level of disparity between them being like the level of disparity between the stars, the sun, and the moon. They support this on the argument that Abraham was too noble to have to see a body disappear before coming to the belief that it could not be his god. Had this body not disappeared (they argue), do you think that he would have taken it to be his god, despite his (prior) knowledge of the impossibility of godhood resting with created bodies? They also ask, "How was it possible for the stars to be the first thing he saw, when the sun is more prominent (than the stars) and is (usually) the first (celestial body) a person sees?" And they point to the fact that God the Exalted mentioned first, "In this way we show Abraham the hidden realities of the heavens and the earth . . ." [al-Anʿām 6:75], after which time Abraham is cited as having spoken the words in the aforementioned verse. How was it possible (they argue) for him to suppose (that these things were his Lord) after the hidden realities had already been revealed to him?

All of these arguments are based on speculative presumption (*zann*), not logical proof (*burhān*).[60] As for their statement, "He was too noble to . . . ," it has been said that Abraham was a youth at the time. And there is nothing incredible about one who is to become a prophet entertaining a notion like this in his youth only to abandon it shortly thereafter. Nor is there anything incredible about his taking the disappearance (of things) to be more of a proof of temporality than are proportionment (*taqdīr*) and corporeality (*jismiya*).

As for his seeing the stars first, it has been related that he had secluded himself in a cave as a youth and emerged (for the first time) at night.

As for the Exalted having stated first, "In this way we show Abraham the hidden realities of the heavens and the earth . . . ," He may simply have mentioned the final stages of this ordeal only to return to the beginning stages subsequently. At any rate, all of these are speculative arguments that are taken to constitute logical proof (*burhān*) by people who know neither what logical proofs really are nor what is required to sustain them.

This is representative of the kind of figurative interpretation in which these people engage. They even figuratively interpret "staff" and "shoes" in God's statement, "Take off your shoes" [Ṭā' Hā' 20:11], and "Throw down what you have in your right hand" [al-Qaṣaṣ 28:19]. And perhaps they should be given the benefit of the doubt regarding such interpretations that are not connected with basic principles of creed, just as we treat (differences over) logical proofs in connection with (questions on) basic principles of creed. They should neither be branded Unbelievers nor deemed guilty of unsanctioned innovation. Granted, if opening the door to this (kind of interpretive activity) leads to confusing the minds of the masses, then charges of unsanctioned innovation should be leveled specifically against those who engage in this activity regarding those views of theirs that have not been handed down on the authority of the Pious Ancestors.

Similar to the above is the view of some of the Bāṭinites[61] to the effect that the "calf" of the Samaritan is a figure of speech [al-Qaṣaṣ 28:87–88], since it is not likely that a large population of people would be devoid of rational individuals who knew that a thing fashioned from gold could not be a god. This too is speculative. For it is not at all impossible for a large group of people to come to such a conclusion, as is attested to by (the existence of entire communities of) idol worshippers. The fact that this is rare yields no certainty whatever (of its impossibility or non-existence).

As for that material that is connected to the fundamental principles of creed, anyone who alters the apparent meaning of a text without a definitive logical proof must be branded an Unbeliever, like those who deny the resurrection of the body and the occurrence of sentient punishment in the Hereafter on the basis of speculative presumptions, suppositions and assumed improbabilities in the absence of any definitive logical proof. Such persons must be branded Unbelievers, absolutely. For there is no logical proof to attest to the impossibility of souls being returned to bodies. Moreover, public proclamations of such beliefs are extremely detrimental to religion. Thus, everyone who attaches himself to such beliefs must be branded an Unbeliever. And this includes most of the philosophers.

Similarly, those who say that God the Exalted knows nothing other than Himself must be branded Unbelievers. Likewise with those who say that He knows only universals, concrete particulars connected with individual things and events falling outside His knowledge. For all of this constitutes an act of deeming what the Prophet taught to be a lie, absolutely. It has nothing to do with what we mentioned regarding the different levels of figurative interpretation. For the evidence contained in the Qur'an and the reports (handed down from the Prophet) teaching of the resurrection of bodies and of God having knowledge of the concrete particulars affecting individuals are too numerous to accommodate figurative interpretation. Moreover, the philosophers admit that they are not engaged in figurative interpretation. Instead, they say: Since it is in the interest of the people to believe in the resurrection of bodies, because of the inability of their minds to grasp the meaning of a noetic resurrection (*ma'ād 'aqlī*), and since it is in their interest to believe that God the Exalted knows what befalls them and that He watches over them so that this can generate hope and fear in their hearts, it was permissible for the Messenger to give them this understanding. And anyone whose aim it is to improve the condition of others by telling them that which promotes their interests cannot (really) be deemed a liar, even if what he teaches them is factually untrue.

This view of theirs is absolutely false, for it amounts to an explicit claim that the Prophet lied, followed by an attempt to cover this up with an excuse that would effectively deny that what he did was properly an act of lying. But the office of prophethood must be raised above such depravity. For truthfulness and the efficacy of reforming people through truth negates any need for lying.

6.4 A Treatise of Martin Luther

Miroslav Volf

Martin Luther (1483–1546) reflects in the treatise "Temporal Authority: To What Extent It Should Be Obeyed" on the relationship between the two realms within which the Christian must live simultaneously: the kingdom of God and the kingdom of this world. The kingdom of this world, governed by the civic authorities, has a proper place in restraining wickedness and maintaining order, but Luther states clearly (here at odds with Augustine's stance on the Donatists) that temporal authority must not be used to enforce the Christian faith. For Luther, that would be to usurp the work of the spirit of God and to deny both divine freedom and human conscience.[62]

Paul's discussion of the believer's response to imperial authority generated a tension in the tradition that is addressed in this treatise by Luther. On the one hand, Christians were enjoined not to avenge themselves; on the other hand, the apostle explains that the government is authorized by God to execute vengeance. This tension becomes acute when those charged with authority belong to the community of faith: If Christians participate in government, how are these two principles to relate to one another? The radicals of the Reformation extricated themselves from this tension, between the claim of Christ to radical obedience and the need for authority to impose constraints, by withdrawing from government. Luther, by contrast, sought to accommodate the tension through a doctrine of "two governments," yet this can only be understood through framing it with his distinction of the "two kingdoms," which are yet simultaneously present with one another.

The spiritual government is exercised by Christ as king over the self, the inner person standing before God. Here God rules by his word of grace, and there is freedom of religion as a consequence of a voluntary and individuating act. The temporal government, where God rules by law enforced by the power of the sword, is mediated by Christ through the rule of princes and regulates the outer person in his or her relationships with others, embracing the sphere of politics, economics, and so on. The commands of Christ speak to the individual directly as a private person; as a public person, the individual is subject to the commands of the ruler.

How are these two governments to be related to one another? Clearly they are in one sense a contrasting pair, yet when set in the context of the distinction between the kingdom of God and the kingdom of the world, both can be seen as ways in which God is establishing his kingdom; governed overall by love, in the temporal sphere that will take the form of care for the neighbor. Luther insists strongly that the temporal may not insert itself into the spiritual, where coercion has no place; equally, the spiritual is not entitled to rule in the temporal, for then gospel would become law. The two are also related more positively, though: The temporal, by guaranteeing peace and creaturely good, provides the conditions in which the spiritual can grow, while the spiritual in turn makes genuine temporal good possible, because righteousness can only truly be effected through a change in the self before God: Without the spiritual, the temporal would be full of hypocrites.

Luther's doctrine of two governments is set within his account of two realms, that of God and that of the world.[63] Those who have embraced Christ belong to the former, while the latter encompasses all the children of Adam. Nevertheless, this distinction cannot be pressed too sharply: Even those who belong to the kingdom of God are, according to Luther's doctrine of justification, also fallen, *simul justus ac peccator*, while even the worldly are also creatures of God. Thus the kingdom of God has something of the world's kingdom in all its citizens, while there is something of God's good creation in the world. The relation between the two kingdoms is thus highly dialectical; it is within this struggle that Luther identifies a divine sanction for temporal government, parallel to, yet distinct from, spiritual government.[64]

Part 2: How Far Temporal Authority Extends

> We come now to the main part of this treatise. Having learned that there must be temporal authority on earth, and how it is to be exercised in a Christian and salutary manner, we must now learn how far its arm extends and how widely its hand stretches, lest it extend too far and encroach upon God's kingdom and government. It is essential for us to know this, for where it is given too wide a scope, intolerable and terrible injury follows; on the other hand, injury is also inevitable where it is restricted too narrowly. In the former case, the temporal authority punishes too much; in the latter case, it punishes too little. To err in this direction, however, and punish too little is more tolerable, for it is always better to let a scoundrel live than to put a godly man to death. The world has plenty of scoundrels anyway and must continue to have them, but godly men are scarce.

It is to be noted first that the two classes of Adam's children—the one in God's kingdom under Christ and the other in the kingdom of the world under the governing authority, as was said above—have two kinds of law. For every kingdom must have its own laws and statutes; without law no kingdom or government can survive, as everyday experience amply shows. The temporal government has laws which extend no further than to life and property and external affairs on earth, for God cannot and will not permit anyone but himself to rule over the soul. Therefore, where the temporal authority presumes to prescribe laws for the soul, it encroaches upon God's government and only misleads souls and destroys them. We want to make this so clear that everyone will grasp it, and that our fine gentlemen, the princes and bishops, will see what fools they are when they seek to coerce the people with their laws and commandments into believing this or that.

When a man-made law is imposed upon the soul to make it believe this or that as its human author may prescribe, there is certainly no word of God for it. If there is no word of God for it, then we cannot be sure whether God wishes to have it so, for we cannot be certain that something which he does not command is pleasing to him. Indeed, we are sure that it does not please him, for he desires that our faith be based simply and entirely on his divine word alone. He says in Matthew 18, "On this rock I will build my church" [Matt. 16:18]; and in John 10, "My sheep hear my voice and know me; however, they will not hear the voice of a stranger, but flee from him" [John 10:27, 5]. From this it follows that with such a wicked command the temporal power is driving souls to eternal death. For it compels them to believe as right and certainly pleasing to God that which is in fact uncertain, indeed, certain to be displeasing to him since there is no clear word of God for it. Whoever believes something to be right which is wrong or uncertain is denying that truth, which is God himself. He is believing in lies and errors, and counting as right that which is wrong.

Hence, it is the height of folly when they command that one shall believe the Church, the fathers, and the councils, though there be no word of God for it. It is not the church but the devil's apostles who command such things, for the church commands nothing unless it knows for certain that it is God's word. As St Peter puts it: "Whoever speaks, let him speak as the word of God" [1 Pet. 4:11]. It will be a long time, however, before they can ever prove that the decrees of the councils are God's word. Still more foolish is it when they assert that kings, princes, and the mass of mankind believe thus and so. My dear man, we are not baptized into kings, or princes, or even into the mass of mankind, but into Christ and God himself. Neither are we called kings, princes, or common folk, but Christians. No one shall or can command the soul unless he is able to show it the way to heaven; but this no man can do, only God alone. Therefore in matters which concern the salvation of souls nothing but God's word shall be taught and accepted.

Again, consummate fools though they are, they must confess that they have no power over souls. For no human being can kill a soul or give it life, or conduct it to heaven or hell. If they will not take our word for it, Christ himself will attend to it strongly enough where he says in the tenth chapter of Matthew, "Do not fear those who kill the body, and after that have nothing that they can do; rather fear him who after he has killed the body, has power to condemn to hell" [Matt. 10:28]. I think it is clear enough here that the soul is taken out of all human hands and is placed under the authority of God alone.

Now tell me: How much wit must there be in the head of a person who imposes commands in an area where he has no authority whatsoever? Would you not judge the person insane who commanded the moon to shine whenever he wanted [it] to? How well would it go if Leipzigers were to impose laws on us Wittenbergers, or if, conversely, we in Wittenberg were to legislate for the people of Leipzig! They would certainly send the lawmakers a thank-offering of hellebore to purge their brains and cure their sniffles. Yet our emperor and clever princes are doing just that today. They are allowing pope, bishop, and sophists to lead them on—one blind man leading the other—to command their subjects to believe, without God's word, whatever they please. And still they would be known as Christian princes, God forbid!

Besides, we cannot conceive how an authority could or should act in a situation except where it can see, know, judge, condemn, change, and modify. What would I think of a judge who should blindly decide cases which he neither hears nor sees? Tell me then: How can a mere man see, know, judge, condemn, and change hearts? That is reserved for God alone, as Psalm 7 says: "God tries the hearts and reins" [Ps. 7:9]; and, "The Lord judges the peoples" [Ps. 7:8]. And Acts 10 says, "God knows the hearts";[65] and Jeremiah: "Wicked and unsearchable is the human heart; who can understand it? I the Lord, who search the heart and reins" [Jer. 17:9–10]. A court should and must be quite certain and clear about everything if it is to render judgment. But the thought and inclinations of the soul can be known to no one but God. Therefore, it is futile and impossible to command or compel anyone by force to believe this or that. The matter must be approached in a different way. Force will not accomplish it. And I am surprised at the big fools, for they themselves all say: *De occultis non iudicat Ecclesia*, the church does not judge secret matters.[66] If the spiritual rule of the church governs only public matters, how dare the mad temporal authority judge and control such a secret, spiritual, hidden matter as faith.

Furthermore, every man runs his own risk in believing as he does, and he must see to it himself that he believes rightly. As nobody else can go to heaven or hell for me, so nobody else can believe or disbelieve for me; as nobody else can open or close heaven or hell to me, so nobody else can drive me to belief or unbelief. How he believes or disbelieves is a matter for the conscience of each individual, and since this takes nothing away from temporal authority the latter should be content to attend to its own affairs and let men believe this or that as they are willing, and constrain no one by force. For faith is a free act, to which no one can be forced. Indeed, it is a work of God in the spirit, not something which outward authorities should compel or create. Hence arises the common saying, found also in Augustine, "No one can or aught to be forced to believe."[67]

Moreover, the blind, wretched fellows fail to see how utterly hopeless and impossible a thing they are attempting. For no matter how harshly they lay down the law, or how violently they rage, they can do no more than force an outward compliance of the mouth and the hand; the heart they cannot compel, though they work themselves to a frazzle. For the proverb is true: "Thoughts are tax free." Why do they persist in trying to force people to believe from the heart when they see that it is impossible? In so doing they only compel weak consciences to lie, to disavow, and to utter what is not in their hearts. They thereby load themselves down with dreadful *alien sins*, for all the lies and false confessions which such weak consciences utter fall back upon him who compels them.[68] Even if their subjects were in error, it would be much easier simply to let them err than to compel them to lie and to utter what is not in their hearts. In addition, it is not right to prevent evil by something even worse.

Would you like to know why God ordains that the temporal princes must offend so frightfully? I will tell you. God has given them to a base mind [Rom. 1:28] and will make an end of them just as he does of the spiritual nobility. For my ungracious lords, the pope and the bishops, are supposed to be bishops and preach God's word. This they leave undone, and have become temporal princes who govern with laws which concern only life and property. How completely they have turned things topsy-turvy! They are supposed to be ruling souls inwardly by God's word; so they rule castles, cities, lands, and people outwardly, torturing souls with unspeakable outrages.

Similarly, the temporal lords are suppose[d] to govern lands and people outwardly. This they leave undone. They can do no more than strip and fleece, heap tax upon tax and tribute upon tribute, letting loose here a bear and there a wolf. Besides this, there is no justice, integrity, or truth to be found among them. They behave worse than any thief or scoundrel, and their temporal rule has sunk quite as low as that of the spiritual tyrants. For this reason God so perverts their minds also, that they rush on into the absurdity of trying to exercise a spiritual rule over souls, just as their counterparts try to establish temporal rule. They blithely heap alien sins upon themselves and incur the hatred of God and man, one scoundrel with the other. Then they lay all the blame on the gospel, and instead of confessing their sin they blaspheme God and say that our preaching has brought about that which their perverse wickedness has deserved—and still unceasingly serves—just as the Romans did when they were destroyed. Here then you have God's decree concerning the high and mighty. They are not to believe it, however, lest this stern decree of God be hindered by their repentance.

But, you say: Paul said in Romans 13 that every soul [*seele*] should be subject to the governing authority [Rom. 13:1]; and Peter says that we should be subject to every human ordinance [1 Pet. 2:13]. Answer: Now you are on the right track, for these passages are in my favor. St Paul is speaking of the governing authority. Now you have just heard that no one but God can have authority over souls. Hence, St Paul cannot possibly be speaking of any obedience except where there can be corresponding authority. From this it follows that he is not speaking of faith, to the effect that temporal authority should have the right to command faith. He is speaking rather of external things, that they should be ordered and governed on earth. His words too make this perfectly clear, where he prescribes limits for both authority and obedience, saying, "Pay all of them their dues, taxes to whom taxes are due, revenue to whom revenue is due, honour to whom honour is due, respect to whom respect is due" [Rom. 13:7]. Temporal obedience and authority, you see, apply only externally to taxes, revenue, honor, and respect. Again, where he says, "The governing authority is not a terror to good conduct, but to bad" [Rom. 13:3], he again so limits the governing authority that it is not to have the mastery over faith or the word of God, but over evil works.

This is also what St Peter means by the phrase, "human ordinance" [1 Pet. 2:13]. A human ordinance cannot possibly extend its authority into heaven and over souls; it is limited to the earth, to external dealings men have with one another, where they can see, know, judge, evaluate, punish, and acquit.

Christ himself makes this distinction, and summed it all up very nicely when he said in Matthew 22, "Render to Caesar the things that are Caesar's and to God the things that are God's" [Matt. 22:21]. Now, if the imperial power extended into God's kingdom and authority, and were not something separate, Christ would not have made this distinction. For, as has been said, the soul is not under the authority of Caesar; he can neither teach it nor guide it, neither kill it nor give it life, neither bind it or loose it, neither judge nor condemn it, neither hold it fast nor release it. All this he would have to do, had he the authority to command it and to impose laws upon it. But with respect to body, property, and honor he has indeed to do these things, for such matters are under his authority.

David too summarized all this long ago in an excellent brief passage, when he said in Psalm 113, "He has given heaven to the Lord of heaven, but the earth he has given to the sons of men" [Ps. 115:16]. That is, over what is on earth and belongs to the temporal, earthly kingdom, man has authority from God; but whatever belongs to heaven and to the eternal kingdom is exclusively under the Lord of heaven. Neither did Moses forget this when he said in Genesis 1, "God said, 'Let us make man to have dominion over the beasts of the earth, the fish of the sea, and the birds of the air'" [Gen. 1:26]. There only external dominion is ascribed to man. In short, this is the meaning as St Peter says in Acts 4, "We must obey God rather than men" [Acts 5:29]. Thereby, he clearly sets a limit to the temporal authority, for if we had to do everything that the temporal authority wanted there would have been no point in saying, "We must obey God rather than men."

If your prince or temporal ruler commands you to side with the pope, to believe thus and so, or to get rid of certain books, you should say, "It is not fitting that Lucifer should sit at the side of God. Gracious sir, I owe you obedience in body and property; command me within the limits of your authority on earth, and I will obey. But if you command me to believe or to get rid of certain books, I will not obey; for then you are a tyrant and overreach yourself, commanding where you have neither the right or the authority," etc. Should he seize your property on account of this and punish such disobedience, then blessed are you; thank God that you are worthy to suffer for the sake of the divine word. Let him rage, fool that he is; he will meet his judge. For I tell you, if you fail to withstand him, if you give in to him and let him take away your faith and your books, you have truly denied God.

Let me illustrate. In Meissen, Bavaria, the Mark, and other places, the tyrants have issued an order that all copies of the New Testament are everywhere to be turned in to the officials. This should not turn in a single page, not even a letter, on pain of losing their salvation. Whoever does so is delivering Christ up into the hands of Herod, for these tyrants act as murderers of Christ just like Herod. If their homes are ordered searched and books or property taken by force, they suffer it to be done. Outrage is not to be resisted but endured; yet we should not sanction it, or lift a little finger to conform, or obey. For such tyrants are acting as worldly princes are supposed to act, and worldly princes they surely are. But the world is God's enemy; hence, they too have to do what is antagonistic to God and agreeable to the world, that they may not be bereft of honor, but remain worldly princes. Do not wonder, therefore, that they rage and mock at the gospel; they have to live up to their name and title.

You must know that since the beginning of the world a wise prince is a mighty rare bird, and an upright prince ever rarer. They are generally the biggest fools or the worst scoundrels on earth; therefore, one must constantly expect the worst from them and look for little good, especially in divine matters which concern the salvation of souls. They are God's executioners and hangmen; his divine wrath uses them to punish the wicked and to maintain outward peace. Our God is a great lord and ruler; this is why he must also have such noble, highborn, and rich hangmen and constables. He desires that everyone shall copiously accord them to riches, honor, and fear in abundance. It pleases his divine will that we call his hangmen gracious lords, fall at their feet, and be subject to them in all humility, so long as they do not ply their trade too far and try to become shepherds instead of hangmen. If a prince should happen to be wise, upright, or a Christian, that is one of the great miracles, the most precious token of divine grace upon that land. Ordinarily the course of events is in accordance with the passage from Isaiah 3, "I will make boys their princes and gaping fools shall rule over them" [Isa. 3:4]; and in Hosea 13, "I will give you a king in my anger, and take him away in my wrath" [Hosea 13:11]. The world is too wicked, and does not deserve to have many wise and upright princes. Frogs must have their storks.

Again you say: "The temporal power is not forcing men to believe; it is simply seeing to it externally that no one deceives the people by false doctrine; how could heretics otherwise be restrained?" Answer: This the bishops should do; it is a function entrusted to them and not to the princes. Heresy can never be restrained by force. One will have to tackle the problem in some other way, for heresy must be opposed and dealt with otherwise than with the sword. Here God's word must do the fighting. If it does not succeed, certainly the temporal power will not succeed either, even if it were to drench the world in blood. Heresy is a spiritual matter which you cannot hack to pieces with iron, consume with fire, or drown in water. God's word alone avails here, as Paul says in II Corinthians, "Our weapons are not carnal, but mighty in God to destroy every argument and proud obstacle that exalts itself against the knowledge of God, and to take every thought captive in the service of Christ" [2 Cor. 10:4–5].

Moreover, faith and heresy are never so strong as when men oppose them by sheer force, without God's word. For men count it certain that such force is for a wrong cause and is directed against the right, since it proceeds without God's word and knows not how to further its cause except by naked force, as brute beasts do. Even in temporal affairs force can be used only after the wrong has been legally condemned. How much less possible it is to act with force, without justice and God's word, in these lofty spiritual matters! See, therefore, what fine, clever nobles they are! They would drive out heresy, but set about it in such a way that they only strengthen the opposition, rousing suspicion against themselves and justifying the heretics. My friend, if you wish to drive out heresy, you must find some way to tear it first of all from the heart and completely turn men's wills away from it. With force you will not stop it, but only strengthen it. What do you gain by strengthening heresy in the heart, while weakening only its outward expression and forcing the tongue to lie? God's word, however, enlightens the heart, and so all heresies and errors vanish from the heart of their own accord.

This way of destroying heresy was proclaimed by Isaiah in his eleventh chapter where he says, "He shall smite the earth with the rod of his mouth, and with the breath of his lips he shall slay the wicked" [Isa. 11:4]. There you see that if the wicked are to be slain and converted, it will be accomplished with the mouth. In short, these princes and tyrants do not realize that to fight against heresy is to fight against the devil, who fills men's hearts with error, as Paul says in Ephesians 6, "We are not contending against flesh and blood, but against spiritual wickedness, against the principalities which rule this present darkness" [Eph. 6:12]. Therefore, so long as the devil is not repelled and driven from the heart, it is agreeable to him that I destroy his vessels with fire of sword; it is as if I were to fight lightning with a straw. Job bore abundant witness to this when in his forty-first chapter he said that the devil counts iron as straw, and fears no power on earth.[69] We learn it is also from experience, for even if all Jews and heretics were forcibly burned no one ever has been or will be convinced or converted thereby.

Nevertheless, such a world as this deserves such princes, none of whom attends to his duties. The bishops are to leave God's word alone and not use it to rule souls; instead they are to turn over to the worldly princes the job of ruling souls with the sword. The worldly princes, in turn, are to permit usury, robbery, adultery, murder, and other evil deeds, and even commit these offences themselves, and then allow the bishops to punish with letters of excommunication. Thus, they neatly put the shoe on the wrong foot: they rule the souls with iron and the bodies with letters, so that worldly princes rule in a spiritual way, and spiritual princes rule in a worldly way. What else does the devil have to do on earth than to masquerade and play the fool with his people? These are our Christian princes, who defend the faith and devour the Turk! Fine fellows, indeed, whom we may well trust to accomplish something by such refined wisdom, namely, to break their necks and plunge land and people into misery and want.

I would in all good faith advise these blind fellows to take heed to a little phrase that occurs in Psalm 107: *Effundit contemptum super principes*.[70] I swear to you by God that if you fail to see that this little text is applicable to you, then you are lost, even though each one of you be as mighty as the Turk; and your fuming and raging will avail you nothing. A goodly part of it has already come true. For there are very few princes who are not regarded as fools or scoundrels; that is because they show themselves to be so. The common man is learning to think, and the scourge of princes (that which God calls *contemptum*) is gathering force among the mob and with the common man. I fear there will be no way to avert it, unless the princes conduct themselves in a princely manner and begin again to rule decently and reasonably. Men will not, men cannot, men refuse to endure your tyranny and wantonness much longer. Dear princes and lords be wise and guide yourselves accordingly. God will no longer tolerate it. The world is no longer what it once was, when you hunted and drove people like game. Abandon therefore your wicked use of force, give thought to dealing justly, and let God's word have its way, as it will anyway and must and shall; you cannot prevent it. If there is heresy somewhere, let it be overcome, as is proper, with God's word. But if you can continue to brandish the sword, take heed lest someone come and compel you to sheathe it—and not in God's name!

But you might say: "Since there is to be no temporal sword among Christians, how then are they to be ruled outwardly? There certainly must be authority even among Christians." Answer: Among Christians there shall and can be no authority; rather all are alike subject to one another, as Paul says in Romans 12: "Each shall consider the other his superior" [Rom. 12:10]; and Peter says in 1 Peter 5: "All of you be subject to one another" [1 Pet. 5:5]. This is also what Christ means in Luke 14: "When you are invited to a wedding, go and sit in the lowest place" [Luke 14:10]. Among Christians there is no superior but Christ himself, and him alone. What kind of authority can there be where all are equal and have the same right, power, possession, and honor, and where no one desires to be the other's superior, but each the other's subordinate? Where there are such people, one could not establish authority even if he wanted to, since in the nature of things it is impossible to have superiors where no one is able or willing to be a superior. Where there are no such people, however, there are no real Christians either.

What, then, are the priests and bishops? Answer: Their government is not a matter of authority or power, but a service and an office, for they are neither higher nor better than other Christians. Therefore, they should impose no law or decree on others without their will and consent. Their ruling is rather nothing more than the inculcating of God's word, by which they guide Christians and overcome heresy. As we have said, Christians can be ruled in faith, not with outward works. Faith, however, can come through no word of man, but only through the word of God, as Paul says in Romans 10, "Faith comes through hearing, and hearing through the word of God" [Rom. 10:17]. Those who do not believe are not Christians; they do not belong to Christ's kingdom, but to the worldly kingdom where they are constrained and governed by the sword and by outward rule. Christians do every good thing of their own accord and without constraint, and find God's word alone sufficient for them. Of this I have written frequently and at length elsewhere.

Notes to Part II

1. For a discussion of these texts and the events they describe, see Omid Safi, *The Politics of Knowledge in Premodern Islam: Negotiating Ideology and Religious Inquiry* (Chapel Hill: University of North Carolina Press, 2006), xliv, 1–2.
2. Ibid., 4.
3. Ibid., 6.

4. Ibid., 19.
5. Ibid., 102.
6. Ibid., 53–54.
7. Cf. the extract and discussion that follows.
8. John Rawls, *A Theory of Justice*, rev. ed. (Cambridge, MA: Belknap Press of Harvard University Press, 1999), 117.
9. See, e.g., Alasdair MacIntyre, *Whose Justice, Which Rationality* (Notre Dame, IN: University of Notre Dame Press, 1988), esp. the chapter titled "Aristotle on Justice," 103–23. For Aristotle, justice was based on ratios, not on equivalences. These ratios govern the principle of fairness in distributive justice and retributive justice (or "justice as rectification"). See Aristotle, *Nicomachean Ethics*, trans. Martin Oswald (1962; repr., Indianapolis: Bobbs-Merrill, 1981), bk. 5, 111–30.
10. See Vincent J. Cornell, "Practical Sufism: An Akbarian Foundation for a Liberal Theology of Difference," *Journal of the Muhyiddin ibn 'Arabi Society* 36 (2004): 59–84.
11. Cited in Jeremy Waldron, introduction to *Theories of Rights*, ed. Jeremy Waldron (Oxford: Oxford University Press, 1984), 4.
12. Wesley Newcomb Hohfeld, *Fundamental Legal Conceptions as Applied in Judicial Reasoning*, originally published in the *Yale Law Journal*, 1913 and 1917; new ed. by Walter Wheeler Cook (New Haven, CT: Yale University, 1964).
13. Bernard Lewis, *The Jews of Islam* (Princeton, NJ: Princeton University Press, 1984), 14–15.
14. Cf. the following further for text and discussion of ibn Lubb's debate with a *dhimmī*.
15. Victor E. Makari, *Ibn Taymiyyah's Ethics: The Social Factor* (Chico, CA: Scholars Press, 1983), 127–31.
16. Ibid., 128.
17. Ibid., 130.
18. Ibid., 218n63; this ḥadīth is translated inaccurately on 129–30, where *mu'ahid* (covenanter) is replaced by *dhimmī*.
19. Ibid., 128.
20. Ibid., 129.
21. Al-Ghazālī's *Fayṣal al-Tafriqa* is chosen for discussion later for just such a reason.
22. See Sayyid Qutb, *Social Justice in Islam*, trans. John B. Hardie and rev. Hamid Algar (Oneonta, NY: Islamic Publications International, 2000), 53–67.
23. *Discours pour la majorité de Charles IX et trois autres discours*, ed. Robert Descimon (Paris: Imprimerie Nationale, 1993), 71–89. Michel de l'Hôpital was

in fact an influential leader of the party of the *politiques*, who sought a pragmatic solution to the conflicts of the time by recognizing that, despite the value of religious uniformity, attempts to impose it by force could be disastrous. In an address in 1562, he insisted that the fundamental issue "is not about the maintenance of religion (*consituenda religione*) but about the maintaining of the commonwealth (*constituenda respublica*)"—the enforcement of unity "may be good in itself," but "experience has shown it to be impossible." Ibid.

24. De l'Hôpital describes the adage as *un vieux proverbe français*. However, it cannot be traced back earlier than the sixteenth century.
25. Joseph Lecler, *Toleration and the Reformation* (New York: Longmans, 1960), 2:42.
26. The title *Rex Christianissimus*, not originally restricted to the kings of France, was assigned by Paul II to Louis XI and his successors in perpetuity in 1469.
27. Following a massacre ordered by the emperor at Thessalonica, Ambrose in 390 forbade him to enter the Cathedral of Milan; the rebuke is set out in *Ep. LI* (Migne, PL16, 1159C–1164B).
28. *Auctoritas sacrata potificum et regalis potestas*, Denzinger-Schönmetzer, 347.
29. E.g., *Codex iuris canonici*, 130, states: *Potestas regiminis de se exercetur pro foro externo, quandoque tamen pro solo foro interno.*
30. "Il y a en Angleterre soixante sects différentes, et une seule sauce"; the aphorism is also attributed to the Marquis Francesco Caraccioli, Neapolitan ambassador in London.
31. Extracts from the translation of Letter XCIII by J. G. Cunningham, from *Library of the Nicene and Post-Nicene Fathers of the Christian Church, Series I*, vol. 1, *The Confessions and Letters of St Augustine, with a Sketch of His Life and Work*, ed. Philip Schaff (Edinburgh: T. & T. Clark, 1886). For each of the following extracts, references are provided for the Latin texts in J. P. Migne's *Patrologia Latina*, vol. 33.
32. The schismatics particularly objected to Caecilian, bishop of Carthage 311–45, on the grounds that he had been consecrated by the *traditor* Felix of Aptunga.
33. The schism was named for Donatus, consecrated by Numidian bishops as a rival bishop to Caecilian in the see of Carthage.
34. Letter XCIII is addressed to Vincentius, Bishop of Cartennae, a member of a moderate subsect of the Donatists called the Rogatists, and former friend of Augustine, who addresses him as "dearly beloved brother" (*dilectissimus frater*).
35. *Enarrationes in Psalmos* 95.11, drawing the contrast between the extremely limited world of Donatism and the genuinely universal horizon of Catholi-

cism: "The clouds of heaven thunder out throughout the world that God's house is being built; and the frogs cry from the marsh (*clamant ranae de palude*), 'We alone are Christians (*Nos soli sumus Christiani*).'"

36. *De civitate Dei* 5.26. The praise of Theodosius is the more striking in that it immediately follows a rather factual, even tepid, account of the archetypal Christian hero Constantine.
37. Migne, *Patrologia Latina*, 33, 325–26.
38. Ibid., 33, 329–30.
39. Ibid., 33, 345–46.
40. The manuscript is from Biblioteca de El Escorial, Spain, no. 1810, 147–55v; text and some notes provided by Professor Hayat Kara of Université Mohammed V, Rabat, Morocco. This translation is by Professor Vincent Cornell.
41. As a close associate of the *Qāḍī al-Jamā'a*, who had control over religious appointments, property, and teaching in Granada, ibn Lubb would have been the second most important religious figure in a centralized kingdom with tight church–state links.
42. This is particularly the import of his quotation from al-Anbiyā' 21:22 in the following text.
43. The *dhimmī* in this case is a Jew—there were hardly any Christians in Granada at this time, as they had been ordered to leave by church authorities.
44. This is a play on words. The Arabic verb *dhamma*, the root of *dhimmī*, means "to blame." Thus the phrase *dhimmiyu dinikum*, which is used in the poem, can mean both "a non-Muslim whom your religion protects" and "one whom your religion blames."
45. The Arabic term *shaqwatī* literally means "my unhappiness." In the present context, "my damnation" is more appropriate.
46. Ibn Lubb's first response is in verse; a more extensive prose version follows.
47. "Community" here translates from *milla*. The text reflects a situation in which Muslims and Jews are assumed to be in separate communities, with little interaction.
48. "General" here means "nonspecific" rather than "universal."
49. This seems to be a reference to al-Mā'ida 5.48: "We have assigned a law and a path to each of you." Ibn Lubb turns this Qur'ānic verse against the *dhimmī* in a way that shows he is far from understanding it as pluralist in meaning.
50. Ibn Lubb adds a further section to his response after seeing a counter statement from another Islamic scholar, whose identity is not now known.
51. *Sunan Abu Dawud* 4/232 number 4694.

52. The Prophet's pagan uncle.
53. The translation is taken from Sherman A. Jackson, *On the Boundaries of Theological Tolerance in Islam: Abu Humid al Ghazālī's* Fayal al Tafriqa (Oxford: Oxford University Press, 2002), 104–10.
54. *Burhān* has the restricted technical sense of a syllogism but more generally indicates any inductive proof that is convincing and conclusive: "argumentation probante, démonstration, quelle que soit sa forme." Farid Jabre, *Essai sur la Lexique de Ghazali* (Beirut: Université Libanaise, 1970), 24–27.
55. The reference is to interpretive disputes over the *Istawā* verse, "[God] ascended (*istawā*) his throne" (al-A'rāf 7:54), which raised for theologians the question of anthropomorphism.
56. "The Just Balance," al-Ghazālī's polemical work against the Ismā'īlīs.
57. *Tajrībī* indicates experience as a basis for knowledge, as distinct from reason and analogy. Jabre, *Essai sur la Lexique de Ghazali*, 49–50.
58. *Tawāturī* reports are those with more than one chain leading back to a source; the term is used particularly in the classification of aḥādīth, but al-Ghazālī's sense here is wider. Jabre, *Essai sur la Lexique de Ghazali*, 269.
59. "The Touchstone of Reasoning," one of al-Ghazālī's works on logic.
60. *Zann* refers to an inductive logic that may be largely correct but is not conclusive; here al-Ghazālī contrasts it polemically as "speculation," with the assurance of *burhān*.
61. The Ismā'īlīs, so called because of their emphasis on esoteric (*bāṭin*) exegesis.
62. The English translation of the treatise is provided by Gary Mann on the "Luther Project" website, www.uoregon.edu/~sshoemak/323/texts/luther~1.htm (accessed April 4, 2009).
63. The two pairs are sometimes conflated in shorthand accounts of the "two kingdoms" theory, but the *Zwei Reiche* should be distinguished from the *Zwei Regimente*.
64. In this dialectical approach, Luther distinguished himself from other Reformation theologians such as Melanchthon, who argued instead for the principle of *cura religionis*, that the civil magistrate had a responsibility, as custodian of both "tables of the Law," to regulate the right order of true religion. It has been suggested, though, that in later life Luther came closer to Melanchthon's position. Cf. James Estes, "The Role of Godly Magistrates in the Church: Melanchthon as Luther's Interpreter and Collaborator," *Church History* 67, no. 3 (1998): 463–84.
65. The reference seems to be to Acts 1:24.
66. This is a recognized proposition of the canonists (cf. Gratian) applied to specific pastoral situations. It is adopted, for example, in the Council of

Trent's canons on marriage (Denzinger no. 1814), where the issue is that of the interior motivation of the couple. Luther here extends its juridical scope dramatically.

67. Cf. *In Joann.* 25 (PL 35, 1607). However, as St. Thomas Aquinas points out (*ST* 2a 2ae 10, 8 *ad* 3), Augustine did defend the use of force to compel right belief in some cases, such as those involving heretics or schismatics who had once held the Catholic faith (e.g., Donatists).
68. The scholastic category of *peccata aliena* included various kinds of personal involvement in another party's sin: by, e.g., counseling, approving, or even failing to criticize.
69. Job 41:27, 33. The biblical reference is in fact to Leviathan.
70. Psalm 107:40: "He pours contempt upon princes."

PART III

THE MODERN WORLD

Although its roots can be traced further back in both religious and secular thinking, it is in the twentieth century that the discourse of human rights comes to dominate the way that justice is understood in many human societies and globally. Among the human rights generally recognized and affirmed by a growing international consensus is that of freedom of religion, and Malcolm Evans's essay provides an eloquent overview of the tensions and challenges involved in translating this general affirmation into the particular contexts of religious practice.

The four Christian and Islamic texts that follow address in different ways the relationship between religious commitment and state power, and the grounding of the language of rights in religious faith. The Barmen declaration and the writings of Imam Khomeini, both emerging in times of immense turmoil in society, propose radically disparate approaches from the faithful to issues of political governance. *Dignitatis humanae* and the two Islamic documents differ more subtly in the ways that they link the affirmation of rights for humans with the primacy of obligations to God.

Chapter 7

Human Rights and the Freedom of Religion

Malcolm Evans

I approach this topic as an international lawyer interested and involved in the protection of religious freedom by and through the means and mechanisms of international law, and particularly through the means and mechanisms of international human rights law. My central point here is that I believe human rights law is developing in a fashion that is likely to hinder rather than assist the realization of the goals of tolerance and religious pluralism. There are two reasons for this. First, the entire human rights approach to religious liberty is increasingly geared toward a form of "neutrality" that is inimical to religious liberty. Second, that approach tends to bear more harshly on some religious traditions than others, undermining the very values that it is said to reflect. To my mind, this increases the need for dialogue between religious communities on such questions. It also means that religious communities, while being fully alive to the need to respect human rights values, should be questioning the direction in which human rights thinking is inclining. I do not think it should be assumed that human rights approaches to questions concerning the relationship of religious believers, as individuals and as communities, to the societies in which they live are necessarily to be preferred or privileged over other conceptions of that relationship.

I should make it clear at the outset that I view human rights as a tool, a methodology for addressing the tensions that arise within the governance of a society. I see human rights as a means of policing the boundaries between the public and the private space, ensuring that the assertion of the authority of the state does not overreach the bounds of legitimacy, while also recognizing that, to a degree, human rights impose minimum requirements upon states for positive assertions of authority in order to ensure that these rights are indeed properly realized. I do not see the international human rights instruments as constituting an ethical code, although they are frequently perceived as such. Indeed, the manner in which human rights obligations come into being, through a tortuous process of negotiation and political compromise, emphasizes their instrumental rather than their transcendental qualities. Theologians will tend to understand human rights in a different fashion from a domestic lawyer, a domestic lawyer may well understand them differently from an international lawyer, and so on. It is, however, worth reminding ourselves that, no matter how much mystique is generated around them, human rights instruments are the product of varying inputs, many highly contentious, often largely political, and are the product of intense negotiation. They are not the distillation of any particular form of wisdom. They are the product of a pragmatic progress and have to be engaged with as such, as important statements of how the international community believes it can and should configure itself, but not in any sense as moral absolutes. They are tools with which we work.

I do not think that freedom of religion and belief has fared particularly well within the human rights framework. Despite the role of religious belief as being one of the wellsprings from which human rights protection flowed in its earliest days, it rapidly became something of a Cinderella within the protective framework. Despite its appearing in President Roosevelt's "four freedoms," and its figuring as an "easy case" for inclusion as Article 18 of the Universal Declaration of Human Rights, it remains the only one of the key rights identified that has not been developed into a specialist, legally binding instrument.[1] Although there have been attempts to draft an international convention on religious liberty, these stalled in 1967 after the first article had been drafted, and the general view is that it is still premature to return to the exercise. The very fact that it is still seen as so difficult an issue tells us something significant about the relationship between human rights and religious belief. Indeed, it has been a struggle to get the United Nations to address the issue from the perspective of the freedom of religion and belief at all. Although this is the approach of the principal human rights instruments, in 1981 the United Nations adopted a rather different tack in adopting its "Declaration on the Elimination of All Forms of Intolerance and of Discrimination Based on Religion or Belief." Although this Declaration now tends to be projected as a summation of UN engagement with the freedom of religion and belief, it was originally more focused on questions of nondiscrimination on the basis of religion or belief, and this was reflected in the original title of the mandate of the UN Special Rapporteur, established in 1986 to monitor its implementation.[2]

The legally binding human rights instruments adopt a common approach to the freedom of religion, and this is exemplified by Article 9 of the European Convention on Human Rights (ECHR), which provides the following:

> (1) Everyone has the right to freedom of thought, conscience and religion; this right includes freedom to change his religion or belief, either alone or in community with others and in public or private, to manifest his religion or belief, in worship, teaching, practice and observance.
>
> (2) Freedom to manifest one's religion shall be subject to only such limitations as are prescribed by law and are necessary in a democratic society in the interests of public safety, for the protection of public order, health or morals, or for the protection of the rights and freedoms of others.

This is a classic human rights formulation. It sets out what appears to be a very clear right—that everyone enjoys the freedom of thought, conscience, and religion. This is generally referred to as the *forum internum*, the sphere of inner belief that is inviolable but that permits little more (if anything) than the freedom to believe what one wishes. When it comes to doing something on the basis of one's beliefs, then this is protected only to the extent that it might be a protected form of "manifestation," and the European Court of Human Rights has not wavered from the view, first expressed by the European Commission on Human Rights back in 1981, that not all actions that are motivated by a belief are protected forms of manifestation of that belief.[3]

Assuming that the individual has been manifesting his or her religion or belief, the next question is whether there has been an "interference" with that manifestation in a fashion that is attributable to the state. Thus, in the recent judgment of *Begum v. Denbigh High School*, the majority of the House of Lords thought that the freedom of religion of a fourteen-year-old girl had not been interfered with at all in the sense of Article 9 when she was not allowed to attend school wearing a *jilbāb* (which contravened the school's policy on uniforms) because she remained free to attend other schools where she might do so, and, as Lord Hoffman put it, "people sometimes have to suffer some inconvenience for their beliefs."[4] Even if all these hurdles were passed, protected forms of manifestation may be trenched upon by the state provided that its actions are prescribed by law, are necessary in a democratic society for the safeguarding of the interests set out in Article 9(2), and are a proportionate response. In assessing the legitimacy of the interference, the state is accorded a not inconsiderable margin of appreciation.[5]

It is worth stressing that the human rights framework expressly envisages that there will be clashes between the practice of religion and the application of a human rights framework: The human rights framework itself implies that this will be so. Thus, when religious believers seek to act in accordance with their conscience by, for example, refusing to sell contraceptives in pharmacies in France, and the legitimacy of the response of the French authorities is called into question, the result is a debate concerning the extent to which human rights thinking protects the freedom of believers to manifest their beliefs in the manner in which they run their businesses.[6] When teachers wish to wear headscarves while teaching, or students while being taught, and the state, acting in the name of the rights and freedoms of others, seeks to prevent them from doing so, there is a clash of values.[7] Why pretend it can be otherwise? The key point is that, in the outworking of this, the vision of the judicial body concerning the role of religion in the life of the individual and in the life of the nation is critical.

The very first case in which the European Court of Human Rights addressed these questions directly illustrates the point. The case concerned the legitimacy of a Jehovah's Witness's being convicted in Greece for the criminal offence of improper proselytism. In this case, the court set out what remains its fundamental statement concerning the freedom of religion, emphasizing that "freedom of thought, conscience and religion is one of the foundations of a 'democratic society' within the meaning of the Convention. It is, in its religious dimension, one of the most vital elements that go to make up the identity of believers and their conception of life, but it is a precious asset for atheists, agnostics, sceptics and the unconcerned. The pluralism indissociable from a democratic society, which has been dearly won over the centuries, depends on it."[8]

In the context of the case, the court itself avoided "taking sides" by retreating into proceduralism, emphasizing the failure of the domestic court properly to apply the law.[9] Individual judges, though, saw the matter rather more starkly, Judge Martens arguing that this was a matter from which the state should retreat as far as possible and leave contestation on matters of religion to religious believers. Judge Valticos, in one of the more colorful pieces of judicial prose ever penned, firmly upheld the right of the state to prevent the religious beliefs of its citizens from being disturbed by the proselytizing activities of others. Subsequent cases tended to support the right of the state to protect believers from forms of expression that failed to evidence "respect" for the views of others (and particularly when such a lack of respect involved offensive portrayals of objects of religious veneration) but did not require them to do so.[10]

Looking back at these cases, we can see that they all proceed from an assumption that the state had no direct role to play in the religious life of believers. The bulk of the cases concerned claims by individuals that their ability to act in accordance with their beliefs had been negatively impacted by the actions of the state in some fashion or that their capacity to enjoy their religion had been disturbed by what others had said about them. The role of the court was to ensure that in such cases the boundaries of proper respect had not been crossed, bearing in mind the situation in which the issue arose and the rights and freedoms of others that might be at stake.

A major shift in approach has, however, now taken place, largely as a result of the expansion of the Council of Europe to embrace the countries of central and eastern Europe. This has led to a spate of cases that raised questions concerning the registration and official recognition of religious leaders, communities, and churches, and as a result the court has come to see the role of the state in very different terms, describing it as being the "neutral organiser of religious life within the State."[11] At one level, this may appear wholly benign, as the approach is still built on the same ideas of ensuring respect, pluralism, and tolerance. However, it has become increasingly apparent that this is no longer understood to mean respect by others for religion as much as respect by religions for others. More and more, religious manifestation is seen as permissible only to the extent that it is compatible with the underpinnings of the ECHR system, these being democracy and human rights. The court today seems to identify democracy and human rights with tolerance and pluralism and is apt to construe any forms of religious manifestation that do not show these virtues as posing a threat to central values. Moreover, the court expressly asserts the view that, while secularism is compatible with democracy and human rights, some forms of religious expression simply are not. The most dramatic example of this can be found in the *Refah Partisi* case, in which the Grand Chamber said:

> The Court concurs in the Chamber's view that Sharī'a is incompatible with the fundamental principles of democracy, as set forth in the Convention. Like the Constitutional Court, the Court considers that Sharī'a, which faithfully reflects the dogmas and divine rules laid down by religion, is stable and invariable. Principles such as pluralism in the political sphere or the constant evolution of public freedoms have no place in it. The Court notes that, when read together, the offending statements, which contain explicit reference to the introduction of Sharī'a, are difficult to reconcile with the fundamental principles of democracy, as conceived in the Convention taken as a whole. It is difficult to declare one's respect for democracy and human rights while at the same time supporting a regime based on Sharī'a, which clearly diverges from Convention values, particularly with regard to its criminal law and criminal procedure, its rules on the legal status of women, and the way it intervenes in all spheres of private and public life in accordance with religious precepts. . . . In the Court's view, a political party whose actions seem to be aimed at introducing Sharī'a in a State party to the Convention can hardly be regarded as an association complying with the democratic ideal that underlies the whole of the Convention.[12]

Such statements from the European Court of Human Rights are not likely to encourage those seeking to find space for the expression of faith in the political society of which they form a part. Once again, according to the court, the human rights approach is to ensure that followers of a religion might believe as they wish and that they might be free to practice the rituals of their faith provided that this is compatible with the general public good, but the state is to rise above religion, ordering and policing its practice but not embracing or reflecting particular tenets of belief.

Against this background, the most recent of this line of cases, *Sahin v. Turkey*, seems an almost inevitable decision. *Sahin* concerned a prohibition on the wearing of headscarves and beards while attending university classes and examinations in Turkey. The court concluded that, although this amounted to a restriction on the manifestation of a religious belief, that restriction was justified in ECHR terms. This has attracted considerable criticism on many grounds, but I wish to highlight the general point that the court seriously distorts Article 9 and the freedom of religion to the extent that it now appears to be as much a tool for the repression of religious liberty as a means of upholding it.[13] It is true that the court is merely repeating what it has always said when it argues that freedom of religion is "primarily" a matter of individual conscience, when it emphasizes the element of "inner belief" by claiming that the freedom of religion merely "implies" a right to manifest, and when it reiterates that not every act motivated by a religion is a legally recognized manifestation of that religion.[14]

This approach dates back to the very first case, that of *Kokkinakis*, in which the court said that "whilst religious freedom is primarily a matter of individual conscience, it also implies, *inter alia*, freedom to 'manifest [one's] religion.'"[15] However, in *Kokkinakis*, the court followed this by saying, "Bearing witness in words and deeds is bound up with the existence of religious convictions," and went on to find a violation of the freedom of religion in the criminal conviction of a Jehovah's Witness for proselytism. In other words, it served as a preface to a broadening of the concept. In *Sahin*, those selfsame words are used as a preface to the limiting of the freedom to bear witness, this being brought about by the stress placed by the court on the role of the state as being to "reconcile the interests of the various groups" and to "ensure" respect between believers and between believers and nonbelievers.[16] It even suggests that there is a positive obligation of the state to ensure that this is the case. I find the idea of the state's being under a positive legal obligation to ensure that religious believers demonstrate respect for each other and for nonbelievers an almost impossible notion. In contrast, the idea that the state might be able to ensure that appropriate processes are in place in order to enhance the prospect of tolerance and mutual respect seems to me to be a more attainable objective, and more in accord with the concept of positive obligations, which work best when they are addressed to means rather than ends.[17]

This was not the route followed in the *Sahin* case, however, and at the end of the day the court proceeds on little more than an assertion of the need to preserve general public order and religious pluralism through the eradication of a particular form of public manifestation of religious belief in state-run institutions. Indeed, the need to restrict the manifestation of religion in order to secure pluralism and tolerance between religions is becoming something of a counterintuitive mantra in human rights circles.[18] In adopting such a stance, the court is not acting in an evenhanded fashion, as it is embracing a form of "secular fundamentalism" that is incompatible with its self-professed role as the overseer of the state as the "neutral and impartial organizer" of the system of beliefs within the state. This is deeply problematic for all religious believers.

It is also deeply problematic on another level. As I have already indicated, the court today stresses the role of the state as the neutral and impartial organizer of religious life. In many states—like it or not—religious difference is seen as a threat to public order. Many states use their laws regarding religious associations as a means to differentiate between those forms of religion that are politically welcome and those that are not. It is very difficult to explain to states that they are bound to strive for religious toleration and pluralism through a policy of strict neutrality between all forms of religion and belief, while at the same time insisting that it is quite legitimate for the state to prohibit public forms of religious manifestation that the state considers to undermine its essential political foundations.

Moreover, where does this leave those believers from religious traditions that seek to order their life in the public space in a different way, based on, for example, the tenets of their faith. Why should they be denied the opportunity to do so? The answer that the court provides is that states need to order their affairs in the interests of all within their jurisdiction rather than in accordance with the views and beliefs of some, be they a majority or a minority—and tolerance, respect, and pluralism are difficult values to cross swords with.

Yet these values are not neutral: They are vehicles for the legitimation of a very real set of assumptions concerning the proper reach of religion in the public sphere. Even advancing these claims of human rights through the instrumentality of international law has the effect of validating the interstate system, with its rather peculiar and eminently contestable way of conceiving the ordering of human society.[19] Moreover, it is arguable that the entire way in which we conceive of human rights has the effect of privileging certain forms of religious belief. It is clearly more difficult for what may be called "fringe" religions or new religious movements to benefit from human rights protections than it is for more mainstream religious traditions to do so.[20] Beyond this, it seems to me that the practical application of human rights approaches to the freedom of religion is structurally biased toward those forms of religious belief that are essentially private and individualist—one might say, pietistic—rather than communitarian in organizational orientation. This is not, perhaps, surprising, as the more communitarian-oriented religious traditions tend to challenge the state's ordering of society in a manner that more individualistically focused religions do not. It is not an accident that Western Christianity has found it easier to cohabit with plural liberal democracies than some other forms of religious traditions, though it appears that this is becoming increasingly difficult as human rights thinking concerning the freedom of religion moves away from liberal secularism to what has been described as a form of fundamentalist secularism. This has the perhaps unexpected consequence of increasing the space for religious communities to come together in order to forge their own distinctive contribution to the realization of the freedom of religion or belief, and to do so in a fashion that seeks to challenge, rather than to conform to, human rights law.

In recent times, religious folk have tended to leave the realization of the freedom of religions to the application of human rights law. I believe that there is an increasing realization that it is necessary for the voice of religious believers to be better heard and better understood by the human rights community if freedom of religion is to continue to be best pursued through the application of human rights law in the modern world. There is an equally pressing need for religious communities to refrain from using the legal regulation of religious life to deny freedom of religion to those whose views do not accord with their own, because this merely serves to reinforce the views of those who seek to limit the role of religion in the life of the community as a whole and to place restrictions on the life of religious communities themselves. As a lawyer, I feel there is a need to recapture a vision of law as the just ordering of society in the light of existing conceptions, and that means taking those conceptions as our starting point rather than imposing increasingly alien solutions to questions upon believers in the name of human rights on the mistaken assumption that it is the only acceptable conception.

Chapter 8

Modern Texts

8.1 The Barmen Declaration

Miroslav Volf

The Theological Declaration of Barmen was addressed in 1934 by the "confessing" church to the German Christians who were seeking to achieve a synthesis between Nazism and Christianity. By contrast, the Barmen declaration insists that, while in the purposes of God the state has a positive role to maintain justice and peace, it must not seek to become "the sole and total order of human life and so fulfill the vocation of the Church as well." For its part, the church must resist pressure to reshape its message according to "the prevailing ideological and political convictions of the day." It should be noted that the declaration insists on the commission, rather than the right, of the church to maintain a steadfast witness to the Gospel of Jesus Christ.[21]

The Barmen declaration can be seen as a direct response to one distorted pattern of political implementation of Luther's "two kingdoms" doctrine—that led by the party of the German Christians, headed by Bishop Ludwig Müller. In opposition to his subordination of church to state, the resistance party within the German churches, uniting theologians of Calvinist and Lutheran confessions, came together to agree to a text drafted by Karl Barth (1882–1968) that, while accepting the principle that spiritual and temporal governments were united as coming from God, emphasized the possibility of their disjunction also. In the context of Germany in the 1930s, indeed, this possibility had become an undoubted reality. Over the centuries, the interpretation of Luther's distinction of "gospel" and "law" had shifted with the gradual process of secularization, so that the latter had come to be seen as the positive law of the state rather than God's law. This enabled the state to usurp more and more of the realm Luther had designated for the church, so that Christianity could be restricted to a "spiritual" space only. Under Nazi rule, this could be expressed in the slogan "Christ for the soul, Hitler for the people."

It is to this challenge that the Barmen declaration responds, by asserting the integrity of the church as mandated by God. The influence of Barthian theology is strong, with the assertion of Christ's authority over all aspects of life and the rejection of any sense of revelation in creation or in history other than the word of God in Jesus Christ; indeed, for this reason it was criticized by some leading Lutheran theologians.[22] The primacy of the text's focus on the ordering of the church is shown by its very form as a successive condemnation of seven "false doctrines" (*falsche Lehre*)—in other words, an anathematization of heresy.[23] Theologians of the confessing church such as Dietrich Bonhoeffer thus insisted that, following its proclamation, they were no longer an "opposition" within the church, but rather constituted the church itself: "The Barmen Declaration was a true confession to the Lord Jesus effected through the Holy Spirit. . . . [I]ts character is one that shapes and divides the Church."[24]

The Barmen declaration has proved an inspiration for Christians in other situations of state-imposed oppression: The idea of "confessing church," for example, resonated strongly in apartheid-era South Africa. As against the mere possibility of passive disobedience, its theological stance seemed to many to provide a basis for active resistance. At the same time, it is a text closely related to the particular context of 1930s Germany, and questions will always be raised about the propriety of borrowing language from that time to apply to another.[25] It remains true that, despite its undoubted emphasis on ecclesial integrity, the Barmen declaration also points to a church faithfully and freely discharging its divine commission as being a sign of hope of the transformation that God intends and that he can bring to the realm of the state also.

I An Appeal to the Evangelical Congregations and Christians in Germany

The Confessional Synod of the German Evangelical Church met in Barmen, May 29–31, 1934. Here representatives from all the German Confessional Churches met with one accord in a confession of the one Lord of the one, holy, apostolic Church. In fidelity to their confession of faith, members of Lutheran, Reformed, and United Churches sought a common message for the need and temptation of the Church in our day. With gratitude to God they are convinced that they have been given a common word to utter. It was not their intention to found a new Church or to form a union. For nothing was farther from their minds than the abolition of the confessional status of our Churches. Their intention was, rather, to withstand in faith and unanimity the destruction of the Confession of Faith, and thus of the Evangelical Church in Germany. In opposition to attempts to establish the unity of the German Evangelical Church by means of false doctrine, by the use of force and by insincere practices, the Confessional Synod insists that the unity of the Evangelical Churches in Germany can come only from the Word of God in faith through the Holy Spirit. Thus alone is the Church renewed.

Therefore the Confessional Synod calls upon the congregations to range themselves behind it in prayer, and steadfastly to gather around those pastors and teachers who are loyal to the Confessions.

Be not deceived by loose talk, as if we meant to oppose the unity of the German nation! Do not listen to the seducers who pervert our intentions, as if we wanted to break up the unity of the German Evangelical Church or to forsake the Confessions of the Fathers!

Try the spirits whether they are of God! Prove also the words of the Confessional Synod of the German Evangelical Church to see whether they agree with Holy Scripture and with the Confessions of the Fathers. If you find that we are speaking contrary to Scripture, then do not listen to us! But if you find that we are taking our stand upon Scripture, then let no fear or temptation keep you from treading with us the path of faith and obedience to the Word of God, in order that God's people be of one mind upon earth and that we in faith experience what he himself has said: "I will never leave you, nor forsake you." Therefore, "Fear not, little flock, for it is your Father's good pleasure to give you the kingdom."

II Theological Declaration Concerning the Present Situation of the German Evangelical Church

According to the opening words of its constitution of July 11, 1933, the German Evangelical Church is a federation of Confessional Churches that grew out of the Reformation and that enjoy equal rights. The theological basis for the unification of these churches is laid down in Article 1 and Article 2 (1) of the constitution of the German Evangelical Church that was recognized by the Reich Government on July 14, 1933:

- Article 1. The inviolable foundation of the German Evangelical Church is the gospel of Jesus Christ as it is attested for us in Holy Scripture and brought to light again in the Confessions of the Reformation. The full powers that the Church needs for its mission are hereby determined and limited.
- Article 2 (1). The German Evangelical Church is divided into member Churches (*Landeskirchen*).

We, the representatives of Lutheran, Reformed, and United Churches, of free synods, Church assemblies, and parish organizations united in the Confessional Synod of the German Evangelical Church, declare that we stand together on the ground of the German Evangelical Church as a federation of German Confessional Churches. We are bound together by the confession of the one Lord of the one, holy, catholic, and apostolic Church.

We publicly declare before all evangelical Churches in Germany that what they hold in common in this Confession is grievously imperiled, and with it the unity of the German Evangelical Church. It is threatened by the teaching methods and actions of the ruling church party of the "German Christians" and of the church administration carried on by them. These have become more and more apparent during the first year of the existence of the German Evangelical Church. This threat consists in the fact that the theological basis on which the German Evangelical Church is united has been continually and systematically thwarted and rendered ineffective by alien principles, on the part of the leaders and spokesmen of the "German Christians" as well as on the part of the church administration. When these principles are held to be valid, then, according to all the Confessions in force among us, the Church ceases to be the Church and the German Evangelical Church, as a federation of Confessional Churches, becomes intrinsically impossible.

As members of Lutheran, Reformed, and United Churches we may and must speak with one voice in this matter today. Precisely because we want to be and to remain faithful to our various confessions, we may not keep silent, since we believe that we have been given a common message to utter in a time of common need and temptation. We commend to God what this may mean for the interrelations of the Confessional Churches.

In view of the errors of the "German Christians" of the present Reich Church government which are devastating the Church and also therefore breaking up the unity of the German Evangelical Church, we confess the following evangelical truths:

1. "I am the way, and the truth, and the life; no one comes to the Father, but by me" [John 14:6]. "Truly, truly, I say to you, he who does not enter the sheepfold by the door, but climbs in by another way, that man is a thief and a robber . . . I am the door; if anyone enters by me, he will be saved" [John 10:1, 9].

Jesus Christ, as he is attested for us in Holy Scripture, is the one Word of God which we have to hear and which we have to trust and obey in life and in death.

We reject the false doctrine, as though the Church could and would have to acknowledge as a source of its proclamation, apart from and besides this one Word of God, still other events and powers, figures and truths, as God's revelation.

2. "Christ Jesus, whom God has made our wisdom, our righteousness and sanctification and redemption" [1 Cor. 1:30].

As Jesus Christ is God's assurance of the forgiveness of all our sins, so, in the same way and with the same seriousness he is also God's mighty claim upon our whole life. Through him befalls us a joyful deliverance from the godless fetters of this world for a free, grateful service to his creatures.

We reject the false doctrine, as though there were areas of our life in which we would not belong to Jesus Christ, but to other lords—areas in which we would not need justification and sanctification through him.

3. "Rather, speaking the truth in love, we are to grow up in every way into him who is the head, into Christ, from whom the whole body [is] joined and knit together" [Eph. 4:15, 16].

The Christian Church is the congregation of the brethren in which Jesus Christ acts presently as the Lord in Word and sacrament through the Holy Spirit. As the Church of pardoned sinners, it has to testify in the midst of a sinful world, with its faith as with its obedience, with its message as with its order, that it is solely his property, and that it lives and wants to live solely from his comfort and from his direction in the expectation of his appearance.

We reject the false doctrine, as though the church were permitted to abandon the form of its message and order to its own pleasure or to changes in prevailing ideological and political convictions.

4. "You know that the rulers of the Gentiles lord it over them, and their great men exercise authority over them. It shall not be so among you; but whoever would be great among you must be your servant" [Matt. 20:25, 26].

The various offices in the Church do not establish a dominion of some over the others; on the contrary, they are for the exercise of the ministry entrusted to and enjoined upon the whole congregation.

We reject the false doctrine, as though the Church, apart from this ministry, could and were permitted to give itself, or allow to be given to it, special leaders vested with ruling powers.

5. "Fear God. Honour the emperor" [1 Pet. 2:17].

Scripture tells us that, in the as yet unredeemed world in which the Church also exists, the State has by divine appointment the task of providing for justice and peace. [It fulfils this task] by means of the threat and exercise of force, according to the measure of human judgment and human ability. The Church acknowledges the benefit of this divine appointment in gratitude and reverence before Him. It calls to mind the Kingdom of God, God's commandment and righteousness, and thereby the responsibility both of rulers and of the ruled. It trusts and obeys the power of the Word by which God upholds all things.

We reject the false doctrine, as though the State, over and beyond its special commission, should and could become the single and totalitarian order of human life, thus fulfilling the Church's vocation as well.

We reject the false doctrine, as though the Church, over and beyond its special commission, should and could appropriate the characteristics, the tasks, and the dignity of the State, thus itself becoming an organ of the State.

6. "Lo, I am with you always, to the close of the age" [Matt. 28:20]. "The Word of God is not fettered" [2 Tim. 2:9].

The Church's commission, upon which its freedom is founded, consists in delivering the message of the free grace of God to all people in Christ's stead, and therefore in the ministry of his own Word and work through sermon and sacrament.

We reject the false doctrine, as though the Church in human arrogance could place the Word and work of the Lord in the service of any arbitrarily chosen desires, purposes, and plans.

The Confessional Synod of the German Evangelical Church declares that it sees in the acknowledgement of these truths and in the rejection of these errors the indispensable theological basis of the German Evangelical Church as a federation of Confessional Churches. It invites all who are able to accept its declaration to be mindful of these theological principles in their decisions in church politics. It entreats all whom it concerns to return to the unity of faith, love, and hope.

8.2 Writings of Imam Khomeini

Seyed Amir Akrami

The religious state in Iran was born out of a particular interpretation of Islam put forward by Ayatollah Khomeini (1902–89). Although his idea of *vilāyat-e-faqīh* (the "Governance of the Jurisconsult")[26] was not in itself a unique one in Shī'ism, or in some ways even in Sunnī Islam, Khomeini's interpretation, expansion, and implementation of it represented a radical departure.[27]

Shī'ite theories of governance in relation to religious leadership in Iran are diverse and can be seen to have evolved over four main periods. From the tenth to the sixteenth centuries, the development of *fiqh* was predominantly focused on personal life, with little or no elaboration on the relationship between religion and politics. From the sixteenth to the nineteenth centuries, though, hints of the doctrine of *vilāyat-e-faqīh* begin to appear, under the Safavid and Qajar dynasties, though tensions with the ruling authorities mean that these were never fully developed. In the early twentieth century, the constitutional movement saw new concepts introduced into Iranian political thought, with a critical attitude manifested toward religious despotism. The fourth phase of evolution is the *vilāyat-e-faqīh* theory as promoted by Khomeini in his writings and speeches, mostly before the Iranian Revolution of 1978–79, and then to some extent implemented by him following that event.[28]

Khomeini's theory rests on two main assertions. First, if Islam, as a divine law, is to be implemented, this will require the establishment of a government that can put the law into practice. Political power must thus be subordinated to Islamic precepts, criteria, values, and regulations. Second, following the occultation of the twelfth imam, there is no divinely guided and infallible spiritual leader in succession to the Prophet.[29] Islamic government in this period must therefore involve the guardianship or governance of just jurisconsults (*fuqahā'*), who have all the rights and responsibilities that the Prophet and the imams had at their times; this is the doctrine of *vilāyat-e-faqīh*. Khomeini stresses that the spiritual qualities of the just *faqīh* should function as a safeguard against his abuse of the power entrusted to him: Being morally just, in Islamic terminology, means being free from pursuing one's own worldly material desires.

Article 5 of the Constitution of the Islamic Republic of Iran refers to the idea of the "Guardianship of the jurisconsult," giving the leadership of the nation to "the just and pious *faqīh*."[30] However, the doctrine has been criticized by many scholars, among whom the most prominent is Ayatollah Hosein 'Ali Montazeri, Khomeini's originally intended successor.[31] Although Montazeri supported the inclusion of *vilāyat-e-faqīh* in the constitution, he maintained that it led to many unintended negative practical consequences, contending that the absolute concentration of power in the hands of the *faqīh* opened the door to dictatorship and overburdened one person with the weight of its business. He suggested both that the *faqīh* should be elected, not appointed, and that the exercise of *vilāyat* should be limited to supervision, not active interference. In practice in postrevolutionary Iran, the need to find a way of mediating between the elected Parliament and the Council of Guardians has meant that the principle of *maṣlahā*, "public good," is increasingly invoked to ensure successful government.[32]

Islamic government is necessary for the implementation of Islamic law[33]

A body of laws alone is not sufficient for a society to be reformed. In order for law to ensure the reform and happiness of man, there must be an executive power and an executor. For this reason, God Almighty, in addition to revealing a body of law (i.e., the ordinances of the Sharī'a), has laid down a particular form of government together with executive and administrative institutions.

The Most Noble Messenger (peace and blessings be upon him) headed the executive and administrative institutions of Muslim society. In addition to conveying the revelation and expounding and interpreting the articles of faith and the ordinances and institutions of Islam, he undertook the implementation of law and the establishment of the ordinances of Islam, thereby bringing into being the Islamic state. He did not content himself with the promulgation of law; rather, he implemented it at the same time, cutting off hands and administering lashings and stonings. After the Most Noble Messenger, his successor had the same duty and function. When the Prophet appointed a successor, it was not for the purpose of expounding articles of faith and law; it was for the implementation of law and the execution of God's ordinances. It was this function—the execution of law and the establishment of Islamic institutions—that made the appointment of a successor such an important matter that the Prophet would have failed to fulfill his mission if he had neglected it. For after the Prophet, the Muslims still needed someone to execute laws and establish the institutions of Islam in society, so that they might attain happiness in this world and the hereafter.[34]

By their very nature, in fact, law and social institutions require the existence of an executor. It has always and everywhere been the case that legislation alone has little benefit: legislation by itself cannot assure the well-being of man. After the establishment of legislation, an executive power must come into being, a power that implements the laws and the verdicts given by the courts, thus allowing people to benefit from the laws and the just sentences the courts deliver. Islam has therefore established an executive power in the same way that it has brought laws into being. The person who holds this executive power is known as the *vali-e-amr*.

The Sunna and path of the Prophet constitute a proof of the necessity for establishing government. First, he himself established a government, as history testifies. He engaged in the implementation of laws, the establishment of the ordinances of Islam, and the administration of society. He sent out governors to different regions; both sat in judgment himself and appointed judges; dispatched emissaries to foreign states, tribal chieftains, and kings; concluded treaties and pacts; and took command in battle. In short, he fulfilled all the functions of government. Second, he designated a ruler to succeed him, in accordance with divine command. If God Almighty, through the Prophet, designated a man who was to rule over Muslim society after him, this is in itself an indication that government remains a necessity after the departure of the Prophet from this world. Again, since the Most Noble Messenger promulgated the divine command through his act of appointing a successor, he also implicitly stated the necessity for establishing government.

It is self-evident that the necessity for enactment of the law, which necessitated the formation of a government by the Prophet (upon whom be peace), was not confined or restricted to his time, but continues after his departure from this world. According to one of the noble verses of the Qur'ān, the ordinances of Islam are not limited with respect to time or place; they are permanent and must be enacted until the end of time. They were not revealed merely for the time of the Prophet, only to be abandoned thereafter, with retribution and the penal code of Islam no longer to be enacted, or the taxes prescribed by Islam no longer collected, and the defense of the lands and people of Islam suspended. The claim that the laws of Islam may remain in abeyance or are restricted to a particular time or place is contrary to the essential creedal bases of Islam. Since the enactment of laws, then, is necessary after the departure of the Prophet from this world, and indeed, will remain so until the end of time, the formation of a government and the establishment of executive and administrative organs are also necessary. Without the formation of a government and the establishment of such organs to ensure that through enactment of the law, all activities of the individual take place in the framework of a just system, chaos and anarchy will prevail and social, intellectual, and moral corruption will arise. The only way to prevent the emergence of anarchy and disorder and to protect society from corruption is to form a government and thus impart order to all the affairs of the country.

Both reason and divine law, then, demonstrate the necessity in our time for what was necessary during the lifetime of the Prophet and the age of the Commander of the Faithful, ʿAlī ibn Abī Ṭālib (peace be upon them)—namely the formation of a government and the establishment of executive and administrative organs.

In order to clarify the matter further, let us pose the following questions: From the time of the Lesser Occultation down to the present (a period of more than twelve centuries that may continue for hundreds of millennia if it is not appropriate for the Occulted Imam to manifest himself), is it proper that the laws of Islam be cast aside and remain unexecuted, so that everyone acts as he pleases and anarchy prevails? Were the laws that the Prophet of Islam labored so hard for twenty-three years to set forth, promulgate, and execute valid only for a limited period of time? Did God limit the validity of His laws to two hundred years? Was everything pertaining to Islam meant to be abandoned after the Lesser Occultation? Anyone who believes so, or voices such a belief, is worse situated than the person who believes and proclaims that Islam has been superseded or abrogated by another supposed revelation.

Islamic government involves the governance of the jurisconsult[35]

The qualifications essential for the ruler derive directly from the nature and form of Islamic government. In addition to general qualifications like intelligence and administrative ability, there are two other essential qualifications: knowledge of the law and justice.

After the death of the Prophet (upon whom be peace), differences arose concerning the identity of the person who was to succeed him, but all the Muslims were in agreement that his successor should be someone knowledgeable and accomplished; there was disagreement only as to his identity.

Since Islamic government is a government of law, knowledge of the law is necessary for the ruler, as has been laid down in tradition. Indeed such knowledge is necessary not only for the ruler, but also for anyone holding a post or exercising some government function. The ruler, however, must surpass all others in knowledge. In laying claim to the Imamate, our Imams also argued that the ruler must be more learned than everyone else. The objections raised by the Shīʿī *ʿulamā'* are also to the same effect. A certain person asked the caliph a point of law and he was unable to answer; he was therefore unfit for the position of leader and successor to the Prophet. Or again, a certain act he performed was contrary to the laws of Islam; hence he was unworthy of his high post.

Knowledge of the law and justice, then, constitute fundamental qualifications in the view of the Muslims. Other matters have no importance or relevance in this connection. Knowledge of the nature of the angels, for example, or of the attributes of the Creator, Exalted and Almighty, is of no relevance to the question of leadership. In the same vein, one who knows all the natural sciences, uncovers all the secrets of nature, or has a good knowledge of music does not thereby qualify for leadership or acquire any priority in the matter of exercising government over those who know the laws of Islam and are just. The sole matters relevant to rule, those that were mentioned and discussed in the time of the Most Noble Messenger (upon whom be peace) and our Imams (upon whom be peace) and were, in addition, unanimously accepted by the Muslims, are: first, the knowledgeability of the ruler or caliph, i.e., his knowledge of the provisions and ordinances of Islam; and second, his justice, i.e., his excellence in belief and morals.

Reason also dictates the necessity for these qualities because Islamic government is a government of law, not the arbitrary rule of an individual over the people, or the domination of a group of individuals over the whole people. If the ruler is unacquainted with the contents of the law, he is not fit to rule; for if he follows the legal pronouncements of others, his power to govern will be impaired, but if, on the other hand, he does not follow such guidance, he will be unable to rule correctly and implement the rules of Islam. It is an established principle that "the *faqīh* has authority over the ruler." If the ruler adheres to Islam, he must necessarily submit to the *faqīh*, asking him about the laws and ordinances of Islam in order to implement them. This being the case, the true rulers are the *fuqahā'* themselves, and rulership ought officially to be theirs, to apply to them, not to those who are obliged to follow the guidance of the *fuqahā'* on account of their own ignorance of the law.

Of course, it is not necessary for all officials, provincial governors, and administrators to know all the laws of Islam and be *fuqahā'*; it is enough that they should know the laws pertaining to their functions and duties. Such was the case in the time of the Prophet and the Commander of the Faithful (peace be upon them). The highest authority must possess the qualities mentioned—comprehensive knowledge and justice—but his assistants, officials, and those sent to the provinces need know only the laws relevant to their own tasks; on other matters they must consult the ruler.

The ruler must also possess excellence in morals and belief; he must be just and untainted by major sin. Anyone who wishes to enact the penalties provided by Islam (i.e., to implement the penal code), to supervise the public treasury and the income and expenditures of the state, and to have God assign to him the power to administer the affairs of His creatures must not be a sinner. God says in the Qur'ān: "My covenant does not embrace the wrong-doer" [al-Baqara 2:124]; therefore, He will not assign such functions to an oppressor or sinner.

If the ruler is not just in granting the Muslims their rights, he will not conduct himself equitably in levying taxes and spending them correctly and in implementing the penal code. It becomes possible then for his assistants, helpers, and confidants to impose their will on society, diverting the public treasury to personal and frivolous use.

Given the contingencies with which Islam has surrounded the operation of this principle, it cannot harm anyone. Particular attributes have been set down as necessary for the "holder of authority" (*vali-e-amr*) and the *faqīh*, and they are attributes that prevent him from going astray. If he utters a single lie, or takes a single wrong step, he forfeits his claim to governance. The whole purpose of the clause in the Constitution relating to the governance of the *faqīh* is to prevent tyranny and despotism.[36]

8.3 The Second Vatican Council on Religious Freedom

Carolyn Evans

The Declaration on Religious Freedom, *Dignitatis humanae*, was one of the most influential documents to emerge from the Second Vatican Council of 1962–65. *Dignitatis humanae* argues strongly that the freedom to follow one's conscience in religious matters is a God-given right that states should uphold even if, in the view of the Catholic Church, a person's conscience is in error.[37]

In October 1958 Cardinal Angelo Giuseppe Roncalli was elected pope. He took the name John XXIII, making a self-deprecating joke that all the other popes named John had had brief reigns.[38] He too was expected to be a transitional pope. Already an old man and of generally traditional views, his pontificate was expected to last only a couple of years and to be a relatively uneventful period of rebuilding in the church.

In the event, he did hold office for only five years before he died, but that period saw a great transformation begin within the Catholic Church.[39] John XXIII saw the need for the church to be open to change and renewal—*aggiornamento*, as he called it—to enable it to respond to the "signs of the times." The change came in many ways, but one of the most important steps taken by John was the calling of a council of all the bishops of the Catholic Church throughout the world—which at the time included more than two thousand men.[40] There had only been twenty-one such general councils in the whole of the church's history, and their purpose was often to condemn error, to strength doctrine, or to reinforce the hierarchy. The First Vatican Council, for example, held in 1869–70, proclaimed the doctrine of papal infallibility, thus reinforcing the hierarchy of the church.

But neither John's personality nor his theology was inclined toward condemnations or the calling down of anathemas, and he warned the church and the world against prophets of doom. He wanted a more positive council that would engage with the many real problems that the world and the church were facing, giving guidance and encouragement to the people of God.[41]

At the time that the council was called, the official position of the church was still one that was opposed to religious liberty. The maxim that there is no right in error was held by a strong group within the Vatican, and the church more generally. Anti-Semitism was still a problem, with several bishops condemning John's moves toward a closer relationship with the Jewish community by arguing that Jews were guilty of deicide because of the Jewish people's role in the crucifixion two thousand years earlier.[42] When John proposed a Commission for Christian Unity and allowed observers from other Christian churches to sit in on council discussions, he caused white-lipped fury among the more traditional grouping in the Vatican.[43]

Against this backdrop of centuries of hostility to religious freedom and condemnation of even mild ecumenical movements toward other Christian groups—let alone people of other faiths such as Muslims—the work of the Vatican Council on religious freedom begun under John XXIII and completed under Pope Paul VI was truly extraordinary.[44]

Set in the context of international law, however, it was a belated (if important) recognition of developments that were already well established elsewhere. It is instructive to compare briefly *Dignitatis humanae*, as the primary document that emerged from the council dealing with religious freedom, with the first major international instrument that specified a right to religious freedom, Article 18 of the Universal Declaration of Human Rights.

Article 18 sets out the right to religious freedom in these terms: "Everyone has the right to freedom of thought, conscience and religion; this right includes freedom to change his religion or belief, and freedom, either along or in community with others and in public or private, to manifest his religion or belief in teaching, practice, worship and observance."[45]

There are a number of similarities between the two documents. Both were drafted after years of contestation, debate, and redrafting in times that were both difficult and hopeful. The Universal Declaration was accepted by the General Assembly in 1948—a time of hope for a peaceful world after the travails of two world wars, but also a time in which the Cold War was beginning to exercise its malign influence on international politics.[46] The Second Vatican Council began during a time when the Cold War had become hot during the Cuban missile crisis and when the threat of nuclear annihilation was a very real one for many people. Yet there was also some hope that the Kennedy and Khrushchev governments might be able to move to a period of better relations than had existed in the past between the two superpowers. Both documents therefore were not mere intellectual exercises or abstract documents but were created with a sense of some urgency as a response to the complex times in which they were written. They were composed with a desire to build on that which was hopeful in the world and to play a part in resolving the serious problems that faced humanity.

They were both also written—despite the contrary sometimes being claimed of the Universal Declaration—by people from a wide variety of countries and after much international consultation.[47] This was particularly important in the case of *Dignitatis humanae* because the traditional sources of power within the Vatican—who under normal circumstances wielded enormous power and influence over developments within the church—found that the wider body of bishops had a far more liberal view of religious freedom than did the traditionalists. Some participants, such as many of the American bishops, had experienced the benefit of living as a religious minority in a country where religious freedom was valued and wanted to remind the bishops from Catholic countries of the importance of such liberty.[48] American bishops were loath to take the hypocritical position that they were deserving of religious toleration as a minority in a predominantly Protestant country but that predominantly Catholic countries were justified in oppressing the liberty of the Protestant or other religious minorities who dwelt there.

Thus both documents were a product of their times and the people who drafted them. It is useful to compare them in a little more detail in relation to a few key issues: first, the source of the right to religious freedom; second, the nature of that right, particularly its implications for religious truth; and third, the questions of who bears obligations and who benefits from religious freedom.

First, the philosophical debate over the source of human rights generally or religious freedom specifically within the international community has proved enduring and has resulted in some concern about the moral strength of the foundations of the international legal system for the protection of human rights. It is sometimes noted that in the United Nations context we can all agree about human rights as long as we do not have to explain why we agree.

By contrast, the drafters of *Dignitatis humanae* had the benefit of a far more cohesive philosophical outlook than did the drafters of the Universal Declaration. *Dignitatis humanae* confidently and regularly makes reference to the divine underpinnings of religious freedom. Yet the document is consciously aiming to reach beyond a narrowly Catholic audience—though the extent to which it succeeds is more questionable. The key passage about the source of religious freedom is the second paragraph of Article 2: "The council further declares that the right to religious freedom has its foundation in the very dignity of the human person as this humanity is known through the revealed word of God and by reason itself." In this passage we see the duality of its underlying reasoning—reasoning that is partly religious and partly secular. *Dignitatis humanae* places the dignity of the human person as the foundation of the right to religious freedom (a similar position to that of the Universal Declaration, which begins with a recognition of "the inherent dignity and of equal and inalienable rights of all members of the human family"). But, unlike the Universal Declaration, it gives two explanations for human beings' possessing this dignity. The first is that the word of God has revealed this inherent dignity. *Dignitatis humanae* points to the example of Jesus and the apostles in their ministry. Article 11 notes that "Christ is at once our Master and our Lord and also meek and humble of heart. In attracting and inviting his disciples He used patience. He wrought miracles to illuminate his teaching and to establish its truth, but His intention was to rouse faith in His disciples, not to exert coercion on them." He was not a political messiah and rejected temporal authority. The apostles too rejected force or deception in making converts, and thus *Dignitatis humanae* concludes confidently that in "faithfulness therefore to the truth of the Gospel, the church is following the way of Christ and the apostles when she recognizes and gives support to the principle of religious freedom." The source of the right is thus clear and, for believers, strong.

However, for those who are not believers in God or indeed in this particular understanding of God, this justification of religious freedom appears to be no foundation at all. For them, therefore, and following in the well-established natural law tradition of the church, comes the role of reason. Even those without the faith that allows them to accept the divine origins of human dignity should be able through reason alone to come to the same conclusion. It must be said that the way in which such reason operates or details of what it reveals are far sketchier than those about the theological underpinnings of this dignity.[49]

Second, this conception of religious freedom, with its strong reliance on religious doctrine, was hard for many of those outside the Catholic (or at least Christian) community to accept as convincing. But the conception was also hard for many of the more traditional thinkers within the church itself.

The individual drafters of the Universal Declaration did hold particular religious or philosophical beliefs, but it was acknowledged (after some debate) that the declaration itself could not refer to God or to any particular religious belief. The Universal Declaration is agnostic on whether there is a God or gods and whether any particular religion is true. It would have been impossible to draft a concept of religious freedom that implicitly or explicitly gave priority or approval to a particular religious belief in a document that was intended to be for all peoples of all faiths in all countries and was drafted by people with a variety of beliefs, including the strong atheist lobby from the Soviet states.

For the Catholic Church, however, there could be no such separation of the personal religious beliefs of those taking part in the council and the outcomes of that council. The church could not be expected to remain agnostic about the true religion or to say that any religious belief is the equal of any other. To even suggest that would be to undermine the most basic teachings of the church. So the traditionalists argued that there was no point and much danger in allowing people to search for the truth in matters of religion. The truth was known—it was an objective fact—and thus it was better for people not to be confused by any suggestion from religious or secular authorities that other religions might have some value or validity.[50]

Again, we can see two strands of reasoning in response to these concerns—one religious, the other more secular. The first is to emphasize that "true" religion is not a matter of compulsion. Indeed compulsion undermines the capacity for an authentically religious response. There is a moral obligation to seek religious truth, and man is "bound to follow his conscience in order that he may come to God, the end and purpose of his life" (Article 3).[51] As Article 2 puts it, people cannot discharge the obligation to seek the truth "unless they enjoy immunity from external coercion as well as psychological freedom." So the human conscience must be given a sphere in which to operate with integrity—otherwise the strength of the beliefs that result will be diminished. In some of the most famous words in the declaration, the council states that "the truth cannot impose itself except by virtue of its own truth, as it makes its entrance into the mind at once quietly and with power."[52]

The other key element of the reasoning is that religious freedom is not about undermining religious truth. Instead it "has to do with immunity from coercion in civil society. It therefore leaves untouched traditional Catholic doctrine on the moral duty of men and societies towards the true religion and toward the one Church of Christ."[53] The final sentence proved very controversial outside the church, but for those within the church, the council neatly sidestepped some controversial issues.[54] In the moral realm, the truth of the teachings of the church remains untouched. The declaration is primarily juridical—it is about the proper role of the state and the impropriety of coercion rather than about the truth or falsity of any particular religious belief.[55] In both *Dignitatis humanae* and other documents of the church developed around this time, most importantly John's encyclical *Pacem in Terris*, there is a growing recognition by the church that a certain degree of freedom in civil society, together with a government that respects human rights, is the best environment in which human beings can respond to God.[56] Long connected with monarchies and authoritarian governments, the church was slowly accepting the need for democracies and limited scope to state power.[57]

This juridical turn assists some of those who might otherwise find it difficult to accept a doctrine that seemed to give equal status to all religions. It situates itself in what is described as the recently developed doctrine of popes on the "inviolable of rights of the human person and the constitutional order of society." (While it does recognize that changes in the world have been part of the impetus for the developments in religious freedom within the church, the authorities cited are almost exclusively religious and draw heavily on papal encyclicals.)

Controversially for those accustomed to conceptions of religious freedom that rely on separation of church and state, the council also concluded that the government "ought indeed to take account of the religious life of the citizenry and show it favor, since the function of government is to make provision for the common welfare."[58] While no particular religion was to be favored, religion itself was valuable and deserved promotion (not merely protection) by the state for the benefit of all. For those who hold to the importance of separation of church and state, this admittedly somewhat vague injunction is very disturbing. It suggests that the juridical turn is only partial and that the commitment of the church to religious truth means that it will want the state to give too much protection to religions at the expense of other beliefs.[59]

Third, the conception of the constitutional order of society that underlies the juridical turn in *Dignitatis humanae* is broader and more inclusive than that in the Universal Declaration. This is one way in which the church moved ahead of the international community rather than simply catching up.[60] Traditional international law concepts hold that states are the subject of international law. Indeed, states are bound to adhere to human rights obligations, and individual human beings benefit from those rights.[61] We see something similar in domestic constitutional systems, for example, the First Amendment of the U.S. Constitution, which says that "Congress shall pass no law" interfering with religious liberty or establishing a religion. These types of conceptions of religious freedom leave untouched many important social institutions outside the state. *Dignitatis humanae*, however, in Article 6, is much broader and deeper in its conception of what is required to create a society in which people can achieve their own perfection in following God. It states that the "care of the right to religious freedom devolves upon the whole citizenry, upon social groups, upon the government, and upon the Church and other religious communities, in virtue of the duty of all toward the common welfare, and in the manner proper to each."[62] In many societies today religious freedom and the capacity to live out one's religious beliefs with integrity is threatened by other religious groups, by private social or commercial forces, and by civil unrest that does not always originate with the government. In those circumstances, the recognition that respect for the religious freedom of all people is the responsibility of all people and not just governments is of great significance.

If the church learned from the international community about the issue of religious freedom more generally then, this is an area in which the international community can learn from the church. The communal aspect of religious freedom, the sense of religion as a communal enterprise and of society as more than a set of individuals, imbues *Dignitatis humanae* and allows it to deal with religious freedom in a more sophisticated and challenging manner than does the Universal Declaration, which is primarily concerned with the state and the individual.[63]

Within *Dignitatis humanae* religious freedom is not merely a right but has an element of duty.[64] Given conditions of religious freedom, people have an obligation to search in good faith for the answers to religious questions. They must act in good faith and follow their conscience where it leads them and respond to God in a manner that is free from fear of punishment from the state or other individuals. It is not freedom for the sake of simply shrugging off burdensome obligations but freedom in which obligations can be taken on as a matter of conscience rather than compulsion.[65] As Cardinal Newman put it, "Conscience has rights because it has duties."

The Universal Declaration sets out the freedom clearly with a greater appeal to universality and perhaps with less ambiguity than *Dignitatis humanae* sometimes engages in. *Dignitatis humanae*, however, sets out a far richer sense of the purpose for the freedom and the communal context in which it will be lived out. It is also an example of one way in which a religious community could embrace religious freedom without compromising its stance on religious truth. These, I believe, are its most significant and enduring contributions.

Declaration on Religious Freedom, Dignitatis Humanae
On the Right of the Person and of Communities to Social and Civil Freedom in Matters Religious[66]

1. A sense of the dignity of the human person has been impressing itself more and more deeply on the consciousness of contemporary man, and the demand is increasingly made that men should act on their own judgment, enjoying and making use of a responsible freedom, not driven by coercion but motivated by a sense of duty.[67] The demand is likewise made that constitutional limits should be set to the powers of government, in order that there may be no encroachment on the rightful freedom of the person and of associations. This demand for freedom in human society chiefly regards the quest for the values proper to the human spirit. It regards, in the first place, the free exercise of religion in society. This Vatican Council takes careful note of these desires in the minds of men. It proposes to declare them to be greatly in accord with truth and justice. To this end, it searches into the sacred tradition and doctrine of the Church—the treasury out of which the Church continually brings forth new things that are in harmony with the things that are old.

First, the council professes its belief that God Himself has made known to mankind the way in which men are to serve Him, and thus be saved in Christ and come to blessedness. We believe that this one true religion subsists in the Catholic and Apostolic Church, to which the Lord Jesus committed the duty of spreading it abroad among all men. Thus He spoke to the Apostles: "Go, therefore, and make disciples of all nations, baptizing them in the name of the Father and of the Son and of the Holy Spirit, teaching them to observe all things whatsoever I have enjoined upon you" [Matt. 28:19–20]. On their part, all men are bound to seek the truth, especially in what concerns God and His Church, and to embrace the truth they come to know, and to hold fast to it.

This Vatican Council likewise professes its belief that it is upon the human conscience that these obligations fall and exert their binding force. The truth cannot impose itself except by virtue of its own truth, as it makes its entrance into the mind at once quietly and with power.

Religious freedom, in turn, which men demand as necessary to fulfill their duty to worship God, has to do with immunity from coercion in civil society. Therefore it leaves untouched traditional Catholic doctrine on the moral duty of men and societies toward the true religion and toward the one Church of Christ.

Over and above all this, the council intends to develop the doctrine of recent popes on the inviolable rights of the human person and the constitutional order of society.

2. This Vatican Council declares that the human person has a right to religious freedom. This freedom means that all men are to be immune from coercion on the part of individuals or of social groups and of any human power, in such wise that no one is to be forced to act in a manner contrary to his own beliefs, whether privately or publicly, whether alone or in association with others, within due limits.

The council further declares that the right to religious freedom has its foundation in the very dignity of the human person as this dignity is known through the revealed word of God and by reason itself.[68] This right of the human person to religious freedom is to be recognized in the constitutional law whereby society is governed and thus it is to become a civil right.

It is in accordance with their dignity as persons—that is, beings endowed with reason and free will and therefore privileged to bear personal responsibility—that all men should be at once impelled by nature and also bound by a moral obligation to seek the truth, especially religious truth. They are also bound to adhere to the truth, once it is known, and to order their whole lives in accord with the demands of truth. However, men cannot discharge these obligations in a manner in keeping with their own nature unless they enjoy immunity from external coercion as well as psychological freedom. Therefore the right to religious freedom has its foundation not in the subjective disposition of the person, but in his very nature. In consequence, the right to this immunity continues to exist even in those who do not live up to their obligation of seeking the truth and adhering to it and the exercise of this right is not to be impeded, provided that just public order be observed.

3. Further light is shed on the subject if one considers that the highest norm of human life is the divine law—eternal, objective and universal—whereby God orders, directs and governs the entire universe and all the ways of the human community by a plan conceived in wisdom and love. Man has been made by God to participate in this law, with the result that, under the gentle disposition of divine Providence, he can come to perceive ever more fully the truth that is unchanging. Wherefore every man has the duty, and therefore the right, to seek the truth in matters religious in order that he may with prudence form for himself right and true judgments of conscience, under use of all suitable means.

Truth, however, is to be sought after in a manner proper to the dignity of the human person and his social nature. The inquiry is to be free, carried on with the aid of teaching or instruction, communication and dialogue, in the course of which men explain to one another the truth they have discovered, or think they have discovered, in order thus to assist one another in the quest for truth.

Moreover, as the truth is discovered, it is by a personal assent that men are to adhere to it.

On his part, man perceives and acknowledges the imperatives of the divine law through the mediation of conscience. In all his activity a man is bound to follow his conscience in order that he may come to God, the end and purpose of life. It follows that he is not to be forced to act in manner contrary to his conscience. Nor, on the other hand, is he to be restrained from acting in accordance with his conscience, especially in matters religious. The reason is that the exercise of religion, of its very nature, consists before all else in those internal, voluntary and free acts whereby man sets the course of his life directly toward God. No merely human power can either command or prohibit acts of this kind.[69] The social nature of man, however, itself requires that he should give external expression to his internal acts of religion: that he should share with others in matters religious; that he should profess his religion in community. Injury therefore is done to the human person and to the very order established by God for human life, if the free exercise of religion is denied in society, provided just public order is observed.

There is a further consideration. The religious acts whereby men, in private and in public and out of a sense of personal conviction, direct their lives to God transcend by their very nature the order of terrestrial and temporal affairs. Government therefore ought indeed to take account of the religious life of the citizenry and show it favor, since the function of government is to make provision for the common welfare. However, it would clearly transgress the limits set to its power, were it to presume to command or inhibit acts that are religious.

4. The freedom or immunity from coercion in matters religious which is the endowment of persons as individuals is also to be recognized as their right when they act in community. Religious communities are a requirement of the social nature both of man and of religion itself.

Provided the just demands of public order are observed, religious communities rightfully claim freedom in order that they may govern themselves according to their own norms, honor the Supreme Being in public worship, assist their members in the practice of the religious life, strengthen them by instruction, and promote institutions in which they may join together for the purpose of ordering their own lives in accordance with their religious principles.

Religious communities also have the right not to be hindered, either by legal measures or by administrative action on the part of government, in the selection, training, appointment, and transferal of their own ministers, in communicating with religious authorities and communities abroad, in erecting buildings for religious purposes, and in the acquisition and use of suitable funds or properties.

Religious communities also have the right not to be hindered in their public teaching and witness to their faith, whether by the spoken or by the written word. However, in spreading religious faith and in introducing religious practices everyone ought at all times to refrain from any manner of action which might seem to carry a hint of coercion or of a kind of persuasion that would be dishonorable or unworthy, especially when dealing with poor or uneducated people. Such a manner of action would have to be considered an abuse of one's right and a violation of the right of others.

In addition, it comes within the meaning of religious freedom that religious communities should not be prohibited from freely undertaking to show the special value of their doctrine in what concerns the organization of society and the inspiration of the whole of human activity. Finally, the social nature of man and the very nature of religion afford the foundation of the right of men freely to hold meetings and to establish educational, cultural, charitable and social organizations, under the impulse of their own religious sense.

5. The family, since it is a society in its own original right, has the right freely to live its own domestic religious life under the guidance of parents. Parents, moreover, have the right to determine, in accordance with their own religious beliefs, the kind of religious education that their children are to receive. Government, in consequence, must acknowledge the right of parents to make a genuinely free choice of schools and of other means of education, and the use

of this freedom of choice is not to be made a reason for imposing unjust burdens on parents, whether directly or indirectly. Besides, the right[s] of parents are violated, if their children are forced to attend lessons or instructions which are not in agreement with their religious beliefs, or if a single system of education, from which all religious formation is excluded, is imposed upon all.

6. Since the common welfare of society consists in the entirety of those conditions of social life under which men enjoy the possibility of achieving their own perfection in a certain fullness of measure and also with some relative ease, it chiefly consists in the protection of the rights, and in the performance of the duties, of the human person.[70] Therefore the care of the right to religious freedom devolves upon the whole citizenry, upon social groups, upon government, and upon the Church and other religious communities, in virtue of the duty of all toward the common welfare, and in the manner proper to each.

The protection and promotion of the inviolable rights of man ranks among the essential duties of government.[71] Therefore government is to assume the safeguard of the religious freedom of all its citizens, in an effective manner, by just laws and by other appropriate means.

Government is also to help create conditions favorable to the fostering of religious life, in order that the people may be truly enabled to exercise their religious rights and to fulfill their religious duties, and also in order that society itself may profit by the moral qualities of justice and peace which have their origin in men's faithfulness to God and to His holy will.[72]

If, in view of peculiar circumstances obtaining among peoples, special civil recognition is given to one religious community in the constitutional order of society, it is at the same time imperative that the right of all citizens and religious communities to religious freedom should be recognized and made effective in practice.

Finally, government is to see to it that equality of citizens before the law, which is itself an element of the common good, is never violated, whether openly or covertly, for religious reasons. Nor is there to be discrimination among citizens.

It follows that a wrong is done when government imposes upon its people, by force or fear or other means, the profession or repudiation of any religion, or when it hinders men from joining or leaving a religious community. All the more is it a violation of the will of God and of the sacred rights of the person and the family of nations when force is brought to bear in any way in order to destroy or repress religion, either in the whole of mankind or in a particular country or in a definite community.

7. The right to religious freedom is exercised in human society: hence its exercise is subject to certain regulatory norms. In the use of all freedoms the moral

principle of personal and social responsibility is to be observed. In the exercise of their rights, individual men and social groups are bound by the moral law to have respect both for the rights of others and for their own duties toward others and for the common welfare of all. Men are to deal with their fellows in justice and civility.

Furthermore, society has the right to defend itself against possible abuses committed on the pretext of freedom of religion. It is the special duty of government to provide this protection. However, government is not to act in an arbitrary fashion or in an unfair spirit of partisanship. Its action is to be controlled by juridical norms which are in conformity with the objective moral order. These norms arise out of the need for the effective safeguard of the rights of all citizens and for the peaceful settlement of conflicts of rights, also out of the need for an adequate care of genuine public peace, which comes about when men live together in good order and in true justice, and finally out of the need for a proper guardianship of public morality.

These matters constitute the basic component of the common welfare: they are what is meant by public order. For the rest, the usages of society are to be the usages of freedom in their full range: that is, the freedom of man is to be respected as far as possible and is not to be curtailed except when and insofar as necessary.

8. Many pressures are brought to bear upon the men of our day, to the point where the danger arises lest they lose the possibility of acting on their own judgment. On the other hand, not a few can be found who seem inclined to use the name of freedom as the pretext for refusing to submit to authority and for making light of the duty of obedience. Wherefore this Vatican Council urges everyone, especially those who are charged with the task of educating others, to do their utmost to form men who, on the one hand, will respect the moral order and be obedient to lawful authority, and on the other hand, will be lovers of true freedom—men, in other words, who will come to decisions on their own judgment and in the light of truth, govern their activities with a sense of responsibility, and strive after what is true and right, willing always to join with others in cooperative effort.

Religious freedom therefore ought to have this further purpose and aim, namely, that men may come to act with greater responsibility in fulfilling their duties in community life.

9. The declaration of this Vatican Council on the right of man to religious freedom has its foundation in the dignity of the person, whose exigencies have come to be fully known to human reason through centuries of experience. What is more, this doctrine of freedom has roots in divine revelation, and for this reason Christians are bound to respect it all the more conscientiously. Revelation does not indeed affirm in so many words the right of man

to immunity from external coercion in matters religious. It does, however, disclose the dignity of the human person in its full dimensions. It gives evidence of the respect which Christ showed toward the freedom with which man is to fulfil his duty of belief in the word of God and it gives us lessons in the spirit which disciples of such a Master ought to adopt and continually follow. Thus further light is cast upon the general principles upon which the doctrine of this declaration on religious freedom is based. In particular, religious freedom in society is entirely consonant with the freedom of the act of Christian faith.

10. It is one of the major tenets of Catholic doctrine that man's response to God in faith must be free: no one therefore is to be forced to embrace the Christian faith against his own will.[73] This doctrine is contained in the word of God and it was constantly proclaimed by the Fathers of the Church.[74] The act of faith is of its very nature a free act. Man, redeemed by Christ the Savior and through Christ Jesus called to be God's adopted son [cf. Eph. 1:5], cannot give his adherence to God revealing Himself unless, under the drawing of the Father [cf. John 6:44], he offers to God the reasonable and free submission of faith. It is therefore completely in accord with the nature of faith that in matters religious every manner of coercion on the part of men should be excluded. In consequence, the principle of religious freedom makes no small contribution to the creation of an environment in which men can without hindrance be invited to the Christian faith, embrace it of their own free will, and profess it effectively in their whole manner of life.

11. God calls men to serve Him in spirit and in truth, hence they are bound in conscience but they stand under no compulsion. God has regard for the dignity of the human person whom He Himself created and man is to be guided by his own judgment and he is to enjoy freedom. This truth appears at its height in Christ Jesus, in whom God manifested Himself and His ways with men. Christ is at once our Master and our Lord [cf. John 13:13] and also meek and humble of heart [cf. Matt. 11:29]. In attracting and inviting His disciples He used patience [cf. Matt. 11:28–30; John 6:67–68]. He wrought miracles to illuminate His teaching and to establish its truth, but His intention was to rouse faith in His hearers and to confirm them in faith, not to exert coercion upon them.[75] He did indeed denounce the unbelief of some who listened to Him, but He left vengeance to God in expectation of the day of judgment [cf. Matt. 11:20–24; Rom. 12:19–20; 2 Thess. 1:8]. When He sent His Apostles into the world, He said to them: "He who believes and is baptized will be saved. He who does not believe will be condemned" [Mark 16:16]. But He Himself, noting that the cockle had been sown amid the wheat, gave orders that both should be allowed to grow until the harvest time, which will come at the end of the world [cf. Matt. 13:30 and 40–42]. He

refused to be a political messiah, ruling by force [cf. Matt. 4:8–10; John 6:15]. He preferred to call Himself the Son of Man, who came "to serve and to give his life as a ransom for the many" [Mark 10:45]. He showed Himself the perfect servant of God [cf. Isa. 42:1–4], who "does not break the bruised reed nor extinguish the smoking flax" [Matt. 12:20].

He acknowledged the power of government and its rights, when He commanded that tribute be given to Caesar: but He gave clear warning that the higher rights of God are to be kept inviolate: "Render to Caesar the things that are Caesar's and to God the things that are God's" [Matt. 22:21]. In the end, when He completed on the cross the work of redemption whereby He achieved salvation and true freedom for men, He brought His revelation to completion. For He bore witness to the truth, but He refused to impose the truth by force on those who spoke against it [cf. John 18:37]. Not by force of blows does His rule assert its claims [cf. Matt. 26:51–53; John 18:36]. It is established by witnessing to the truth and by hearing the truth, and it extends its dominion by the love whereby Christ, lifted up on the cross, draws all men to Himself [cf. John 12:32].

Taught by the word and example of Christ, the Apostles followed the same way. From the very origins of the Church the disciples of Christ strove to convert men to faith in Christ as the Lord; not, however, by the use of coercion or of devices unworthy of the Gospel, but by the power, above all, of the word of God [cf. 1 Cor. 2:3–5; 1 Thess. 2.3–5]. Steadfastly they proclaimed to all the plan of God our Savior, "who wills that all men should be saved and come to the acknowledgment of the truth" [1 Tim. 2:4]. At the same time, however, they showed respect for those of weaker stuff, even though they were in error, and thus they made it plain that "each one of us is to render to God an account of himself" and for that reason is bound to obey his conscience [Rom. 14:12; cf. Rom. 14:1–23; 1 Cor. 8:9–13; 10:23–33]. Like Christ Himself, the Apostles were unceasingly bent upon bearing witness to the truth of God, and they showed the fullest measure of boldness in "speaking the word with confidence" before the people and their rulers [Acts 4:31; cf. Eph. 6:19–20]. With a firm faith they held that the Gospel is indeed the power of God unto salvation for all who believe [cf. Rom. 1:16]. Therefore they rejected all "carnal weapons" [cf. 2 Cor. 10:4; 1 Thess. 5:8–9]: they followed the example of the gentleness and respectfulness of Christ and they preached the word of God in the full confidence that there was resident in this word itself a divine power able to destroy all the forces arrayed against God [cf. Eph. 6:11–17] and bring men to faith in Christ and to His service [cf. 2 Cor. 10:3–5]. As the Master, so too the Apostles recognized legitimate civil authority. "For there is no power except from God," the Apostle teaches, and thereafter commands: "Let everyone be subject to higher authorities . . . He who resists authority resists God's ordinance" [Rom. 13:1–5; cf. 1 Pet. 2:13–17]. At the same time, however, they did not hesitate to speak out against governing powers which set themselves in opposition to the holy will of God: "It is necessary to obey God rather than men" [Acts 5:29; cf. Acts 4:19–20]. This is the way along which the martyrs and other faithful have walked through all ages and over all the earth.

12. In faithfulness therefore to the truth of the Gospel, the Church is following the way of Christ and the apostles when she recognizes and gives support to the principle of religious freedom as befitting the dignity of man and as being in accord with divine revelation. Throughout the ages the Church has kept safe and handed on the doctrine received from the Master and from the apostles. In the life of the People of God, as it has made its pilgrim way through the vicissitudes of human history, there has at times appeared a way of acting that was hardly in accord with the spirit of the Gospel or even opposed to it. Nevertheless, the doctrine of the Church that no one is to be coerced into faith has always stood firm.

Thus the leaven of the Gospel has long been about its quiet work in the minds of men, and to it is due in great measure the fact that in the course of time men have come more widely to recognize their dignity as persons, and the conviction has grown stronger that the person in society is to be kept free from all manner of coercion in matters religious.

13. Among the things that concern the good of the Church and indeed the welfare of society here on earth—things therefore that are always and everywhere to be kept secure and defended against all injury—this certainly is preeminent, namely, that the Church should enjoy that full measure of freedom which her care for the salvation of men requires.[76] This is a sacred freedom, because the only-begotten Son endowed with it the Church which He purchased with His blood. Indeed it is so much the property of the Church that to act against it is to act against the will of God. The freedom of the Church is the fundamental principle in what concerns the relations between the Church and governments and the whole civil order.

In human society and in the face of government the Church claims freedom for herself in her character as a spiritual authority, established by Christ the Lord, upon which there rests, by divine mandate, the duty of going out into the whole world and preaching the Gospel to every creature.[77] The Church also claims freedom for herself in her character as a society of men who have the right to live in society in accordance with the precepts of the Christian faith.[78]

In turn, where the principle of religious freedom is not only proclaimed in words or simply incorporated in law but also given sincere and practical application, there the Church succeeds in achieving a stable situation of right as well as of fact and the independence which is necessary for the fulfillment of her divine mission.

This independence is precisely what the authorities of the Church claim in society.[79] At the same time, the Christian faithful, in common with all other men, possess the civil right not to be hindered in leading their lives in accordance with their consciences. Therefore, a harmony exists between the freedom of the Church and the religious freedom which is to be recognized as the right of all men and communities and sanctioned by constitutional law.

14. In order to be faithful to the divine command, "teach all nations" [Matt. 28:19–20], the Catholic Church must work with all urgency and concern "that the word of God be spread abroad and glorified" [2 Thess. 3:1]. Hence the Church earnestly begs of its children that, "first of all, supplications, prayers, petitions, acts of thanksgiving be made for all men . . . For this is good and agreeable in the sight of God our Saviour, who wills that all men be saved and come to the knowledge of the truth" [1 Tim. 2:1–4]. In the formation of their consciences, the Christian faithful ought carefully to attend to the sacred and certain doctrine of the Church.[80] For the Church is, by the will of Christ, the teacher of the truth. It is her duty to give utterance to, and authoritatively to teach, that truth which is Christ Himself, and also to declare and confirm by her authority those principles of the moral order which have their origins in human nature itself. Furthermore, let Christians walk in wisdom in the face of those outside, "in the Holy Spirit, in unaffected love, in the word of truth" [2 Cor. 6:6–7], and let them be about their task of spreading the light of life with all confidence [cf. Acts 4:29] and apostolic courage, even to the shedding of their blood.

The disciple is bound by a grave obligation toward Christ, his Master, ever more fully to understand the truth received from Him, faithfully to proclaim it, and vigorously to defend it, never—be it understood—having recourse to means that are incompatible with the spirit of the Gospel. At the same time, the charity of Christ urges him to love and have prudence and patience in his dealings with those who are in error or in ignorance with regard to the faith.[81] All is to be taken into account—the Christian duty to Christ, the life-giving word which must be proclaimed, the rights of the human person, and the measure of grace granted by God through Christ to men who are invited freely to accept and profess the faith.

15. The fact is that men of the present day want to be able freely to profess their religion in private and in public. Indeed, religious freedom has already been declared to be a civil right in most constitutions, and it is solemnly recognized in international documents.[82] The further fact is that forms of government still exist under which, even though freedom of religious worship receives constitutional recognition, the powers of government are engaged

in the effort to deter citizens from the profession of religion and to make life very difficult and dangerous for religious communities.

This council greets with joy the first of these two facts as among the signs of the times. With sorrow, however, it denounces the other fact, as only to be deplored. The council exhorts Catholics, and it directs a plea to all men, most carefully to consider how greatly necessary religious freedom is, especially in the present condition of the human family. All nations are coming into even closer unity. Men of different cultures and religions are being brought together in closer relationships. There is a growing consciousness of the personal responsibility that every man has. All this is evident. Consequently, in order that relationships of peace and harmony be established and maintained within the whole of mankind, it is necessary that religious freedom be everywhere provided with an effective constitutional guarantee and that respect be shown for the high duty and right of man freely to lead his religious life in society.

May the God and Father of all grant that the human family, through careful observance of the principle of religious freedom in society, may be brought by the grace of Christ and the power of the Holy Spirit to the sublime and unending and "glorious freedom of the sons of God" [Rom. 8:21].

8.4 Two Islamic Declarations on Human Rights

Fikret Karcic

The Universal Islamic Declaration of Human Rights (UIDHR), a compilation of human rights in Islam, was adopted in 1981 by the Islamic Council, a London-based nongovernmental organization. In terminology and format, it is similar to the United Nations' Universal Declaration of Human Rights (UDHR) of 1948; indeed, it was seen by its compilers as a Muslim equivalent to the UDHR. Conceptually, it is characterized by using Islamic law (Sharīʿa) as a controlling standard for individual and collective rights. The Cairo Declaration is a document adopted by the Organization of the Islamic Conference (OIC) in 1990. It is a political and legal document, expressing the stand of OIC member states with regard to human rights in Islam; it emerged as a consequence of increased interest in human rights in the Muslim world in the 1980s and with the intent to produce a Muslim equivalent to relevant international codifications of human rights, which were seen by some in the Muslim world as a product of Western culture. Like the UIDHR, the Cairo Declaration uses the Sharīʿa as a framework for the interpretation of the rights and freedoms that it stipulates but is less ideologically charged.

During the second part of the twentieth century, and especially from the 1980s onward, many Muslim scholars became engaged in a debate over the relationship between human rights and Islam. This development was generated both by the emergence of human rights discourse in the modern world and by the inclusion of human rights protection clauses in the constitutions of many Muslim countries. As has been observed by Heiner Bielefeldt, four basic positions were taken in this debate.[83]

First, there is what may be called the "Islamization" of human rights, based on the view that human rights have always been part of the Sharīʿa, as divine law provides an absolute foundation for the protection of rights and duties of every person. According to this position, there is a distinctively Islamic concept of human rights, in certain aspects different from a Western one. This position, which can also be labeled as "essentialist," has found expression in a number of official and semiofficial documents, among which are the two presented here—the Universal Islamic Declaration of Human Rights (UIDHR) and the Cairo Declaration on Human Rights in Islam. In these documents, the Sharīʿa is both the frame of reference and the guideline for interpretation of codified text.

Second, some scholars adopt pragmatic approaches, allowing leniency in the praxis of the application of the Sharīʿa. For instance, in this perspective, the validity of certain institutions such as polygamy may remain unchallenged, but in practice their application is restricted to a certain degree to meet a human rights standard of equality.

Third, there is also a position characterized by liberal reconceptualization. Some Muslim scholars propose a reinterpretation of the Sharīʿa in order to bring its provisions into line with contemporary developments. However, their attempts are very often controversial and lack both inner consistency and acceptance by the majority.

Finally, some adopt a clearly secular stance, calling for the secularization of law and the relegation of religion to the realm of private life. This position, however, is not popular and is seen to endorse the acceptance of the Western scheme of human rights into Muslim society.

In terms of this schema, the two texts presented here both adopt an "essentialist" position. UIDHR in its preamble provides that the Holy Qur'ān and the Sunna are the legal and moral frameworks within which human institutions and relations are established. Human rights are decreed by divine law and consequently cannot be curtailed, abrogated, or disregarded by human authorities; moreover, duties and obligations have priorities over rights. The Cairo Declaration stipulates that fundamental rights and freedoms in Islam are an integral part of the Islamic religion. As divine commandments, contained in the revealed books of God, their observance is an act of worship. Every person is individually responsible for their safeguarding, and the Umma is collectively responsible.

Thus these two Muslim documents give great significance to human rights; they are divine commandments, contained in revealed books—an expression that indicates common ground among the revealed religions vis-à-vis human rights. One might infer that human rights, as provided for in the revealed texts, constitute what the Romans called the *lex aeterna* (eternal laws) of humanity. Classical Muslim scholars identified such values as *al-ḍarūriyyāt* ("necessities"), which had to be protected in every human society—these included life, religion, dignity, property, and progeny.[84] In addition, human rights are defined as an integral part of the religion of Islam and their observance as an act of worship. Another distinctive feature of an Islamic perspective is the view that duties and obligations have priority over rights, though this is not further elaborated here.

With respect to possible limitations imposed on human rights, UIDHR provides that the only limitations shall be such "as are enjoined by the Law for the purpose of securing the due recognition of, and respect for, the rights and freedoms of others and of meeting the just requirements of morality, public order and the general welfare of the Community."[85] In fact this is an "Islamized" version of the formulation in the UDHR, with "law" interpreted as "the Sharīʿa," and "a democratic society" replaced by "the Community (Umma)."[86] The Cairo Declaration briefly states in Article 24 that "all rights and freedoms stipulated in this Declaration are subject to Islamic Sharīʿa," and adds that the Sharīʿa is also the only source of reference for the explanation or clarification of any of the articles of the declaration.[87] Provisions like this open questions as to the identity of the authoritative interpreters of the Sharīʿa and consequently can lead to different interpretations of these documents.

The Universal Islamic Declaration of Human Rights[88]

> This is a declaration for mankind, a guidance and instruction to those who fear God. [Āl ʿImrān 3:138]

Foreword

Islam gave to mankind an ideal code of human rights fourteen centuries ago. These rights aim at conferring honour and dignity on mankind and eliminating exploitation, oppression and injustice.

Human rights in Islam are firmly rooted in the belief that God, and God alone, is the Law Giver and the Source of all human rights. Due to their Divine origin, no ruler, government, assembly or authority can curtail or violate in any way the human rights conferred by God, nor can they be surrendered.

Human rights in Islam are an integral part of the overall Islamic order and it is obligatory on all Muslim governments and organs of society to implement them in letter and in spirit within the framework of that order.

It is unfortunate that human rights are being trampled upon with impunity in many countries of the world, including some Muslim countries. Such violations are a matter of serious concern and are arousing the conscience of more and more people throughout the world.

I sincerely hope that this *Declaration of Human Rights* will give a powerful impetus to the Muslim peoples to stand firm and defend resolutely and courageously the rights conferred on them by God.

This *Declaration of Human Rights* is the second fundamental document proclaimed by the Islamic Council to mark the beginning of the 15th

Century of the Islamic era, the first being the *Universal Islamic Declaration* announced at the International Conference on The Prophet Muhammad (peace and blessings be upon him) and his Message, held in London from April 12 to 15, 1980.

The *Universal Islamic Declaration of Human Rights* is based on the Qur'ān and the Sunna and has been compiled by eminent Muslim scholars, jurists and representatives of Islamic movements and thought. May God reward them all for their efforts and guide us along the right path.

Salem Azzam, *Secretary General*[89]

> O men! Behold, We have created you all out of a male and a female, and have made you into nations and tribes, so that you might come to know one another. Verily, the noblest of you in the sight of God is the one who is most deeply conscious of Him. Behold, God is all-knowing, all aware. [al-Ḥujurāt 49:13]

Preamble

Whereas the age-old human aspiration for a just world order wherein people could live, develop and prosper in an environment free from fear, oppression, exploitation and deprivation, remains largely unfulfilled;

Whereas the Divine Mercy unto mankind reflected in its having been endowed with super-abundant economic sustenance is being wasted, or unfairly or unjustly withheld from the inhabitants of the earth;

Whereas Allah (God) has given mankind through His revelations in the Holy Qur'ān and the Sunna of His Blessed Prophet Muhammad an abiding legal and moral framework within which to establish and regulate human institutions and relationships;

Whereas the human rights decreed by the Divine Law aim at conferring dignity and honour on mankind and are designed to eliminate oppression and injustice;

Whereas by virtue of their Divine source and sanction these rights can neither be curtailed, abrogated or disregarded by authorities, assemblies or other institutions, nor can they be surrendered or alienated;

Therefore we, as Muslims, who believe

(a) in God, the Beneficent and Merciful, the Creator, the Sustainer, the Sovereign, the sole Guide of mankind and the Source of all Law;

(b) in the Vicegerency (*Khilāfa*) of man who has been created to fulfil the Will of God on earth;

(c) in the wisdom of Divine guidance brought by the Prophets, whose mission found its culmination in the final Divine message that was conveyed by the Prophet Muhammad (Peace be upon him) to all mankind;

(d) that rationality by itself without the light of revelation from God can neither be a sure guide in the affairs of mankind nor provide spiritual nourishment to the human soul, and, knowing that the teachings of Islam represent the quintessence of Divine guidance in its final and perfect form, feel duty-bound to remind man of the high status and dignity bestowed on him by God;

(e) in inviting all mankind to the message of Islam;

(f) that by the terms of our primeval covenant with God our duties and obligations have priority over our rights, and that each one of us is under a bounden duty to spread the teachings of Islam by word, deed, and indeed in all gentle ways, and to make them effective not only in our individual lives but also in the society around us;

(g) in our obligation to establish an Islamic order:

(i) wherein all human beings shall be equal and none shall enjoy a privilege or suffer a disadvantage or discrimination by reason of race, colour, sex, origin or language;

(ii) wherein all human beings are born free;

(iii) wherein slavery and forced labour are abhorred;

(iv) wherein conditions shall be established such that the institution of family shall be preserved, protected and honoured as the basis of all social life;

(v) wherein the rulers and the ruled alike are subject to, and equal before, the Law;

(vi) wherein obedience shall be rendered only to those commands that are in consonance with the Law;

(vii) wherein all worldly power shall be considered as a sacred trust, to be exercised within the limits prescribed by the Law and in a manner approved by it, and with due regard for the priorities fixed by it;

(viii) wherein all economic resources shall be treated as Divine blessings bestowed upon mankind, to be enjoyed by all in accordance with the rules and the values set out in the Qur'ān and the Sunna;

(ix) wherein all public affairs shall be determined and conducted, and the authority to administer them shall be exercised after mutual consultation (*shūrā*) between the believers qualified to contribute to a decision which would accord well with the Law and the public good;

(x) wherein everyone shall undertake obligations proportionate to his capacity and shall be held responsible *pro rata* for his deeds;

(xi) wherein everyone shall, in case of an infringement of his rights, be assured of appropriate remedial measures in accordance with the Law;

(xii) wherein no one shall be deprived of the rights assured to him by the Law except by its authority and to the extent permitted by it;

(xiii) wherein every individual shall have the right to bring legal action against anyone who commits a crime against society as a whole or against any of its members;

(xiv) wherein every effort shall be made to

(a) secure unto mankind deliverance from every type of exploitation, injustice and oppression,

(b) ensure to everyone security, dignity and liberty in terms set out and by methods approved and within the limits set by the Law;

Do hereby, as servants of Allah and as members of the Universal Brotherhood of Islam, at the beginning of the Fifteenth Century of the Islamic Era, affirm our commitment to uphold the following inviolable and inalienable human rights that we consider are enjoined by Islam.

I Right to Life[90]

(a) Human life is sacred and inviolable and every effort shall be made to protect it. In particular no one shall be exposed to injury or death, except under the authority of the Law.

(b) Just as in life, so also after death, the sanctity of a person's body shall be inviolable. It is the obligation of believers to see that a deceased person's body is handled with due solemnity.

II Right to Freedom[91]

(a) Man is born free. No inroads shall be made on his right to liberty except under the authority and in due process of the Law.

(b) Every individual and every people has the inalienable right to freedom in all its forms—physical, cultural, economic and political—and shall be entitled to struggle by all available means against any infringement or abrogation of this right; and every oppressed individual or people has a legitimate claim to the support of other individuals and/or peoples in such a struggle.

III Right to Equality and Prohibition against Impermissible Discrimination[92]

(a) All persons are equal before the Law and are entitled to equal opportunities and protection of the Law.

(b) All persons shall be entitled to equal wage for equal work.

(c) No person shall be denied the opportunity to work or be discriminated against in any manner or exposed to greater physical risk by reason of religious belief, colour, race, origin, sex or language.

IV Right to Justice[93]

(a) Every person has the right to be treated in accordance with the Law, and only in accordance with the Law.

(b) Every person has not only the right but also the obligation to protest against injustice; to recourse to remedies provided by the Law in respect of any unwarranted personal injury or loss; to self-defence against any charges that are preferred against him and to obtain fair adjudication before an independent judicial tribunal in any dispute with public authorities or any other person.

(c) It is the right and duty of every person to defend the rights of any other person and the community in general (*ḥisba*).

(d) No person shall be discriminated against while seeking to defend private and public rights.

(e) It is the right and duty of every Muslim to refuse to obey any command which is contrary to the Law, no matter by whom it may be issued.

V Right to Fair Trial[94]

(a) No person shall be adjudged guilty of an offence and made liable to punishment except after proof of his guilt before an independent judicial tribunal.

(b) No person shall be adjudged guilty except after a fair trial and after reasonable opportunity for defence has been provided to him.

(c) Punishment shall be awarded in accordance with the Law, in proportion to the seriousness of the offence and with due consideration of the circumstances under which it was committed.

(d) No act shall be considered a crime unless it is stipulated as such in the clear wording of the Law.

(e) Every individual is responsible for his actions. Responsibility for a crime cannot be vicariously extended to other members of his family or group, who are not otherwise directly or indirectly involved in the commission of the crime in question.

VI Right to Protection against Abuse of Power[95]

Every person has the right to protection against harassment by official agencies. He is not liable to account for himself except for making a defence to the charges made against him or where he is found in a situation wherein a question regarding suspicion of his involvement in a crime could be *reasonably* raised.

VII Right to Protection against Torture[96]

No person shall be subjected to torture in mind or body, or degraded, or threatened with injury either to himself or to anyone related to or held dear by him, or forcibly made to confess to the commission of a crime, or forced to consent to an act which is injurious to his interests.

VIII Right to Protection of Honour and Reputation[97]

Every person has the right to protect his honour and reputation against calumnies, groundless charges or deliberate attempts at defamation and blackmail.

IX Right to Asylum[98]

(a) Every persecuted or oppressed person has the right to seek refuge and asylum. This right is guaranteed to every human being irrespective of race, religion, colour and sex.

(b) *al-Masjid al-Ḥarām* (the sacred house of Allah) in Mecca is a sanctuary for all Muslims.

X Rights of Minorities[99]

(a) The Qur'ānic principle "There is no compulsion in religion" shall govern the religious rights of non-Muslim minorities.

(b) In a Muslim country religious minorities shall have the choice to be governed in respect of their civil and personal matters by Islamic Law, or by their own laws.

XI Right and Obligation to Participate in the Conduct and Management of Public Affairs[100]

(a) Subject to the Law, every individual in the community (*umma*) is entitled to assume public office.

(b) Process of free consultation (*shūrā*) is the basis of the administrative relationship between the government and the people. People also have the right to choose and remove their rulers in accordance with this principle.

XII Right to Freedom of Belief, Thought and Speech[101]

(a) Every person has the right to express his thoughts and beliefs so long as he remains within the limits prescribed by the Law. No one, however, is entitled to disseminate falsehood or to circulate reports which may outrage public decency, or to indulge in slander, innuendo or to cast defamatory aspersions on other persons.[102]

(b) Pursuit of knowledge and search after truth is not only a right but a duty of every Muslim.[103]

(c) It is the right and duty of every Muslim to protest and strive (within the limits set out by the Law) against oppression even if it involves challenging the highest authority in the state.[104]

(d) There shall be no bar on the dissemination of information provided it does not endanger the security of the society or the state and is confined within the limits imposed by the Law.

(e) No one shall hold in contempt or ridicule the religious beliefs of others or incite public hostility against them; respect for the religious feelings of others is obligatory on all Muslims.[105]

XIII Right to Freedom of Religion[106]

Every person has the right to freedom of conscience and worship in accordance with his religious beliefs.

XIV Right to Free Association[107]

(a) Every person is entitled to participate individually and collectively in the religious, social, cultural and political life of his community and to establish institutions and agencies meant to enjoin what is right (*ma'rūf*) and to prevent what is wrong (*munkar*).

(b) Every person is entitled to strive for the establishment of institutions whereunder an enjoyment of these rights would be made possible. Collectively, the community is obliged to establish conditions so as to allow its members full development of their personalities.

XV The Economic Order and the Rights Evolving Therefrom[108]

(a) In their economic pursuits, all persons are entitled to the full benefits of nature and all its resources. These are blessings bestowed by God for the benefit of mankind as a whole.

(b) All human beings are entitled to earn their living according to the Law.

(c) Every person is entitled to own property individually or in association with others. State ownership of certain economic resources in the public interest is legitimate.

(d) The poor have the right to a prescribed share in the wealth of the rich, as fixed by *Zakāt*, levied and collected in accordance with the Law.

(e) All means of production shall be utilised in the interest of the community (*umma*) as a whole, and may not be neglected or misused.

(f) In order to promote the development of a balanced economy and to protect society from exploitation, Islamic Law forbids monopolies, unreasonable restrictive trade practices, usury, the use of coercion in the making of contracts and the publication of misleading advertisements.

(g) All economic activities are permitted provided they are not detrimental to the interests of the community (*umma*) and do not violate Islamic laws and values.

XVI Right to Protection of Property[109]
No property may be expropriated except in the public interest and on payment of fair and adequate compensation.

XVII Status and Dignity of Workers[110]
Islam honours work and the worker and enjoins Muslims not only to treat the worker justly but also generously. He is not only to be paid his earned wages promptly, but is also entitled to adequate rest and leisure.

XVIII Right to Social Security[111]
Every person has the right to food, shelter, clothing, education and medical care consistent with the resources of the community. This obligation of the community extends in particular to all individuals who cannot take care of themselves due to some temporary or permanent disability.

XIX Right to Found a Family and Related Matters[112]
(a) Every person is entitled to marry, to found a family and to bring up children in conformity with his religion, traditions and culture. Every spouse is entitled to such rights and privileges and carries such obligations as are stipulated by the Law.

(b) Each of the partners in a marriage is entitled to respect and consideration from the other.

(c) Every husband is obligated to maintain his wife and children according to his means.

(d) Every child has the right to be maintained and properly brought up by its parents, it being forbidden that children are made to work at an early age or that any burden is put on them which would arrest or harm their natural development.

(e) If parents are for some reason unable to discharge their obligations towards a child it becomes the responsibility of the community to fulfil these obligations at public expense.

(f) Every person is entitled to material support, as well as care and protection, from his family during his childhood, old age or incapacity. Parents are entitled to material support as well as care and protection from their children.

(g) Motherhood is entitled to special respect, care and assistance on the part of the family and the public organs of the community (*umma*).

(h) Within the family, men and women are to share in their obligations and responsibilities according to their sex, their natural endowments, talents and inclinations, bearing in mind their common responsibilities toward their progeny and their relatives.

(i) No person may be married against his or her will, or lose or suffer diminution of legal personality on account of marriage.

XX Rights of Married Women[113]

Every married woman is entitled to:

(a) live in the house in which her husband lives;

(b) receive the means necessary for maintaining a standard of living which is not inferior to that of her spouse, and, in the event of divorce, receive during the statutory period of waiting (*'idda*) means of maintenance commensurate with her husband's resources, for herself as well as for the children she nurses or keeps, irrespective of her own financial status, earnings, or property that she may hold in her own rights;

(c) seek and obtain dissolution of marriage (*khul'*) in accordance with the terms of the Law. This right is in addition to her right to seek divorce through the courts.

(d) inherit from her husband, her parents, her children and other relatives according to the Law;

(e) strict confidentiality from her spouse, or ex-spouse if divorced, with regard to any information that he may have obtained about her, the disclosure of which could prove detrimental to her interests. A similar responsibility rests upon her in respect of her spouse or ex-spouse.

XXI Right to Education[114]

(a) Every person is entitled to receive education in accordance with his natural capabilities.

(b) Every person is entitled to a free choice of profession and career and to the opportunity for the full development of his natural endowments.

XXII Right of Privacy[115]

Every person is entitled to the protection of his privacy.

XXIII Right to Freedom of Movement and Residence[116]

(a) In view of the fact that the World of Islam is veritably *Umma Islamia*, every Muslim shall have the right to freely move in and out of any Muslim country.

(b) No one shall be forced to leave the country of his residence, or be arbitrarily deported therefrom without recourse to due process of Law.

Explanatory Notes

1. In the above formulation of Human Rights, unless the context provides otherwise:

(a) [T]he term "person" refers to both the male and female sexes.

(b) [T]he term "Law" denotes the Sharī'a, i.e.[,] the totality of ordinances derived from the Qur'ān and the Sunna and any other laws that are deduced from these two sources by methods considered valid in Islamic jurisprudence.

2. Each one of the Human Rights enunciated in this declaration carries a corresponding duty.

3. In the exercise and enjoyment of the rights referred to above every person shall be subject only to such limitations as are enjoined by the Law for the purpose of securing the due recognition of, and respect for, the rights and the freedom of others and of meeting the just requirements of morality, public order and the general welfare of the Community (Umma).

The Arabic text of this Declaration is the original.

Glossary of Arabic Terms

Ḥisba—Public vigilance, an institution of the Islamic State enjoined to observe and facilitate the fulfillment of right norms of public behavior. The *Ḥisba* consists in public vigilance as well as an opportunity to private individuals to seek redress through it.

'Idda—The waiting period of a widowed or divorced woman during which she is not to re-marry.

Khilāfa—The vicegerency of man on earth or succession to the Prophet, transliterated into English as the Caliphate.

Khul'—Divorce a woman obtains at her own request.

Ma'rūf—Good act.

Munkar—Reprehensible deed.

Sharī'a—Islamic law.

Sunna—The example or way of life of the Prophet (peace be upon him), embracing what he said, did, or agreed to.

Umma Islamia—World Muslim community.

Zakāt—The "purifying" tax on wealth, one of the five pillars of Islam obligatory on Muslims.

The Cairo Declaration on Human Rights in Islam[117]

The Member States of the Organization of the Islamic Conference:[118]

Reaffirming the civilizing and historical role of the Islamic Umma which God made the best nation that has given mankind a universal and well-balanced civilization in which harmony is established between this life and the hereafter and knowledge is combined with faith; and the role that this Umma should play to guide a humanity confused by competing trends and ideologies and to provide solutions to the chronic problems of this materialistic civilization;

Wishing to contribute to the efforts of mankind to assert human rights, to protect man from exploitation and persecution, and to affirm his freedom and right to a dignified life in accordance with the Islamic Sharī'a;

Convinced that mankind which has reached an advanced stage in materialistic science is still, and shall remain, in dire need of faith to support its civilization and of a self-motivating force to guard its rights;

Believing that fundamental rights and universal freedoms in Islam are an integral part of the Islamic religion and that no one as a matter of principle has the right to suspend them in whole or in part or violate or ignore them in as much as they are binding divine commandments, which are contained in the Revealed Books of God and were sent through the last of His Prophets to complete the preceding divine messages thereby making their observance an act of worship and their neglect or violation an abominable sin, and accordingly every person is individually responsible—and the Umma collectively responsible—for their safeguard;

Proceeding from the above-mentioned principles, declare the following:

Article 1

(a) All human beings form one family whose members are united by submission to God and descent from Adam. All men are equal in terms of basic human dignity and basic obligations and responsibilities, without any discrimination on the grounds of race, colour, language, sex, religious belief, political affiliation, social status or other considerations. True faith is the guarantee for enhancing such dignity along the path to human perfection.

(b) All human beings are God's subjects, and the most loved by him are those who are most useful to the rest of His subjects, and no one has superiority over another except on the basis of piety and good deeds.

Article 2

(a) Life is a God-given gift and the right to life is guaranteed to every human being. It is the duty of individuals, societies and states to protect this right from any violation, and it is prohibited to take away life except for a Sharīʿa-prescribed reason.

(b) It is forbidden to resort to such means as may result in the genocidal annihilation of mankind.

(c) The preservation of human life throughout the term of time willed by God is a duty prescribed by Sharīʿa.

(d) Safety from bodily harm is a guaranteed right. It is the duty of the state to safeguard it, and it is prohibited to breach it without a Sharīʿa-prescribed reason.

Article 3

(a) In the event of the use of force and in case of armed conflict, it is not permissible to kill non-belligerents such as old men, women and children. The wounded and the sick shall have the right to medical treatment; and prisoners of war shall have the right to be fed, sheltered and clothed. It is prohibited to mutilate dead bodies. It is a duty to exchange prisoners of war and to arrange visits or reunions of the families separated by the circumstances of war.

(b) It is prohibited to fell trees, to damage crops or livestock, and to destroy the enemy's civilian buildings and installations by shelling, blasting or any other means.

Article 4

Every human being is entitled to inviolability and the protection of his good name and honour during his life and after his death. The state and society shall protect his remains and burial place.

Article 5

(a) The family is the foundation of society, and marriage is the basis of its formation. Men and women have the right to marriage, and no restrictions stemming from race, colour or nationality shall prevent them from enjoying this right.

(b) Society and the State shall remove all obstacles to marriage and shall facilitate marital procedure. They shall ensure family protection and welfare.

Article 6

(a) Woman is equal to man in human dignity, and has rights to enjoy as well as duties to perform; she has her own civil entity and financial independence, and the right to retain her name and lineage.

(b) The husband is responsible for the support and welfare of the family.

Article 7

(a) As of the moment of birth, every child has rights due from the parents, society and the state to be accorded proper nursing, education and material, hygienic and moral care. Both the foetus and the mother must be protected and accorded special care.

(b) Parents and those in such like capacity have the right to choose the type of education they desire for their children, provided they take into consideration the interest and future of the children in accordance with ethical values and the principles of the Sharīʿa.

(c) Both parents are entitled to certain rights from their children, and relatives are entitled to rights from their kin, in accordance with the tenets of the Sharīʿa.

Article 8

Every human being has the right to enjoy his legal capacity in terms of both obligation and commitment. Should this capacity be lost or impaired, he shall be represented by his guardian.

Article 9

(a) The quest for knowledge is an obligation, and the provision of education is a duty for society and the State. The State shall ensure the availability of ways and means to acquire education and shall guarantee educational diversity in the interest of society so as to enable man to be acquainted with the religion of Islam and the facts of the Universe for the benefit of mankind.

(b) Every human being has the right to receive both religious and worldly family, the school, the university, the media, etc., and in such an integrated and balanced manner as to develop his personality, strengthen his faith in God and promote his respect for and defence of both rights and obligations.

Article 10

Islam is the religion of unspoiled nature. It is prohibited to exercise any form of compulsion on man or to exploit his poverty or ignorance in order to convert him to another religion or to atheism.[119]

Article 11

(a) Human beings are born free, and no one has the right to enslave, humiliate, oppress or exploit them, and there can be no subjugation but to God the Most-High.

(b) Colonialism of all types being one of the most evil forms of enslavement is totally prohibited. Peoples suffering from colonialism have the full right to freedom and self-determination. It is the duty of all States and peoples to support the struggle of colonized peoples for the liquidation of all forms of colonialism and occupation, and all States and peoples have the right to preserve their independent identity and exercise control over their wealth and natural resources.

Article 12

Every man shall have the right, within the framework of Sharīʿa, to free movement and to select his place of residence whether inside or outside his country and, if persecuted, is entitled to seek asylum in another country. The country of refuge shall ensure his protection until he reaches safety, unless asylum is motivated by an act which Sharīʿa regards as a crime.

Article 13

Work is a right guaranteed by the State and Society for each person able to work. Everyone shall be free to choose the work that suits him best and which serves his interests and those of society. The employee shall have the right to safety and security as well as to all other social guarantees. He may neither be assigned work beyond his capacity nor be subjected to compulsion or exploited or harmed in any way. He shall be entitled—without any discrimination between males and females—to fair wages for his work without delay, as well as to the holidays, allowances and promotions which he deserves. For his part, he shall be required to be dedicated and meticulous in his work. Should workers and employers disagree on any matter, the State shall intervene to settle the dispute and have the grievances redressed, the rights confirmed and justice enforced without bias.

Article 14

Everyone shall have the right to legitimate gains without monopolization, deceit or harm to oneself or to others. Usury (*ribā*) is absolutely prohibited.

Article 15

(a) Everyone shall have the right to own property acquired in a legitimate way, and shall be entitled to the rights of ownership, without prejudice to oneself, others or to society in general. Expropriation is not permissible except for the requirements of public interest and upon payment of immediate and fair compensation.

(b) Confiscation and seizure of property is prohibited except for a necessity dictated by law.

Article 16

Everyone shall have the right to enjoy the fruits of his scientific, literary, artistic or technical production and the right to protect the moral and material interests stemming therefrom, provided that such production is not contrary to the principles of Sharīʿa.

Article 17

(a) Everyone shall have the right to live in a clean environment, away from vice and moral corruption, an environment that would foster his self-development; and it is incumbent upon the State and society in general to afford that right.

(b) Everyone shall have the right to medical and social care, and to all public amenities provided by society and the State within the limits of their available resources.

(c) The State shall ensure the right of the individual to a decent living which will enable him to meet all his requirements and those of his dependents, including food, clothing, housing, education, medical care and all other basic needs.

Article 18

(a) Everyone shall have the right to live in security for himself, his religion, his dependents, his honour and his property.

(b) Everyone shall have the right to privacy in the conduct of his private affairs, in his home, among his family, with regard to his property and his relationships. It is not permitted to spy on him, to place him under surveillance or to besmirch his good name. The State shall protect him from arbitrary interference.

(c) A private residence is inviolable in all cases. It will not be entered without permission from its inhabitants or in any unlawful manner, nor shall it be demolished or confiscated and its dwellers evicted.

Article 19

(a) All individuals are equal before the law, without distinction between the ruler and the ruled.

(b) The right to resort to justice is guaranteed to everyone.

(c) Liability is in essence personal.

(d) There shall be no crime or punishment except as provided for in the Sharīʿa.

(e) A defendant is innocent until his guilt is proven in a fair trial in which he shall be given all the guarantees of defence.

Article 20

It is not permitted without legitimate reason to arrest an individual, or restrict his freedom, to exile or to punish him. It is not permitted to subject him to physical or psychological torture or to any form of humiliation, cruelty or indignity. Nor is it permitted to subject an individual to medical or scientific experimentation without his consent or at the risk of his health or of his life. Nor is it permitted to promulgate emergency laws that would provide executive authority for such actions.

Article 21

Taking hostages under any form or for any purpose is expressly forbidden.

Article 22

(a) Everyone shall have the right to express his opinion freely in such manner as would not be contrary to the principles of the Sharīʿa.[120]

(b) Everyone shall have the right to advocate what is right, and propagate what is good, and warn against what is wrong and evil according to the norms of Islamic Sharīʿa.[121]

(c) Information is a vital necessity to society. It may not be exploited or misused in such a way as may violate sanctities and the dignity of Prophets, undermine moral and ethical values or disintegrate, corrupt or harm society or weaken its faith.[122]

(d) It is not permitted to arouse nationalistic or doctrinal hatred or to do anything that may be an incitement to any form of racial discrimination.[123]

Article 23

(a) Authority is a trust; and abuse or malicious exploitation thereof is absolutely prohibited, so that fundamental human rights may be guaranteed.

(b) Everyone shall have the right to participate, directly or indirectly in the administration of his country's public affairs. He shall also have the right to assume public office in accordance with the provisions of Sharī'a.

Article 24

All the rights and freedoms stipulated in this Declaration are subject to the Islamic Sharī'a.

Article 25

The Islamic Sharī'a is the only source of reference for the explanation or clarification to any of the articles of this Declaration.

Notes to Part III

1. Roosevelt enunciated the "four freedoms" in a state of the union address on January 6, 1941. The other three were freedom of expression, freedom from want, and freedom from fear. UDHR was adopted by the UN General Assembly in December 1948.
2. See generally Nazila Ghanea, ed., *The Challenge of Religious Discrimination at the Dawn of the New Millennium* (The Hague: Martinus Nijhoff, 2004). It was the Oslo Coalition, a group established in 1988, that led a campaign to change this focus, resulting in a change in the mandate holder's title to "Special Rapporteur on the Freedom of Religion or Belief," thus highlighting the broader question of freedom of religion and belief and treating it as a primary focus.
3. The locus classicus of this remains the decision of the commission in *Arrowsmith v. UK*, App. 7050/75 (1978), 19 *Decisions and Reports*, 5.
4. *Begum v. Denbigh High School*, [2006], UKHL 16 (March 22, 2006), Lord Hoffman, para. 50 (and see also at para. 54). See also Lord Bingham, paras. 23 and 25, and Lord Scott, para. 89.
5. See, e.g., *Wingrove v. UK*, November 25, 1996, *ECHR* 1996-V, and, for a recent example, *IA v. Turkey*, App. 42571/98, Judgment of September 13, 2005. These are all cases in which freedom of expression has been curbed in order to protect the religious sensibilities of others (thus disproving

Lady Hale in *Begum v. Denbigh High School*, para. 98, where she said that the European Court of Human Rights "has never accepted that interference with the right of freedom of expression is justified by the fact that the ideas may offend someone"). Cf. *Murphy v. Ireland*, Judgment, July 10, 2003, *ECHR* 2003-IX; 38 *EHRR* (2004), 13, where the freedom of religious expression through the means of radio broadcasting was curbed in order to protect the freedom of religion of others.

6. *Pichon v. France*, App. 49854/99, decision of October 2, 2001, and see [2002] *EHRLR* 408–9.
7. *Dahlab v. Switzerland*, App. 42393/98, Decision of February 15, 2001, *ECHR* 2001-V; *Leyla Sahin v. Turkey*, App. 44774/98, Judgment of November 10, 2005. For a similar issue before the courts in England and Wales, see *Begum v. Denbigh High School.*
8. *Kokkinakis v. Greece*, Judgment of May 25, 1993, ECHR Ser. A, 260-A, 17 *EHRR* 397 (1994), para. 31.
9. Ibid., para. 49. This makes it particularly difficult to understand Lord Bingham in the *Begum* case (para. 29) where he argues that "the focus at Strasbourg is not and has never been on whether a challenged decision or action is the product of a defective decision-making process."
10. See cases cited in earlier notes and also *Otto-Preminger-Institut v. Austria*, Judgment of October 20, 1994, ECHR, Ser. A, 295-A, 19 *EHRR* 34 (1995), para 47: "The respect for the religious feelings of believers as guaranteed in Article 9 can legitimately be thought to have been violated by provocative portrayals of objects of religious veneration; and such portrayals can be regarded as a malicious violation of the spirit of tolerance, which must also be a feature of democratic society." Cf. also the statements issued in the wake of the "cartoons" issued by the UN Special Rapporteur on Freedom of Religion or Belief and the Special Rapporteur for the Promotion and Protection of the Right to Freedom of Expression (February 8, 2006), reprinted in 1 *Religion and Human Rights* (2006). For lack of requiring the state to protect believers in these types of cases, see, e.g., *Choudhury v. UK*, App. 17439/90 (1991), 12 *HRLJ* 172, in which the European Commission on Human Rights concluded that there was no violation of the freedom of religion where the state did not step in to prevent forms of expression that the applicant considered disrespectful to his or her beliefs. In extreme cases, there might be such a need. However, see *Otto-Preminger-Institut v. Austria*, para. 47: "In extreme cases the effect of a particular method of opposing or denying religious beliefs can be such as to inhibit those who hold such beliefs from exercising their freedom to hold and express them."
11. See, e.g., *Leyla Sahin v. Turkey*, App. 4474/98, Judgment of November 10, 2005, para. 107, citing a long list of authorities on this, dating back to 1996.

12. *Refah Partisi and others v. Turkey*, Apps. 41340/98, 41342/98, 4134/98. 4134/98, Judgment of February 13, 2003. The "Constitutional Court" referred to is that of Turkey.
13. See generally the collection of materials available at www.strasbourg conference.org.
14. *Leyla Sahin v. Turkey*, para. 105.
15. *Kokkinakis v. Greece*, para. 31.
16. *Leyla Sahin v. Turkey*, para. 106.
17. Thus comments such as, "The role of the authorities . . . is not to remove the cause of tension by eliminating pluralism, but to ensure that the competing groups tolerate each other" (*Serif v. Greece, ECHR* 1999-XI, para. 53) might be acceptable if they are understood in a procedural rather than a substantive sense, though this may not be what the court thinks.
18. Cf. *Begum v. Denbigh High School*, Lady Hale, para. 97, who, when upholding the legitimacy of what she sees as interference with the manifestation of religion in that case, commented that "the school's task is also to promote the ability of people of diverse races, religions and cultures to live together in harmony. . . . [A] uniform dress code can play its role in smoothing over ethnic, religious and social divisions."
19. For a radical critique, and a resulting plea for a radical reconceiving of international society, see Philip Allott, *Eunomia: New Order for a New World*, 2nd ed. (Oxford: Oxford University Press, 2001), and *The Health of Nations: Society and Law beyond the State* (Cambridge: Cambridge University Press, 2002).
20. Cf. *Begum v. Denbigh High School*, para. 21: "Any sincere religious belief must command respect, particularly when derived from an ancient and respected religion." See, generally, Carolyn Evans, *Freedom of Religion under the European Convention on Human Rights* (Oxford: Oxford University Press, 2001), 57–59.
21. English translation from Arthur Cochrane, *The Church's Confession under Hitler* (Philadelphia: Westminster, 1962), 237–42.
22. Notably the gifted Paul Althaus, whose interest in the idea of "Christianity as community," arising from his Luther scholarship, led him to become markedly sympathetic to Nazism. See, e.g., Richard Steigmann-Gall, *The Holy Reich: Nazi Conceptions of Christianity, 1919–1945* (Cambridge: Cambridge University Press, 2003), 33.
23. It should also be noted in this regard that part of the declaration in particular places itself in opposition to attempts to impose a new unity on the confessional churches—a reference to the centralizing policies of Bishop Müller's German Christians.

24. Dietrich Bonhoeffer, *Gesammelte Schriften*, II, 259, writing in 1936, cited in Eberhard Bethge, *Dietrich Bonhoeffer* (London: Collins, 1977), 435.
25. E.g., the language of "confessing church" is also sometimes appropriated by particular groups within the churches' current debates over human sexuality; yet the issue here is one purely of intraecclesial dispute rather than of state imposition.
26. *Faqīh* (pl. *fuqahā'*) meaning "jurisconsult."
27. Texts extracted from Khomeini's writings are taken from Hamid Algar, ed. and trans., *Imam Khomeini: Islam and Revolution, Writings and Declarations* (London: KPI, 1985).
28. The revolutionary constitution of 1979, while it clearly embodies the principle of *vilāyat-e-faqīh* (see following discussion), cannot be seen as a simple expression of that theory alone, but rather represents an accommodation between an intended theocracy and the influences of other sources of political legitimation. See, e.g., Asghar Schirazi, *The Constitution of Iran: Politics and the State in the Islamic Republic* (London: I. B. Tauris, 1998).
29. According to Twelver Shī'ism, the twelfth imam, identified with the eschatological Mahdī, who is expected to appear before the end of the world to fill it with justice and free it from corruption and injustice, had two periods of occultation (*ghayba*): in the Lesser Occultation he appeared to four specific deputies (*novvab*) and gave them guidance on different occasions after his first disappearance; in the Greater Occultation, which began after the Lesser, he completely disappeared, and no one can claim to be his appointed deputy.
30. The doctrine reappears in Articles 107–9, dealing with the Leadership Council and the personal qualities its members should possess. Schirazi, *Constitution of Iran*, 35.
31. Montazeri was careful to present his criticisms as directed, not against Khomeini himself, but against misinterpretations of his teaching.
32. Constitutionally, this is effected through the "Council of Expediency," which can arbitrate between the Parliament and the Guardians council.
33. Extract from Khomeini, "Islamic Government," in Algar, *Imam Khomeini*, 40–42.
34. In Shī'ism, there has always been the need for a divinely guided and infallible spiritual leader after the Prophet; this leader is called an "imam."
35. Extract from Khomeini, "Islamic Government," in Algar, *Imam Khomeini*, 59–61.
36. This paragraph from "Interviews," in Algar, *Imam Khomeini*, 342.
37. English text from the Vatican website, www.vatican.va.
38. Peter Hebblethwaite, *John XXIII: Pope of the Council* (London: Geoffrey Chapman, 1984), 286.

39. The importance of this work to him can be seen in John's deathbed words: "Today more than ever, certainly more than in previous centuries, we are called to serve man as such, and not merely Catholics; to defend above all and everywhere the rights of the human person, and not merely those of the Catholic Church." Cited in Hebblethwaite, *John XXIII*, 498.
40. Hebblethwaite, *John XXIII*, chaps. 14–15.
41. In his opening address to the council, John put it this way: "We feel bound to disagree with these prophets of misfortune who are forever forecasting calamity—as though the end of the world was imminent. And yet today Providence is guiding us towards a new order of human relationships which, thanks to human effort and yet far surpassing its hopes, will bring us to the realisation of still higher and undreamed of expectations; in this way even human oppositions can lead to the good of the Church."
42. Wilton Wynn, *Keepers of the Keys: John XXIII, Paul VI and John Paul II: Three Who Changed the Church* (New York: Random House, 1988) 217–18, although note that the document condemning anti-Semitism was approved overwhelmingly (1,763 votes to 250) in the final session of the council in 1965.
43. Before the council, Pope John met with leaders from various Anglican, Episcopal, Baptist, Evangelical, and Orthodox churches. John maintained a particular interest in the Orthodox churches, probably in part because his time as a Vatican diplomat brought him into contact with such churches. Hebblethwaite, *John XXIII*, 376–85. An attempt to cancel a joint Catholic-Protestant prayer service in Rome had to be overruled by Pope John himself to ensure that it could go ahead as planned.
44. See Jerald C. Brauer, "Religious Freedom as a Human Right," in *Religious Liberty: An End and a Beginning*, ed. John Courtney Murray (New York: Macmillan, 1966), 46. "The hard fact is that countless numbers of people were convinced that the Roman Catholic Church, by definition, could not or would not pass a powerful statement concerning religious liberty. This strong document [*Dignitatis humanae*] is eloquent testimony to the spirit of renewal embodied in Vatican Council II."
45. Universal Declaration of Human Rights, UN Doc. A/811 (1948). The Universal Declaration is a General Assembly resolution rather than a treaty and thus, in international law terms, is not a legally binding document. Its moral and political force, however, and its influence on the development of later human rights treaties make it one of the most important statements of internationally accepted human rights.
46. See generally, Mary Ann Glendon, *A World Made New: Eleanor Roosevelt and the Universal Declaration of Human Rights* (New York: Random House, 2001).

47. Ibid.
48. Some of them certainly needed reminding. Cardinal Ottaviani, unofficial leader of the traditionalists within the church, made a public speech arguing, "It is the duty of rulers of a Catholic state to defend the religious unity of its people from disturbing elements. . . . Reason revolts at the thought that, in deference to a small minority, the faith of practically all the people should be injured by those who would foster schism." Cited in Wynn, *Keepers of the Keys*, 78.
49. Murray develops the notion in more detail by linking *Dignitatis humanae* with the objective order—"rooted in the given reality of man as man." John Courtney Murray, "The Declaration on Religious Freedom: A Moment in Its Legislative History," in *Religious Liberty: An End and a Beginning*, ed. John Courtney Murray, 40. However, as Canavan notes, the arguments here are unlikely to "commend itself to many minds outside the natural law tradition." J. Canavan, "The Catholic Concept of Religious Freedom as a Human Right," in *Religious Liberty: An End and a Beginning*, ed. John Courtney Murray, 72.
50. Murray, "The Declaration on Religious Freedom," 31–32; Samuel Gregg, "*Dignitatis Humanae* and the Catholic Human Rights Revolution," www.catholicculture.org/culture/library/view.cfm?recnum=2876 (accessed April 4, 2009).
51. Although see Murray, "The Declaration on Religious Freedom," 26–27, for the problems that the idea of freedom of conscience had as the primary basis for the declaration.
52. *Dignitatis humanae*, Art. 1, para. 3.
53. Ibid., Art. 1, para. 4.
54. Although, of course, it caused considerable offense among other religious groups, with one writer saying that the language "puzzles and annoys non-Catholics" even while defending the ideas behind the text. Canavan, "Catholic Concept of Religious Freedom," 68.
55. Murray, "The Declaration on Religious Freedom," 27–29. In discussing this he concludes, "The object of religious freedom as a juridical conception is not the actualization of the positive value inherent in religious beliefs, professions and practice. These values, as values, are juridically irrelevant, however great their religious, moral and social significance. The object of the right is simply the assure absence of constraints and restraints on individuals and groups in their efforts to pursue freely the positive values of religion" (28).
56. *Pacem in terris*, Arts. 67–78.
57. Although even here it could not bring itself to make the position in favor of democracies entirely clear. Canavan, "Catholic Concept of Religious Freedom," 79.

58. *Dignitatis humanae*, Art. 3.
59. For a strong critique of this element of *Dignitatis humanae*, see Philip D. Denenfeld, "The Conciliar Declaration and the American Declaration," in *Religious Liberty: An End and a Beginning*, ed. John Courtney Murray, 120–32.
60. J. V. Langmead Casserley, "The Need to Affirm Religious Freedom," in *Religious Liberty: An End and a Beginning*, ed. John Courtney Murray, 138, says that *Dignitatis humanae* can be described with some (if not complete) accuracy as "a tardy catching up by the conscience of the Church with the more progressive and developed conscience of the world."
61. The Universal Declaration of Human Rights (1948) does state in its preamble that "every individual and every organ of society" has an obligation to promote human rights, but most international treaties are focused on the obligations of states rather than other social groups.
62. *Dignitatis humanae*, Art. 6.
63. Hilary Charlesworth, "The Challenges of Human Rights Law for Religious Traditions" in *Religion and International Law*, ed. Mark Janis and Carolyn Evans (The Hague: Martinus Nijhoff, 1999), 412.
64. John L. McKenzie, "The Freedom of the Christian," in *Religious Liberty: An End and a Beginning*, ed. John Courtney Murray, 105, puts it bluntly: "In evading freedom Catholics evade responsibility. They permit the character of their Christian fulfilment to be determined by another."
65. Cardinal Bea, who was influential on matters of religious freedom and ecumenism, put the matter thus: "The word conscience, properly understood, also includes the moral law that God has placed in the hearts of all men and without which liberty becomes licence." It should be obvious that in speaking of the freedom to follow one's conscience, Cardinal Bea did not propose to undermine God's sovereignty or to assert complete human autonomy. He was not speaking of just any kind of freedom, but of the freedom to follow one's own conscience.
66. *Dignitatis humanae* was promulgated by Pope Paul VI on December 7, 1965.
67. Cf. John XXIII, encyclical, *Pacem in terris*, April 11, 1963, AAS 55 (1963), 279; and ibid., 265; Pius XII, radio message, December 24, 1944, AAS 37 (1945), 14.
68. Cf. John XXIII, *Pacem in terris*, 260–61; Pius XII, radio message, December 24, 1942, 19; Pius XI, encyclical, *Mit brennender sorge*, March 14, 1937, AAS 29 (1937), 160; Leo XIII, encyclical, *Libertas praestantissimum*, June 20, 1888, Acts of Leo XIII 8 (1888), 237–38.
69. Cf. John XXIII, *Pacem in terris*, 270; Paul VI, radio message, December 22, 1964, AAS 57 (1965), 181–82.

70. Cf. John XXIII, encyclical, *Mater et magistra*, May 15, 1961, AAS 53 (1961), 417; John XXIII, *Pacem in terris*, 273.
71. Cf. John XXIII, *Pacem in terris*, 273–74; Pius XII, radio message, June 1, 1941, AAS 33 (1941), 200.
72. Cf. Leo XIII, encyclical, *Immortale dei*, November 1, 1885, AAS 18 (1885), 161.
73. Cf. CIC, c. 1351; Pius XII, allocution to prelate auditors and other officials and administrators of the tribune of the Holy Roman Rota, October 6, 1946, AAS 38 (1946), 394; Pius XII, encyclical, *Mystici corporis*, June 29, 1943, AAS (1943), 243.
74. Cf. Lactantius, *Divinarum institutionum*, 5.19, CSEL 19, 463–64, 465 (*PL* 6, 614 and 616 [chap. 20]); St. Ambrose, *Epistola ad valentianum imp.*, letter 21 (*PL* 16, 1005); St. Augustine, *Contra litteras petiliani*, 2.83, CSEL 52, 112 (*PL* 43, 315); cf. C. 23, q. 5, c. 33; St. Augustine, letter 23 (*PL* 33, 98); St. Augustine, letter 34 (*PL* 33, 132); St. Augustine, letter 35 (*PL* 33, 135); St. Gregory the Great, *Epistola ad virgilium et theodorum episcopos massiliae galliarum*, Register of Letters 1, 45, MGH ep. 1, 72 (*PL* 77, 510–11 [bk. 1, ep. 47]); St. Gregory the Great, *Epistola ad Johannem episcopum Constantinopolitanum*, Register of Letters 3, 52, MGH letter 1, 210 (*PL* 77, 649 [bk. 3, letter 53]); cf. D. 45, c. 1 (ed. Friedberg, col. 160); Council of Toledo IV, c. 57, Mansi 10, 633; cf. D. 45, c. 5 (ed. Friedberg, col. 161–62); Clement III, X., V, 6, 9 (ed. Friedberg, col. 774); Innocent III, *Epistola ad arelatensem archiepiscopum*, X., III, 42, 3 (ed. Friedberg, col. 646).
75. Cf. Matthew 9:28–29; Mark 9:23–24; 6.5–6; Paul VI, encyclical, *Ecclesiam suam*, August 6, 1964, AAS 56 (1964), 642–43.
76. Cf. Leo XIII, letter, *Officio sanctissimo*, December 22, 1887, AAS 20 (1887), 269; Leo XIII, letter *Ex litteris*, April 7, 1887, AAS 19 (1886), 465.
77. Cf. Mark 16:15; Matthew 28:18–20; Pius XII, encyclical, *Summi pontificatus*, October 20, 1939, AAS 31 (1939), 445–46.
78. Cf. Pius XI, letter, *Firmissimam constantiam*, March 28, 1937, AAS 29 (1937), 196.
79. Cf. Pius XII, allocution, *Ci riesce*, December 6, 1953, AAS 45 (1953), 802.
80. Cf. Pius XII, radio message, March 23, 1952, AAS 44 (1952), 270–78.
81. Cf. John XXIII, *Pacem in terris*, 299–300.
82. Cf. ibid., 295–96.
83. E.g., Heiner Bielefeldt, "Universalism versus Relativism: On the Necessity of Intercultural Dialogue on Human Rights," in *The Islamic World and the West: An Introduction to Political Cultures and International Relations*, ed. Kai Hafez (Leiden: Brill, 2000), 46–56, and in other publications.
84. UIDHR addresses issues of "freedom of religion" in Articles 12 and 13, the Cairo Declaration in Articles 10 and 22. See further the following detailed

notes on those sections. Mohammad Hashim Kamali, *Principles of Islamic Jurisprudence* (Cambridge: ITS, 271).

85. UIDHR, explanatory note 3.
86. UDHR Article 29.2 reads: "In the exercise of his rights and freedoms, everyone shall be subject only to such limitations as are determined by law solely for the purpose of securing due recognition and respect for the rights and freedoms of others and of meeting the just requirements of morality, public order and the general welfare in a democratic society."
87. Cairo Declaration, Art. 24; and ibid., Art. 25.
88. This text of the UIDHR is taken from the website of the Islamic Council, www.alhewar.com. The site provides numerous references to Qur'ānic and traditional sources for each article; these have not been checked in detail but are indicated in the notes that follow.
89. The UIDHR was released by Salem Azzam on September 19, 1981 (Dhu Qaidah 1401).
90. UIDHR gives references to al-Mā'ida 5:32; ḥadīth narrated by Muslim, Abū Dā'ūd, Tirmidhī, Nasā'ī; ḥadīth narrated by al-Bukhārī.
91. UIDHR gives references to ḥadīth narrated by al-Bukhārī, Muslim; the sayings of the caliph 'Umar; al-Shūrā 42:41; al-Ḥajj 22:41.
92. UIDHR gives references to the address of the Prophet; ḥadīth narrated by al-Bukhārī, Muslim, Abū Dā'ūd, Tirmidhī, Nasā'ī; the address of the Caliph Abū Bakr; the farewell address of the Prophet; al-Aḥqāf 46:19; ḥadīth narrated by Aḥmad; al-Mulk 67:15; al-Zalzala 99:7–8.
93. UIDHR gives references to al-Nisā' 4:59; al-Mā'ida 5:49; al-Nisā' 4:148; ḥadīth narrated by al-Bukhārī, Muslim, Tirmidhī; ḥadīth narrated by al-Bukhārī, Muslim; ḥadīth narrated by Muslim, Abū Dā'ūd, Tirmidhī, Nasā'ī; ḥadīth narrated by al-Bukhārī, Muslim, Abū Dā'ūd, Tirmidhī, Nasā'ī; ḥadīth narrated by Abū Dā'ūd, Tirmidhī; ḥadīth narrated by al-Bukhārī, Muslim, Abū Dā'ūd, Tirmidhī, Nasā'ī; ḥadīth narrated by al-Bukhārī.
94. UIDHR gives references to ḥadīth narrated by al-Bukhārī, Muslim; al-Isrā' 17:15; al-Aḥzāb 33:5; al-Ḥujurāt 49:6; al-Najm 53:28; al-Baqara 2:229; ḥadīth narrated by al-Baihaki, Ḥākim; al-Isrā' 17:15; al-Ṭūr 52:21; Yūsuf 12:79.
95. UIDHR gives references to al-Aḥzāb 33:58.
96. UIDHR gives references to ḥadīth narrated by al-Bukhārī, Muslim, Abū Dā'ūd, Tirmidhī, Nasā'ī; ḥadīth narrated by ibn Māja.
97. UIDHR gives references to the Prophet's farewell address; al-Ḥujurāt 49:12; al-Ḥujurāt 49:11.
98. UIDHR gives references to al-Tawba 9:6; Āl 'Imrān 3:97; al-Baqara 2:125; al-Ḥajj 22:25.

99. UIDHR gives references to al-Baqara 2:256; al-Mā'ida 5:42; al-Mā'ida 5:43; al-Mā'ida 5:47.
100. UIDHR gives references to al-Shūrā 42:38; ḥadīth narrated by Aḥmad; the address of the caliph Abū Bakr.
101. UIDHR gives references to al-Aḥzāb 33:60–61; Sabā' 34:46; ḥadīth narrated by Tirmidhī, Nasā'ī; al-Nisā' 4:83; al-An'ām 6:108.
102. As is made clear in the explanatory note appended to the text of UIDHR, the "Law" referred to here is the Islamic Sharī'a. It is an open question as to who will determine what the law prescribes—scholars, contemporary or past authorities, the state, or whomever.
103. The operational consequences of this provision are absent: Who is obliged to provide conditions for the pursuit of knowledge?
104. This is similar to the right to resistance against an oppressive regime recognized in Western culture. It is qualified by the "limits set out by the Law."
105. Note that protection against contempt is provided for "religious belief," while respect is due for the "religious feelings of others." It appears that nonreligious beliefs are not covered by either.
106. UIDHR gives references to al-Kāfirūn 109:6.
107. UIDHR gives references to Yūsuf 12:108; Āl 'Imrān 3:104; al-Mā'ida 5:2; ḥadīth narrated by Abū Dā'ūd, Tirmidhī, Nasā'ī, ibn Māja.
108. UIDHR gives references to al-Mā'ida 5:120; al-Jāthiyya 45:13; al-Shu'arā' 26:183; al-Isrā' 17:20; Hūd 11:6; al-Mulk 67:15; al-Najm 53:48; al-Ḥashr 59:9; al-Ma'ārij 70:24–25; the sayings of the caliph Abū Bakr; ḥadīth narrated by al-Bukhārī, Muslim; ḥadīth narrated by Muslim; ḥadīth narrated by Muslim, Abū Dā'ūd, Tirmidhī, Nasā'ī; ḥadīth narrated by al-Bukhārī, Muslim, Abū Dā'ūd, Tirmidhī, Nasā'ī; al-Muṭaffifīn 83:1–3; ḥadīth narrated by Muslim; al-Baqara 2:275; ḥadīth narrated by al-Bukhārī, Muslim, Abū Dā'ūd, Tirmidhī, Nasā'ī.
109. UIDHR gives references to al-Baqara 2:188; ḥadīth narrated by al-Bukhārī; ḥadīth narrated by Muslim; ḥadīth narrated by Muslim, Tirmidhī.
110. UIDHR gives references to al-Tawba 9:105; ḥadīth narrated by Abū Yala (*Majma al-Zawaid*); ḥadīth narrated by ibn Māja; al-Aḥqāf 46:19; al-Tawba 9:105; ḥadīth narrated by Tabaranī (*Majma al-Zawaid*); ḥadīth narrated by al-Bukhārī.
111. UIDHR gives references to al-Aḥzāb 33:6.
112. UIDHR gives references to al-Nisā' 4:1; al-Baqara 2:228; ḥadīth narrated by al-Bukhārī, Muslim, Abū Dā'ūd, Tirmidhī, Nasā'ī; al-Rūm 30:21; al-Ṭalāq 65:7; al-Isrā' 17:24; ḥadīth narrated by al-Bukhārī, Muslim, Abū Dā'ūd, Tirmidhī; ḥadīth narrated by Abū Dā'ūd; ḥadīth narrated by al-Bukhārī, Muslim; ḥadīth narrated by Abū Dā'ūd, Tirmidhī; ḥadīth narrated by Aḥmad, Abū Dā'ūd.

113. UIDHR gives references to al-Ṭalāq 65:6; al-Nisā' 4:34; al-Ṭalāq 65:6; al-Baqara 2:229; al-Nisā' 4:12; al-Baqara 2:237.
114. UIDHR gives references to al-Isrā' 17:23?24; ḥadīth narrated by ibn Māja; Āl 'Imrān 3:187; the Prophet's farewell address; ḥadīth narrated by al-Bukhārī, Muslim; ḥadīth narrated by al-Bukhārī, Muslim, Abū Dā'ūd, Tirmidhī.
115. UIDHR gives references to ḥadīth narrated by Muslim; al-Ḥujurāt 49:12; ḥadīth narrated by Abū Dā'ūd, Tirmidhī.
116. UIDHR gives references to al-Mulk 67:15; al-An'ām 6:11; al-Nisā' 4:97; al-Baqara 2:21; al-Ḥashr 59:9.
117. The text is taken from the version provided by the International Document Database on Religion and Law, www.religlaw.org/interdocs/docs/cairo hrislam1990.htm.
118. The Cairo Declaration was adopted and issued at the Nineteenth Islamic Conference of Foreign Ministers in Cairo on August 5, 1990.
119. The wording is not clear here. Does it mean that conversion without compulsion or exploitation of poverty and ignorance is acceptable? Is this applicable only to conversions from Islam?
120. Note that the qualification of the use of this right is specified as being in accordance to the "principles of Sharī'a." This is not the Sharī'a in its totality, but its principles, its most fundamental and general norms (*al-mabādī*).
121. This clause enunciates legal protection for the principle of *al-amr bi al-ma'rūf wa al-nahy min al-munkar*, as in Āl 'Imrān 3:110; this should be "in accordance to the norms of Islamic Sharī'a." This leaves open questions as to whether the principle expresses an individual or a collective right and whether it is possible to institutionalize it.
122. The text insists that freedom of expression does not legalize the violation of sanctities (i.e., the basic tenets of religion) or prophets, or of the values of society—which is here understood as a believing society. Reminiscences of the Rushdie affair may be detected here.
123. This clause contains a prohibition of anti-Islamic ideologies such as nationalism and racism. The exclusion of "doctrinal hatred" refers to sectarian animosities, such as between different *madhāhib*.

Index